A Western Horseman Book

Colorado Springs, Colorado

HORSEMAN'S SCRAPBOOK

By Randy Steffen

Edited by Chan Bergen

Illustrations by Randy Steffen

HORSEMAN'S SCRAPBOOK

Published by
The Western Horseman Inc.

3850 North Nevada Ave.
Box 7980
Colorado Springs, CO 80933-7980

Design, Typography, and Production
Western Horseman
Colorado Springs, Colorado

Cover painting of Randy Steffen
By Dwayne Brech

Printing
Williams Printing Inc.
Colorado Springs, Colorado

Fifth Printing: January 1992

ISBN 0-911647-07-4

DEDICATION

This book is dedicated to the memory of the author,
the late Randy Steffen, who enriched this collection
of ideas through his untiring research, artistic talent,
and detailed knowledge of horses and horsemanship.
It is also dedicated to the loyal *Western Horseman*
readers who contributed many of these tips and ideas that
other horsemen might benefit from their discoveries.

CONTENTS

1 INTRODUCTION

It was in the early 1950s when Randy Steffen contacted then *Western Horseman* editor Dick Spencer to discuss the possibility of publishing a series of helpful tips in the magazine. Each tip would include a brief description of the idea and be illustrated with one of Randy's pen-and-ink drawings. The first tips appeared in the January 1953 issue. More followed and each time a tip was published, it seemed to suggest ideas for other helpful tips. Many of the ideas came from

Randy's extensive knowledge of horses and horsemanship, but many more were furnished by enthusiastic readers anxious to share their experiences with other horsemen.

The earliest hints were published pretty much as fillers without benefit of title or head. Later, a brief heading told the subject of the hints and eventually, they also appeared in page form with several tips under a head such as *Hints for Horsemen*, *Horseman's Scrapbook*,

and finally *Handy Hints*.

By the end of the decade the capsule hints that touched on every conceivable subject—fencing, trailering, tack, breaking, horse gear, and more—had become so popular that they became a regular feature in the magazine. For a number of years, nearly every issue of the magazine included Randy's by-line.

As the hints gained in popularity, the magazine constantly received requests for help from subscribers who remem-

Randy Steffen in his California studio. He was recovering from heart surgery when this photo was taken.

Pictured is Randy and the Paso Fino Sin Verquenza.

bered a hint but couldn't locate it in their back issues. Thus, the idea for the first *Scrapbook* came about. Two more books of hints followed and over the years, the three *Scrapbooks* have been right on top of our best-seller list.

After the last *Scrapbook* came off the presses, more than 250 additional hints were published in the magazine. This revision represents the best of the hints previously published in the *Scrapbooks*, plus the hints later published in the magazine that have never appeared in book form. Horsemen will appreciate this collection that combines the best of all those ideas in a single, handy reference.

Randy Steffen was a rarity in the horse world. His background and experience made him uniquely qualified to write and illustrate for the horseman. He was born on a ranch in Maverick County, about 20 miles from Eagle Pass, Texas. His father was half Indian, so Randy guessed that he was "one quarter Indian." His family was involved in ranching and they also operated a store in the Eagle Pass area, and Randy finished high school there.

When he graduated in 1935, he received an appointment to the United States Military Academy at West Point. As was customary, he attended Stanton Preparatory Academy as a prerequisite to attending West Point. During this period, he waited on tables, gave riding lessons at a local public stable, and managed to play some polo.

At the Military Academy Randy discovered he would have to study the French language, a requirement that he soon determined, "I just could not whack

my way through." It didn't take him long to find out that the Naval Academy gave the cadet several other languages to choose from. He was successful in swapping academies with a Naval cadet who wanted to go to West Point. Randy graduated an ensign in 1940 and eventually served in the European Theater of Operations during World War II.

After the war, he entered civilian life in the field of engineering. But he wasn't happy in that occupation, and 1945 found him in Nevada, where he leased a ranch and got involved in training, buying, and selling horses. It was during this period that he became seriously interested in art. He proceeded on his own without benefit of instruction, and managed to sell some of his work locally. It was a start that was to have an important impact on his future.

About this time, he and some others were hired by the government to trap mustangs in Nevada, but when he found out that the government wanted the captured horses shot, Randy quit them. Later, he got a contract to catch wild horses at Death Valley National Monument, a tough job under the toughest of conditions. He and a couple of helpers eventually rounded up about 266 horses in five weeks. Later, when he published some tips on trapping wild horses, he was talking from firsthand experience.

In 1948, Randy left Nevada and moved to Colorado Springs for a few months, where he had been offered the job of designing a new office building for *The*

Randy Steffen, circa 1960.

LES WALSH

On the trail with Dr. Roger Daniels. Randy is riding a Santa Fe saddle.

Western Horseman magazine. Using the Palace of the Governors building in Santa Fe as a model, Randy designed what is perhaps one of the most striking office buildings in the Colorado Springs area (his original design for the building appears on page 144).

Randy was a man of varied talents, and his next job was training polo ponies in California. Then it was back to Cisco, Tex., where he became managing editor of a horse magazine that was in serious trouble. Even the Steffen talents failed to save the publication. Soon he was in Hollywood where he worked as a stunt

Weldon McConnell modeled for Randy for his sculpture titled The Brush Popper.

The Ancient Order of St. Barbara was presented to Randy Steffen by Major General David N. Ott during a meeting of the Company of Military Historians at Fort Sill, Okla., in 1975.

man and stand-in for some well-known western movie idols. It was around this time that he began writing and illustrating the short hints that were to become so popular.

Detailed research was always the Steffen trademark and he began writing definitive articles on a variety of topics. Many remain the best ever written on those subjects. Included were *United States Military Saddles; The Civil War Soldier; The American Sidesaddle; Indian-Fighting Cavalryman; Stagecoach! The Abbot-Downing Story; Saddles Through History; Bits Through History; Horse Equipment of the Plains Indians;* and *The American Stock Saddle.* In commenting on Randy's work,

Randy receives the American Exemplar Award from Rodney M. Guthrie.

Publisher Dick Spencer said:

"Over the years Randy Steffen has earned a reputation as a top western artist, writer, and researcher. . . . The things that interest him are the things that interest other horsemen—and he is gifted in his ability through the pen, the brush, and the written word to pass along these interesting bits of information to other horsemen. . . ."

Steffen's next project would prove the accuracy of the above statement. No exhaustive study had been attempted on the personal gear and horse gear of the United States Cavalry and Randy went to work on the research that would produce a series of four books on the subject. Titled *The Horse Soldier 1776-1943,* the books traced the uniforms, arms, accou-

terments, and equipment of the cavalryman. The series was published in 1977, '78, and '79 by the University of Oklahoma Press, the same press that previously published his *United States Military Saddles—1812-1943.* Both titles have become invaluable references for the collector and the historian.

In the late 1960s, Randy began to seriously work at fine art. His first effort was a bronze, and that led to other pieces and paintings as well. But by the early '70s, failing health had confined him to a wheelchair for periods of time; still, he pursued fine art with his customary zeal.

In 1974, American Airlines gave two Americana Awards, and one of them went to Randy for his work in preserving American history. Then the Dallas area Bicentennial Commission selected Randy to receive its Bicentennial Award for promotion of American history through art and writing. This group also nominated Randy for the Freedom Foundation George Washington Award. The result—he journeyed to Valley Forge, where on February 2, 1976, he was honored with the American Exemplar Award. It was to be a fitting and final triumph to cap the distinguished westerner's career.

Less than a year later, on January 17, 1977, Randy Steffen died. He was 59 years old, and in accordance with his last wish, his ashes were scattered in the Wichita Mountains at the wildlife refuge near Cache, Oklahoma.

Chan Bergen
Executive Editor

FENCING, GATES, LATCHES, AND CATTLE GUARDS 2

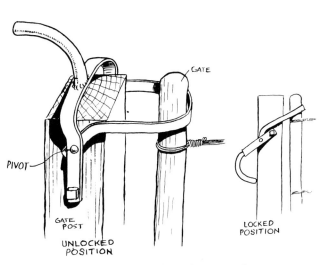

THIS IS WHAT the folks around Lund, Nev., call a Mormon gate latch, according to one of our readers from that area. It's a pretty positive locking device, working on the above-center principle, and should be easy enough to make and install on a wire gate.

HERE'S A MOVABLE electric fence used in a horse pasture close to the highway near Grass Valley, California. The posts are 4x4s, whittled down on one end to fit into concrete building blocks. Two strands of smooth wire are fastened to each post with porcelain insulators. It should be no job at all to move this fence from one location to another as the horses crop the grass short.

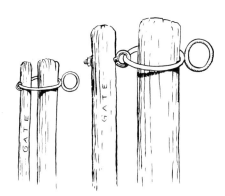

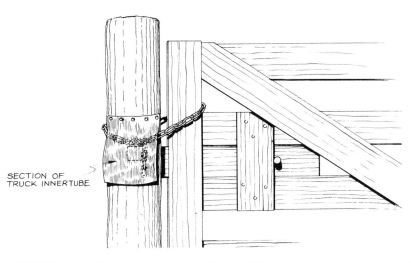

THIS WIRE gate catch comes from a reader in Rapid City, South Dakota. You'll have to weld a ring big enough to get a pretty good-sized fist through, onto a larger ring. Then attach it to the gate with a big staple, as shown at the left, or an eyebolt. The hand-ring gives you something to grasp.

I LIKED this idea from a contributor in Missouri. When it's necessary to hang a chain and padlock on a gate, cut a sheet of rubber from an old inner tube and tack it on the gate post so it completely protects the lock from any moisture.

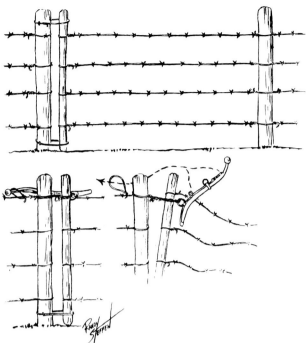

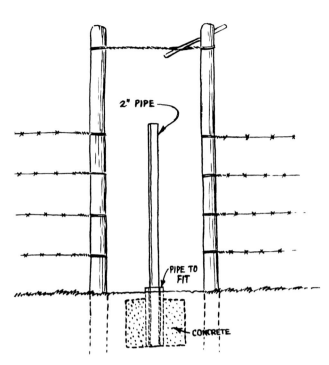

HERE ARE TWO typical cow-country gates . . . easy to make, and husky enough to stand up under wild stock and hard use. The top drawing shows a gate often called a "Texas" gate, although the reason has never been explained. It's a cinch that you'd have a tough time making a gate any simpler than this one. And the drawing should enable you to build one if you've never seen one before. The lower drawing shows a similar gate, but with a latch that utilizes an old harness hame that makes tightening this gate easy compared to the top one. The hame, fastened to the fence post with wire, provides a lot of leverage when it's drawn back toward the loop of wire that secures it in place. These gates are economical to make, and I'll bet you won't find a ranch in Texas that doesn't have several of one type or the other in its fences.

HERE'S A HANDY pasture walk-through gate that can be opened wide enough to allow a horse to be led through. The pipe in the center can be lifted out of its pipe socket to clear the opening enough to admit passage of a horse. With the pipe in place, a man can walk through the opening with ease.

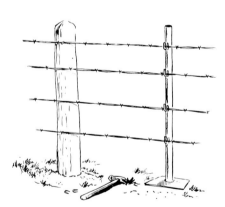

THIS fence-wire gauge will help make your fences neat and evenly spaced. Make the gauge from a piece of pipe welded to a flat steel plate large enough to form a steady base. Small U-shaped pieces of rod are welded to the pipe at the preferred heights. After the wire is stretched, this gauge can be placed close to each post and the wire stapled to the post at the correct intervals.

TO MAKE the spacing of post holes fast and easy, take a hint from the officials at football games. Rig two rods with a chain the correct length; then take a set of markers made from baling wire, as I show here, and you can mark off even spacings for fence posts almost as fast as you can walk. Too bad the holes can't be dug as easily.

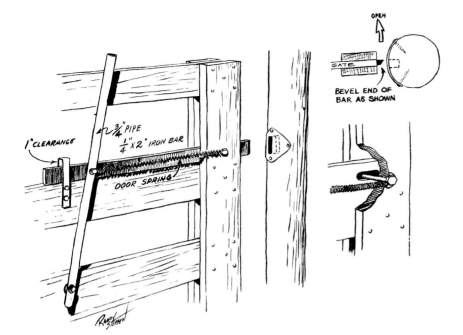

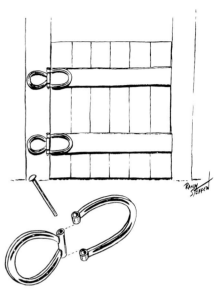

THIS GATE LATCH can be opened or closed without dismounting from your horse. Construction of this latch should be easy to savvy from just the drawings. If the gate is to swing one way only, the end of the iron bar should be beveled on the side away from the direction the gate opens. If it's to swing both ways, then the bar should be beveled on both sides. Some gate-wise horses may be smart enough to work the lever with their noses. If you have this kind of horse on your place, cut the top of the lever off even with, or a little below, the top rail of the gate; it can still be worked easily by a rider, but a horse won't be able to do much with it.

A SUBSCRIBER from Idaho is the originator of this good-looking set of door or gate hinges. He welds small sections of pipe to the ends of the shoes, and uses a bolt for the pin. Notice how the one shoe is spread at the heels while the other is made more narrow. This is one of the best gate-hinge designs I've seen.

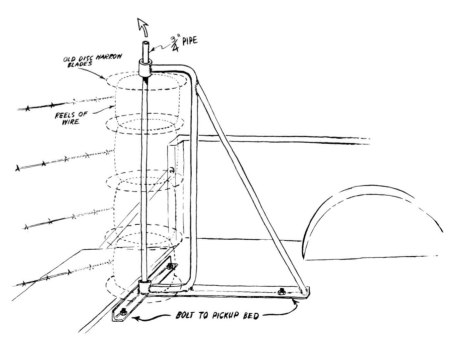

HERE'S A stock-proof gate latch that's easy for a ranch mechanic to make from scrap material usually found in the barn or shop. And ol' Dobbin isn't about to spring this one with his nose. The ring has to be lifted up for the bar on the gate to clear and allow the gate to be opened. But when it's pushed against the ring in closing, the bar pushes the ring aside and effectively latches itself.

AN OLD-TIMER sent me an idea for using disc harrow blades for placing between four rolls of barbed wire when laying out the wire from a pickup. While I was reading the letter, a neighbor dropped in and made a quick sketch of a wire-stringing rig he'd made up a long ways back. Here it is—disc blades to keep the wire from tangling, and the pipe and angle iron holder that bolts to the bed of the pickup. The vertical pipe axle on which the reels of wire revolve lifts straight up to replace empty reels. The bushings in which this axle revolves are short sections of pipe.

9

HERE'S A slick horseshoe-and-chain latch that is easy to make. The shoe is heated and bent hot to the shape shown. The chain, fastened in the eyebolt in the door with a cold shot link, slips over the end of the shoe and proves an effective stop for a door or gate.

A CANADIAN READER saw this type of walk-through gate in pastures in British Columbia and she says it is absolutely foolproof, and works for horses and ponies. She suggests a more acute angle if the gate will be used for very small ponies.

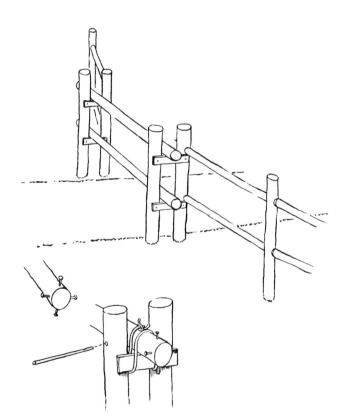

HERE'S A SLIDING rail gate idea that comes from a reader in New Mexico. The rails slide on the flat board supports nailed to the posts. If you have a horse that gets out of anything, just pound four nails into the end of the rail, as shown, and tie it down to the supports with a length of rope. A more positive way to lock this type of gate would be to slip an iron rod into a hole drilled through one post and at least part way through the rail. However, this would mean lining up the hole in the rail with the hole in the post every time the gate was to be locked.

THIS SIMPLE take-down fence idea is a good one for those who have to go through a fence every once in a while where there's no gate. Use three staples on each wire instead of a single staple, arranging them as shown in the drawing. Several large rocks will hold the wire on the ground while you lead your horse across, or drive the pickup over it. It may be best in some cases to prepare two adjacent posts this way so the wire won't be too limp when it's put back up in place. Long staples are really a little better for this job than the shorter, more common ones.

10

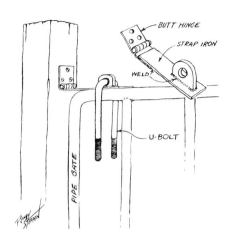

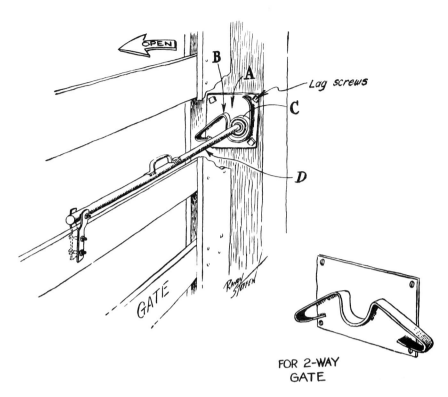

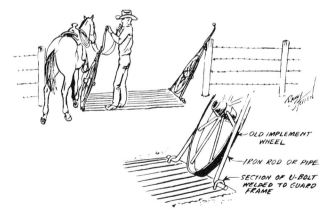

FOR 2-WAY GATE

THIS LATCH, for use with a pipe gate, is virtually horse-proof. And that's saying a lot, for I have a big brown Quarter Horse mare that can and does open blamed near everything I've ever closed her in with . . . short of a padlocked latch. A friend of mine uses this one, and because he operated a pack string in conjunction with his professional hunting operation, he gets more practical horse experience in a week than most of us get in a year. You can see how easy this latch is to make—a little welding, a large butt hinge, some heavy wood screws, and a large eyebolt are all that it takes. An old pony would have to wiggle his lips several directions at once to open this one!

THIS IS a sure-enough good gate latch and the drawing pretty much explains itself. The principal parts are a large ball bearing (an old car transmission bearing works fine), a piece of steel shaft, $1\frac{1}{4}''$ in diameter by 30" long, with a hole drilled at one end as a pivot point, some $\frac{1}{8}''$ sheet iron for the latch plate (8" x 8"), and some stout 1" strap iron for the pivot hangers, and the latch guide (B). The latch guide is welded to the $\frac{1}{8}''$ iron plate and this assembly is fastened to the gate post with lag screws. The bearing is tack-welded to the end of the shaft, and the pivot point is located after making sure the bearing will fit right against the latch plate. This can be made to work well with either a one-way or a double-swinging gate by using a different design guide strap for each, as shown in my drawing.

CATTLE GUARDS are nice to have, but the man who rides a lot either has to build an extra gate alongside his cattle guard to pass his horse through, or build a gadget like the one I've shown here. I saw one similar to this in Oklahoma some time ago, but it didn't have the swinging rod to hold it upright. I've added that detail to the design for what it's worth. This hinged cattle guard wing can be attached to most any cattle guard that has enough space between the ends of the rails or pipes and the fence post. Made from scrap pipe or sucker rod, it's light but effective.

THIS CATTLE guard design is useful as well as good-looking. The implement wheel and pipe ends are hinged on the guard itself, and fold back out of the way to allow a man to lead a saddle horse through either side. A pair of old steel horse collar hames welded to the top of the pipe frame form a distinctive and useful handle.

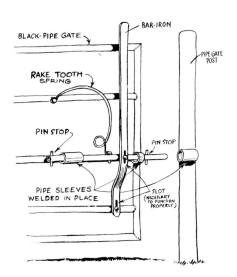

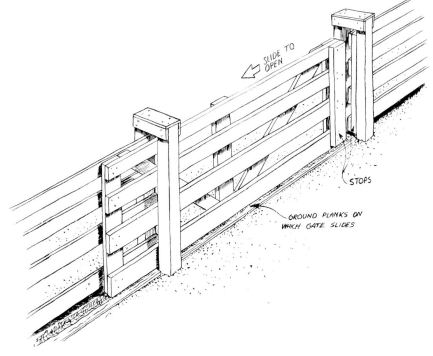

NOW HERE'S a gate latch for a pipe gate that utilizes a tooth from a hay rake as a spring. The ends of the tooth should first be heated so they can be bent easily for attachment to the gate and the sliding pipe latch. The rest of the parts are simple pipe sleeves welded in place as shown. The handle is a bar, bent to clear the latch, and slotted at the pivot and at the latch attachment.

THIS SLIDING GATE is quite common on ranches in the Saltillo area in the Mexican state of Coahuila. Made without hinges or metal hardware of any kind, except the nails used to hold the gate boards together, it slides on a greased plank surface. While some of the wild Mexican cattle will attempt to jump a pole gate, they rarely try this one.

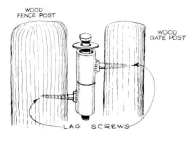

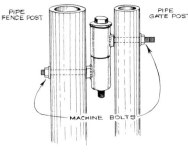

BUILDING ANY kind of fence in cow country can prove to be back-breaking, sweaty work. Any method that will make this chore a bit easier will prove to be welcome news to any ranch's fence crew. This tip will save some effort when building a fence with steel posts. For a two-man crew, one man packs the heavy steel post driver on his shoulder between the posts that have been placed in position on the ground, while the second man bends down, picks up the post, and slips it under the driver. When the man carrying the driver gets tired they change about; a lot of posts can be set in a day using this method.

THESE stout gate hinges are ideal for stock gates. Both types are made by welding sections of pipe to either lag screws or machine bolts, and mounting on gate or fence posts as shown. A washer and bolt form the hinge pin arrangement for both types.

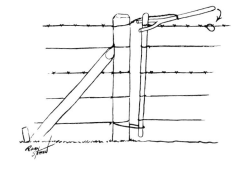

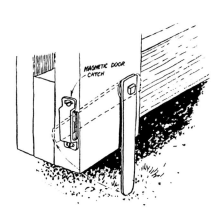

THIS IDEA comes from Australia and it's sure-'nuf a simple latch to fix on a wire gate. It uses a stout forked stick about three feet long, a simple wire attachment to the gate post, and a wire loop at the right position on the top strand of the gate. Note how the Australians brace a gate post. The brace is sharpened and mortised slightly into the main post. The other end is snugged up against a stout stake driven into the ground.

THIS GATE stop utilizes a magnetic door catch fastened to the bottom of the gate. A swinging, strap-iron stop, attached to the gate with a lag screw and one or two washers, makes it free-swinging. The door catch keeps the stop up, out of the way when the gate is opened or closed normally. A nudge with the toe of your boot lets the stop swing down and holds the gate open in any desired position.

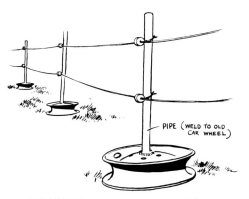

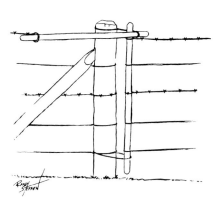

TO MAKE a temporary or movable electric fence, weld pipe to an old car wheel to form an easily moved standard. This will provide a firm support on most any surface.

HERE'S another gate latch from Australia that is similar to our Texas gate latch. A three-foot stick will do the trick.

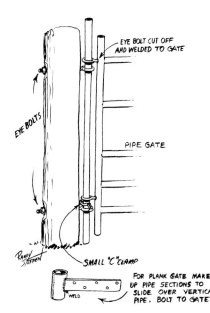

IF YOU live in snow country, this tip will save a lot of digging to free gates that have been snowed in. It's adjustable through the use of a small C-clamp on the pipe between the gate and the gate post. This pipe can be as long as necessary to accommodate the deepest snow. The clamp, locked to the pipe below the lower gate eye, keeps the gate at any desired height.

ANOTHER VERSION of a gate latch is made with an old car spring. My drawing explains how it is put together. This idea from the Nebraska Sandhills requires some welding, but is worth the effort.

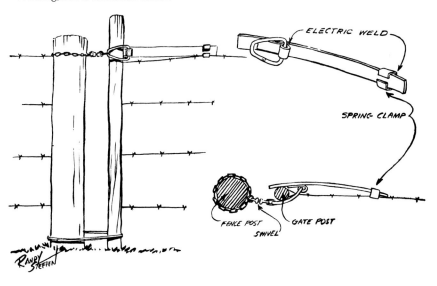

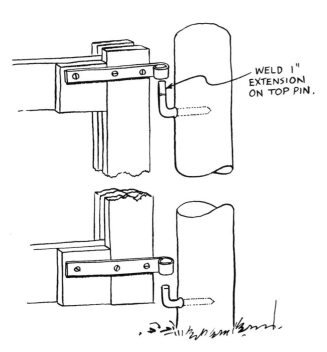

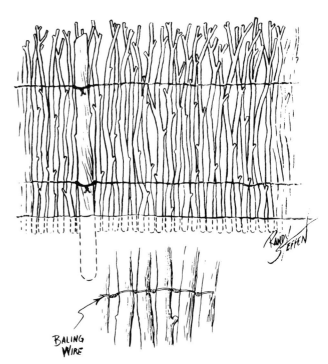

THE READER who submitted this idea has had some experience in hanging gates, I can see that. And if you've ever struggled with a new gate equipped with this type of hinge, you'll know exactly what I'm talking about. He welds a short extension to the top pin of the hardware on the gate post. Then, when he fits the top hinge sleeve over the top pin, he has no trouble keeping it there while he lines up the bottom one.

THE OLD Southwestern picket-pole corral is a picturesque part of the great cow country; and for you folks who'd like to have one on your place, the drawing shows how very simple they are to make. The only materials you'll need will be enough two-inch mesquite, cedar, oak, or most any kind of poles, crooked or otherwise, long enough to stand up as high or as low as you want. You'll also need all the old baling wire you've probably been cussing ever since you started feeding baled hay to your horses. You should set fairly stout posts every eight or ten feet to support the lighter picket fence. Be sure you tie the fence to these posts, top and bottom, with more baling wire. This kind of fence, while extremely rough, presents a rustic and pleasing appearance around anybody's horse lot.

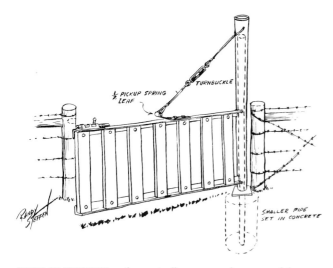

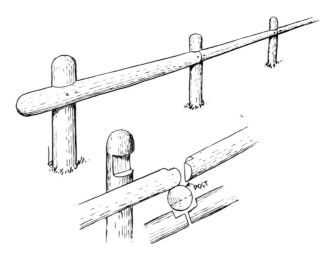

FREE-SWINGING and practically sag-proof are two of the features found in this gate. Angle-iron is welded to a large diameter pipe that fits over a smaller pipe set in concrete. A flat metal plate welded to the smaller pipe at ground level provides a low-friction surface for the gate to swing on. Two-inch lumber bolted to top and bottom angle-irons form a barrier that stock won't break up quickly, and you can use your favorite bolt or latch design to keep the gate closed. The cable, turnbuckle, and spring assembly keep the gate from sagging.

HERE'S HOW to make a single-rail, pine-pole border fence that is simple and good-looking. Care must be taken to cut each post to fit the size of the rail that will be used with it. Each post and rail should be marked so there will be a neat fit when the fence is ready for final assembly. Several coats of a preservative are necessary if you want the rails and posts to retain a bright finish. Untreated poles will turn dark in a hurry.

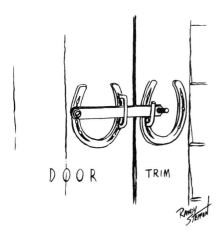

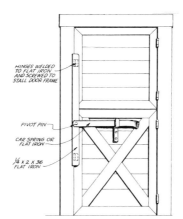

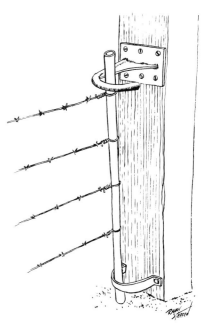

HERE'S A real western gate or cabinet latch that can be made up from a couple of old shoes and odd pieces of rod and strap. The finished latch can be nailed to the gate or door with horseshoe nails of the right size. A coat of flat, black paint will make this look real classy.

THIS stall door latch or fastener is similar to the type often found on horse trailer doors. It should be simple to make, and it is completely foolproof on any hinged stall door. It can be opened with one hand or even an elbow if your hands are full.

I WAS on a hunting trip in the California Sierras and had to go through a big ranch on the way to the hunting area; this is the type of gate latch I found on the ranch. It's easy to open and close and, above all, it's rugged. The latch is a piece of rod about $3/4$ inch in diameter, welded to a $1/8$-inch gusset; the whole assembly is welded to a boiler-plate base that has been drilled for fastening to the gate post with lag screws. The holder for the bottom of the pipe gate post was formed from heavy strap iron and fastened with lag screws as shown.

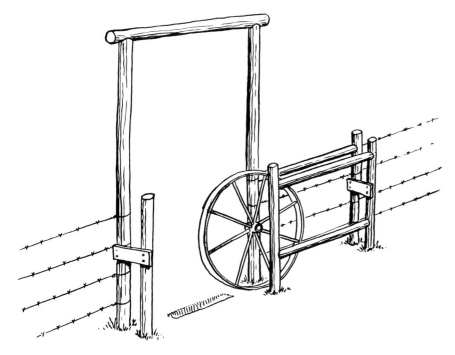

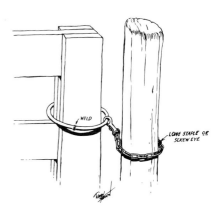

HERE'S AN UNUSUAL gate that is easy enough for a man on horseback to open and close without dismounting. Most any type of old iron wheel will work, providing it is the right size. A low depression under the center of the gate prevents the wheel from rolling except when it is pushed. But while horseback, it can easily be rolled aside.

THIS GATE latch is an easy one to make and will defy any horse or cow to open it. The easiest way to make this is to weld a ring of $3/8$-inch steel and assemble it as shown when building the gate. A suitable snap is fastened to a length of chain to permit securing the gate. A large staple or a long-shanked screw eye fastens the chain securely to the post so it can be handled easily from either side.

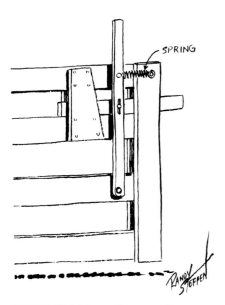

A FRIEND had a problem with horses trying to jump a cattle guard on his San Bernardino ranch, and here's the way he licked the problem. A green cowhide was stretched out on the side of a barn, held in place with nails, and allowed to dry flat. When dry, it was cut in half down the back, and a half hide was nailed to each side of the slanted wood side-pieces of the cattle guard. The sight and smell of the hides kept the horses completely away from the vicinity, and there was no more problem.

HERE'S AN old standby-type of gate latch that's made up of all wood parts, except for the spring. The slot that's shown in the hardwood handle is necessary, so be sure to include it. A friend of mine in Auburn, Calif., had a number of gate latches like this on a ranch he managed.

HERE'S A Texas bumper gate design that works both ways. This one's easy to make, but as with any mechanical design, some thought and care must be used while building it. The gate should be ten feet wide and five feet high, made from two-inch material, and braced as shown with vertical and diagonal two-inch planks. The gate-support pole should be a length of four-inch pipe for the best operation, but a treated wood pole can be made to work. One of the most important factors in building this gate is placing the pole firmly in the ground; setting it in concrete is the safest and surest bet.

The swinging action is provided by the iron straps bent to fit around the pole and bolted securely to the gate frame. These straps should be about 3/8 inch thick and five inches wide. Notice the flange welded to the pole below each strap—these are to keep the gate from dragging on the ground. Be sure to set your guy wire, or cable, solidly; a utility company "deadman" does this job best. When you're ready to mount the chains on your bumper gate, fasten them temporarily until you're sure they're exactly the right length to swing your gate to the center post each time. Then fasten them permanently.

The two small fence posts and wire at the opening end of the gate will keep stock from nosing through the gate during a big blow, when the gate is bound to swing a little. And a final word of precaution—when you're ready to drive your car through this gate, ease up to it and nudge it open if you don't want a fender repair bill. The little sign, "Hit Me Easy," is a good thing to paint on each side. It should keep your friends from being peeved at you over damage to their cars.

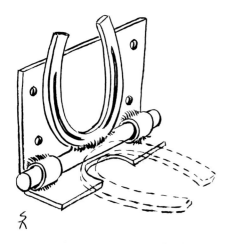

THIS HORSESHOE swinging latch is a stout one for gates on places where stock is handled. Two short sections of pipe are welded to a piece of boiler plate and shaped and drilled as shown. The rod must be slipped into the pipe sections before the shoe is welded to it. While this type of latch works best on a pipe-frame gate, you can spread the shoe to make it work on a wood gate.

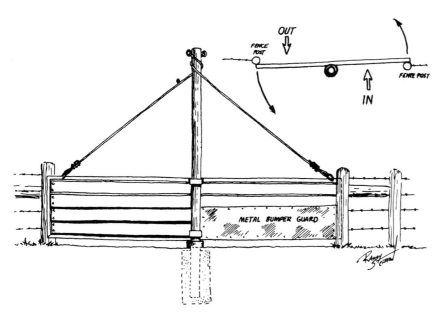

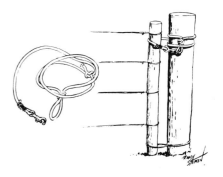

THIS IS another example of a Texas bump gate and a typical one. You just ease up to it in your car, nudge it open a foot or so, and boil right on through. The steel cables go to the top of the six-inch or heavier pipe post in the middle coil around the pole, then uncoil to close the gate with a clang after you're well in the clear with your rear bumper. I've run at these gates enough to where I can breeze on through them with a horse trailer behind the car; but there have been several times when I wasn't quick enough on the throttle and the trailer got a pretty sound banging on the side. Moral: have someone get out and hold the gate open if you're dragging a trailer. If you're by yourself, pour the coal to 'er pardner, and keep your fingers crossed that your judgment hasn't slipped.

A READER from Salem, Ore., cooked up this gate latch idea, tried it, and found that the idea worked real well. Heavy nylon rope will work best since it will last longer when exposed to the elements.

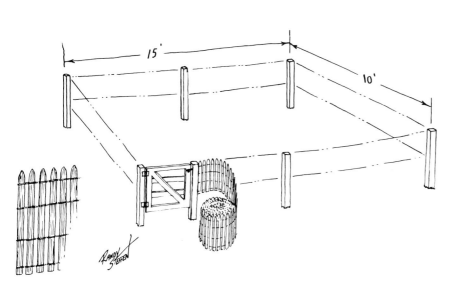

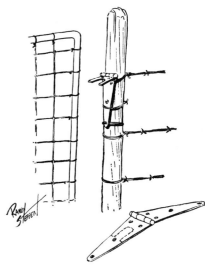

I REMEMBER seeing a horse in a dandy temporary corral. It was 10x15 feet in size with a gate made of 2x4s large enough to walk a horse through. The corral posts were 4x4 redwood, on which was wired a roll of 24-inch picket snow fence. This comes in 50-foot rolls and is available from lumber yards. It was high enough for a horse, and the sharp ends of the pickets discouraged his leaning over the fence to crop grass on the outside. While I wouldn't want to rely on this for a permanent corral, it's certainly good enough for a short period of time, is cheap, and goes up with a minimum of time and effort.

IF YOU have some gates on your place with pipe frames, here's a latch that will work as well as any and can be made in a few minutes with a hacksaw and a file. As the drawing shows, use a fairly large strap hinge. Cut one ear so it will slip freely over the pipe gate frame when wired to the post as shown. If your post is solid enough, use a couple of large wood screws to keep it from slipping up and down, then wire it securely.

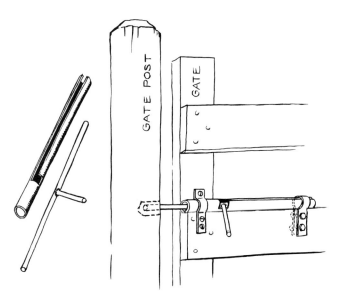

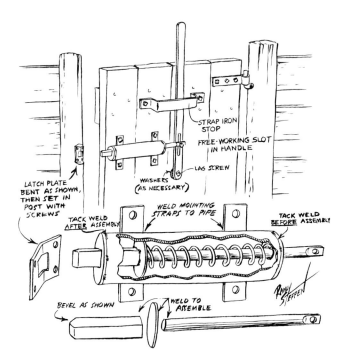

A READER sent me this idea along with a note explaining that he uses this same type of latch on several gates at his place. His experience has been that it is virtually impossible for horses or cattle to rub this type of latch open. It is made from an 18-inch-long section of 1-inch pipe. A slot is cut in the pipe with a hacksaw and the welded-up rod is put in place before the latch is bolted to the gate. Strap iron is used to hold the latch in place, and a hole drilled in the fence post provides an effective stop for the bolt. These latches are inexpensive to make and if extra security is needed on a large gate, you might consider mounting two of them, one at the top and one near the bottom of the gate.

THIS LATCH is designed primarily for a set of pens where it's necessary for a mounted man to frequently open and close a gate while separating cattle or other livestock. Many ranches have welding shops, but if you don't have one available, your local welder can help you with it. I show no dimensions here because I don't know what size scrap materials you'll be able to find on your place. But I believe you can readily adapt this design to whatever materials you can find.

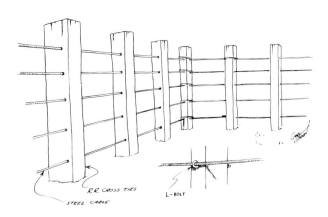

THIS IS a good way to make a water gap in a fence that goes across a stream or waterway of any kind. A reader in Tahoe City built one like this in his lakeside pasture where a small stream runs into Lake Tahoe. The wooden structure pivots on the pipe that's fastened to the fence posts with U-bolts so that a rise in the stream floats it out and away from the fence. When the water level goes down, it settles down to its original position.

HERE'S A CORRAL that is buffalo bull strong. Made of old railroad cross-ties set firmly in the ground, and utility-company-discarded steel cable threaded through holes drilled in the ties, it will hold anything you put in it that is not little enough to crawl between the strands. If you want, you can fasten the cable to the face of the ties with L-bolts, but this is much more costly and isn't a bit more satisfactory than the drilled holes. It would be a good idea to use a turnbuckle on each strand, somewhere around the circumference of the corral, so you can pull the cables tight enough to eliminate any sagging.

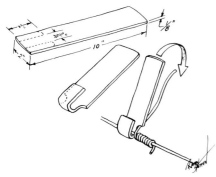

A WIRE SPLICER is a handy thing to have around any place with fences to keep up. While there is one almost identical to this on the market, they are hard to find so you may want to have your blacksmith make one. Sure saves wear and tear on hands and gloves, and makes a mighty neat job on wire fences.

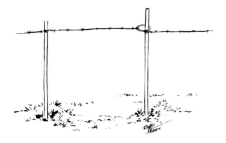

HERE IS a temporary fence with a gate for anyone who has a horse with enough respect for a single strand of wire to stay inside it without a fuss. The cinch ring, or ring from a big work-horse snaffle, is easy to slip over one of the metal posts and makes a gate that is easy to open.

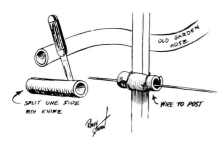

WHEN I had to move about 100 feet of electric fence, I broke a few of the insulators. I improvised by using a length of an old rubber garden hose cut into six-inch lengths. It was easy to slit the pieces down one side with a pocket knife, slip them over the fencing as shown, and wire them to the posts.

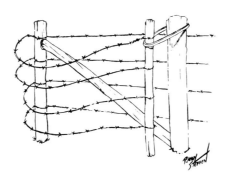

THIS IDEA will save a lot of aggravation when moving bunches of stock from one pasture to another. No matter how a wire gate is propped open—when you need it open and away from the gate opening to keep horses or cattle from tangling in the wire—the blamed thing seems to flop down at the wrong moment. Many's the time I've seen a spooky bunch turn back and fairly run over the herders when a gate flopped down under their noses. An old car fan belt looped over the gate post between the two top wires will enable you to secure the gate to a post and keep it there until you are ready to close it.

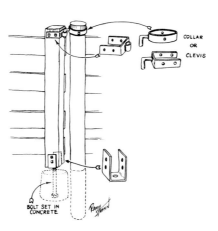

HERE'S one way to hang a big, heavy gate, such as the type found on bucking chutes in a rodeo arena, or large corral gates. A reader told me that this was a design he came up with one time when he had to hang a big gate and had no big store hinges with which to do it. He says the gate swings easily and smoothly, supported mainly on the large bolt set in concrete at the bottom. He advises being liberal with grease in the hole the bolt fits into so it won't wear the wood excessively.

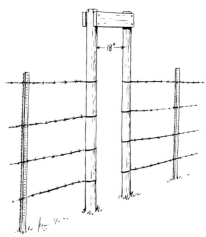

THIS IS a simple walk-through gap for a wire fence that I've seen used in a jillion places. The two small posts are set firmly in the ground, and fastened together at the top by a couple of braces. Then the wire is wrapped and fastened as shown. The distance between the two posts can vary, but should be just wide enough for a man to slip through sideways.

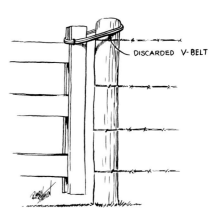

THERE ARE almost as many types of ranch gate fasteners as there are ranch gates, but every once in a while I come across one that is worthy of passing on to you folks, and this is one of those. I spotted this one on a ranch in Nevada. It is nothing more than a discarded V-belt stapled to a gate as I've shown here. It was a simple matter to swing it up over the fence post to open; and it was just as easy to lift it up and over the top of the post to close and secure the gate. The way I show it, a horse could nudge the belt up and open the gate, but it would be a simple matter to wire a snap to the belt so the snap could be hooked to the top strand of wire on the fence. No horse could open it then!

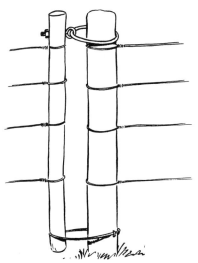

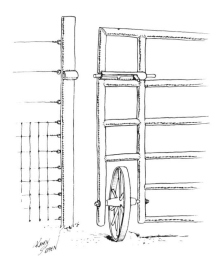

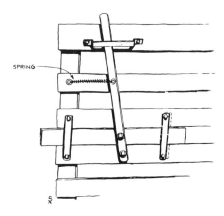

ANOTHER IDEA for a gate latch is this simple design that comes from Eastland, Texas. The big ring is inserted into the eye after a cold chisel is used to pry the eye open. A few smart shots with a hammer close it again and it's ready for mounting on the nearest gate.

HERE'S A cure for the large pipe gates that almost invariably sag after a relatively short period of use. One of our California readers rigged up this iron wheelbarrow wheel on one of his gates and eliminated the possibility of sagging.

THIS IS the old tried-and-true gate latch that has graced the gates of a thousand cow outfits from the Missouri to the Pacific for a hundred years or more. The latch is easy to make and is ideal for a horse outfit. The addition of a spring to keep the latch closed makes this design a little better than the old style.

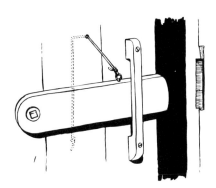

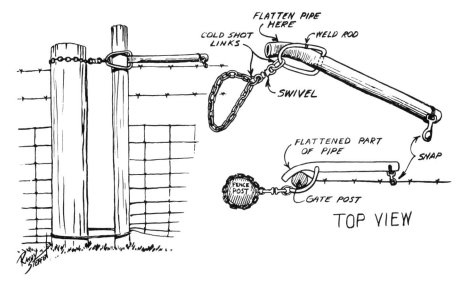

THE OLD expression, *the latch string is always out,* is pretty much lost on today's generation. I know, because my studio doors are equipped with old-time latches and latch strings, and half the people trying to open my doors have to be told how to pull the latch string. At any rate, this type of latch is easy to make and it is a mighty effective way to keep the door closed. The drawing shows how you can make one of your own.

STILL ANOTHER DESIGN for a pasture gate latch is this one from a reader in Nebraska. It is easy to make with an acetylene welding torch, a piece of one-inch pipe, some scrap iron rod, a short piece of chain, some cold-shot chain links, a harness snap, and a swivel. The result is a stout, permanent latch. I believe the drawing is clear enough to let you make this up without a long-winded set of instructions from me.

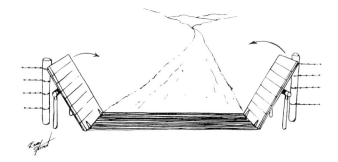

AN OLD FRIEND from Ash Meadows, Nev., uses this slick arrangement on the cattle guard at the entrance to his home place. The panels are made of stout, two-inch lumber, and are hinged at the bottom so that they can be lowered over the cattle guard to allow solid footing when horses or cattle are to be driven across. The panels are of such size that they meet in the center and afford a solid crossing.

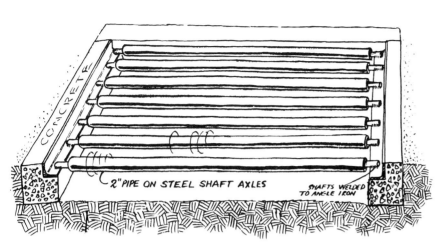

2" PIPE ON STEEL SHAFT AXLES

SHAFTS WELDED TO ANGLE IRON

NOW HERE'S the prize of all handy hints and it comes from a ranch in Nevada. It's a cattle guard that really should discourage any livestock from more than placing one foot on it—provided it is built wide enough to keep horses or cattle from jumping its span. Two-inch pipe is slipped over steel shafting, so that the pipe can revolve when anything steps on it. When the shafting is welded to the end pieces as shown here, this arrangement makes the most practical cattle guard I have ever seen. No animal would do more than test it before backing away in a hurry.

I AM constantly surprised with new gate latch ideas and this one comes from a reader in the East who owned a horse that was a whiz at opening gates. This one is about as foolproof as they come and no smart-aleck horse is likely to worry it open with his nose. The latch is made by removing the pin from a large T-hinge, substituting another pin made from a piece of rod bent to the shape shown, and fastening this pin to the gate post with a length of small chain.

RANCHERS and working cowboys will appreciate this idea. If you've never had to maintain wire fences closing in a good-sized piece of grassland, you may not appreciate how handy this little digging-bar end could be. Small and light enough to go in a saddle pocket easily, it converts to a man-sized tool when a green stick is whittled to fit snugly inside the heavy-wall tube, welded to the hardened steel spud end. Wherever stock is wild and wood fence posts are used, there'll be need for replacing posts that rot off or are knocked over.

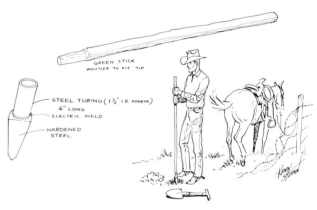

GREEN STICK
WHITTLED TO FIT TIP

STEEL TUBING (1½" I.D. APPROX)
4" LONG
ELECTRIC WELD

HARDENED STEEL

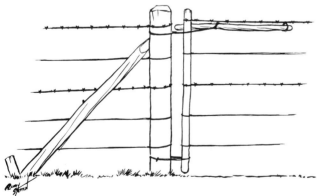

WE'VE HAD a few ideas from Australia and here's another—a wire gate latch that is common in the cattle country down there. While it's very similar to some types used here, it is a little different, and well worth passing on to you.

WHEN I needed a new gate for one of my pastures, I made up one that is similar to gates I remembered from a horse ranch in California. It can be knocked together in nothing flat with light lumber, all of the same dimension, and clinched nails hold it as securely as any type of hardware. The best hinges to use are similar to those I have shown in the drawing. Believe me, this is as sagproof a gate design as you'll find.

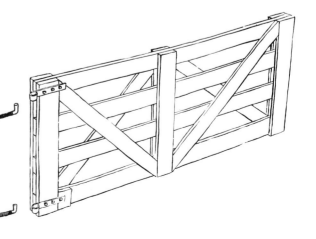

21

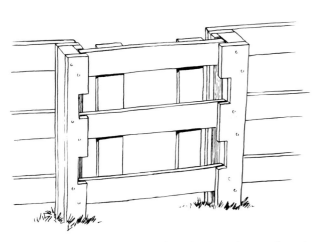

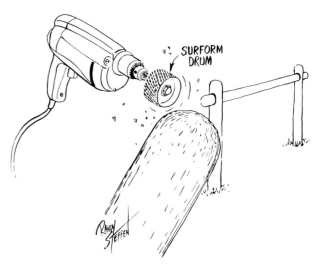

HERE's a husky gate that's just the ticket for a place in a board fence that needs going through only occasionally. A friend uses this design for a spot in his yearling pasture. The drawing shows the construction clearly enough to enable you to make one up from whatever dimension lumber you might have on hand.

I SURE LIKE the looks of peeled pine pole fences, railings, furniture, hitch racks, or anything this good-looking native material might be used for. I used to gripe about the job of rounding the ends of these poles since it took a long time by hand. Then I learned about a device called a *surform* drum, mounted it on my electric drill, and believe me, it did the job in nothing flat. Try it!

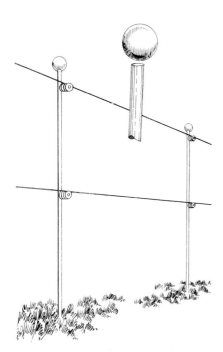

ANOTHER IDEA to cure a sagging gate comes from a Montana reader. He used a swivel wheel that was discarded from the front jack of an old trailer. Mounting it on a corral gate as shown, he held it firmly in place with a couple of U-bolts and a wood back nailed at the top to keep it in position. He says it rolls easily over the ground, and makes it so much easier to open and close. This one is on his arena gate.

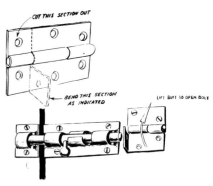

THIS IS an important tip that old-time cowmen all over the West agree on: when your pasture fences are made with all wooden posts, be sure to ground each wire of the fence with a steel post at least once per mile of fence. Cattle have a tendency to drift before a storm, and sometimes will bunch against a fence. A single bolt of lightning could kill the whole bunch if it were to hit an ungrounded fence line anywhere near them.

A HORSE that itches seems to delight in scratching himself on every sharp object in sight, so he often sports scratches and cuts that certainly don't enhance his appearance. A reader in Ontario keeps her horse in a pasture fenced with two strands of electric wire on steel posts. In order to keep the horse's head from becoming scratched from his rubbing on the tops of the steel posts, she uses small, hollow rubber balls with a small slit cut in each to cover the post ends.

WE'VE ALL seen horses that have a special genius for opening latches of most any type. Well, here's a latch that's simple enough to make and an ol', sly horse would need at least two noses to open it. The reader who sent this one uses an ordinary butt hinge, cuts off one end section on one side, bends the lower end section at right angles, then mounts the hinge with two screws in line with the closed bolt. Gravity makes the stop fall into position unless it's held up at the same time the bolt is slid open.

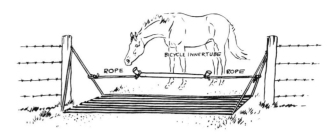

I SAW THIS neat wagon wheel gate at a horse ranch in Bedford, Texas. The frame members are 2x4s, with doweled and glued joints, and the wheels are bolted to the frame with lag screws through drilled holes. Oversize holes were drilled in the iron wagon tires to allow the lags to be screwed in without damage to the threads. Regular heavy-duty gate hinge hardware was used to hang the gates on cedar posts.

SOME CATTLE and horses don't have much respect for a cattle guard. This is another idea that should slow 'em down some while permitting a car to drive over. The bicycle tube will stretch enough to allow the wheels to pass but you will have to experiment some on the right height to prevent snagging.

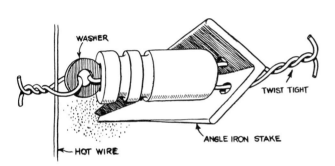

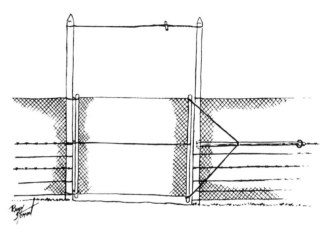

THIS IS a method for stringing electric wire on temporary angle iron stakes. The washer affords a good, stout anchorage for the insulated wire that holds the porcelain insulator to the iron stake. The drawing shows a view looking down on one of the stakes.

NOW THIS IS a dandy style for a corral gate—or for any gate where the gate posts are wired together at the top. This one is from Australia and while we show a woven wire fence, the same arrangement could be used with smooth or barbed wire on a common wire gate. You can bet this gate lever would stretch the wire until it sang like a harp. Notice that the end of the lever is mortised into the post. These levers as used in Australia are usually about nine feet long.

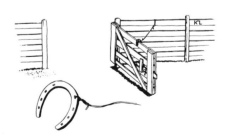

IF YOU have trouble making your horses or cattle respect a cattle guard, here's a gimmick you can add easily enough. It will help to keep them from jumping or walking across. Fluttering bits of cloth are spooky to both horses and cattle. I'd suggest using strips of plastic ribbon as they'll last a long time. Ordinary nylon or similar rope tied to the wire connecting the two posts will make a rig that should last a long time.

WHILE AN old friend who trains cutting horses was visiting us, we talked about horses that were smart enough, or ornery enough, to open most any kind of a stall latch. My friend told me that he had to use one of these chain latches on the stall of an Arabian he once owned. This latch stopped him from meandering around the rancho at will.

HORSESHOES have a number of uses and here's another. The shoes can be utilized as shown to hold open gates while working cattle or moving them from one pen to another. Baling wire, twine, or even a light chain can be used to fasten the horseshoe to the corral fence. This idea works equally well on plain or pole gates.

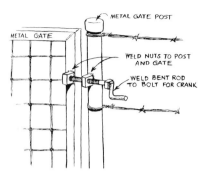

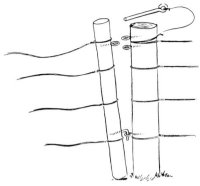

HERE'S another gate latch that's pretty much stock-proof and it shouldn't be hard to make up. You will have to do a little welding on this one, but that makes it ideal for metal gates. My drawing pretty much explains how to put this neat idea together.

I THOUGHT I had seen every variety of backwoods wire gate there ever was, but on a recent research trip to the East, I bumped into this one. It has four large screw eyes, an eyebolt, and a long lag screw that had been bent in an L-shape with its head cut off. This gate works just as good as any of the Utah, Mormon, Oklahoma, Texas, and Oregon gates you ever saw.

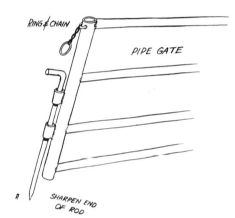

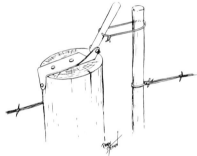

EVER TRY to straighten and tamp a sagging fence post by yourself? It's a job that makes you wish you had a couple of extra hands. Well, here's a method that will allow you to accomplish the feat by yourself. First, pike a mound of dirt near the bottom of the post on the same side it leans. Now stomp a shallow hole in the ground with your boot heel—about $2\frac{1}{2}$- or 3-feet from the base of the post on the same side. Insert the end of the shovel handle in the heel mark, and while straightening the post with one hand, place the point of the shovel against it with the other. The point of the shovel will bite into the wood enough to hold it upright. Use your foot to scrape the pile of dirt into the hole and tamp it firmly with your bar.

HERE'S AN outfit that's easy to rig on any pipe gate that will allow you to peg it open in any position you desire. The ring and chain fastened at the top allow you to hold the sharpened end of the iron stake clear of the ground, if you want the gate to swing free.

A READER from Smithers, British Columbia, sent us this idea to keep a gate closed. It is simple but effective and easy to make. He uses a piece of strap iron, cuts it to the shape shown, bends up a fulcrum tab, and drills it for a pivot bolt. The handle is a piece of smooth wood, drilled for the wire gate loop. This acts as an effective above-center catch that will lock very effectively, and certainly eliminates fumbling with other hard-to-close arrangements.

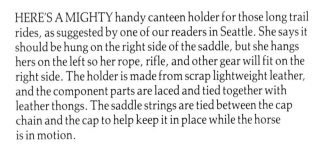

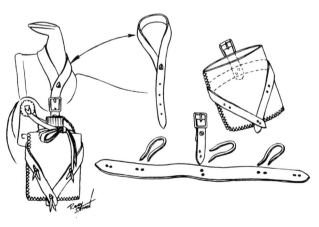

HERE'S A MIGHTY handy canteen holder for those long trail rides, as suggested by one of our readers in Seattle. She says it should be hung on the right side of the saddle, but she hangs hers on the left so her rope, rifle, and other gear will fit on the right side. The holder is made from scrap lightweight leather, and the component parts are laced and tied together with leather thongs. The saddle strings are tied between the cap chain and the cap to help keep it in place while the horse is in motion.

Fencing for the Horseman

ONE OF THE biggest problems facing the modern horseman is fencing. No horse owner is immune from this necessary part of horse ownership. While horsemen ordinarily have a wide choice of types of fences and the materials that go into them, the construction of woven-wire fences offers many advantages besides speed of building and economy. And, since the building of woven-wire fences offers more serious technical problems than most any other type of fencing, a few examples of the best practices, and some of the standards arrived at by the combined knowledge and cooperation of the Federal government, consumer representatives, and wire manufacturers, would make fence building a little easier for the horseman.

But first a word of caution. Horses and barbed wire do not mix any better than little boys and loaded guns; they are an accident waiting to happen. And the smaller the enclosure, the greater chance of injuries from barbed wire. If you're lucky enough to have pastures several hundred acres or larger in size, there is less chance of injury, especially if there are no horses on the other side of the fences that your horses might argue with.

Thousands of horsemen today use woven wire, or double-twisted barbless wire, also referred to as just smooth wire. Because horses do not have the respect for smooth wire that they do for barbed wire, they lean on it, over it, and through it more readily, necessitating more frequent repairs. But most horsemen prefer this to risking having a horse torn up on barbed wire.

If you use woven wire and it's not high enough to prevent horses leaning over it to graze on the other side, you might run a strand of barbed wire along the top. However, many horsemen use smooth wire for this. If the woven wire doesn't reach clear down to the ground, some horsemen also run a strand of smooth wire along the bottom, as shown in Fig. 1. Barbed wire on the bottom is decidedly more dangerous than on the top because horses have a habit of pawing at a fence, or striking out when squabbling with a neighbor over the fence. Either way, a horse can get a foot hung up in that barbed wire.

Going to Fig. 1 . . . the first woven-wire style, using 47-inch wire, is practical for horses. Height to the top of the woven wire is a couple of inches shy of four-and-a-half feet . . . plenty good for anything short of a fence-climbing stud. I show the other types in detail for the benefit of any horse owners who are also in the cow business.

Of course, nothing beats a stout wooden or pipe fence for corrals, but this heavy woven wire, 47 inches wide, makes a good corral, too. The heavier gauge is best, and requires far less maintenance. In case you didn't know, this type fencing is available in 8, 11, 12$\frac{1}{2}$, and 14$\frac{1}{2}$ gauge. The larger the numbers, the lighter the gauge.

WOVEN WIRE

One of the most common types of horse fencing is woven wire. The rectangular mesh is the most common, but the V-mesh style is also very popular and practical. Safety is a primary consideration when selecting wire, and several types of woven fencing designed specifically for horses are available. Most fencing designed for horses has a tight weave that will keep an animal from getting a hoof stuck in the wire.

Woven wire suitable for horses comes in a variety of sizes ranging from 47 inches to 72 inches in width. The wire is often sold in lengths of 10 and 20 rods (a rod is 16$\frac{1}{2}$ feet, in case you were about to look it up), but some sources offer wire in lengths as short as 100 feet. Farm and ranch supply stores and many lumber yards offer good selections of woven-wire horse fencing. These sources will usually specify the wire gauge, or thickness, with the top and bottom wires being the heaviest and the stay and line wire being slightly lighter. For example,

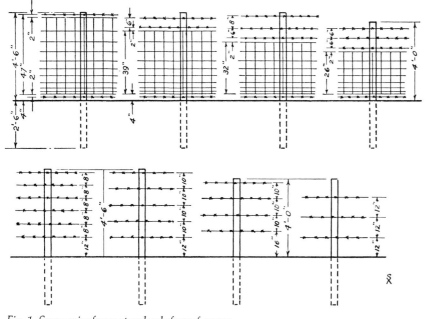

Fig. 1. Some wire fence standards for reference.

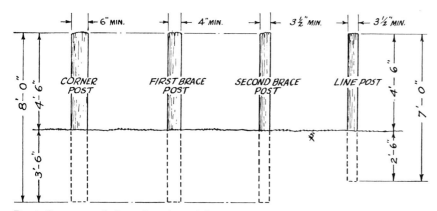

Fig. 2. Recommended post lengths and diameters.

25

one company offers horse fencing with 8-gauge top and bottom wires with all other wires being 10-gauge.

FENCE POSTS

The most common types of fence posts in use today are wood and metal. Some ranch supply houses offer special, $2^1/_2$-inch galvanized, 6-gauge staples for attaching woven wire to wooden posts. If steel posts are preferred, fencing may be wired to the post or bead welded. Steel posts come in different lengths, and will last a lifetime. However, for the purpose of this article, we will consider only wooden fence posts.

Osage orange (bois d'arc), black locust, white and red cedar, white oak, and catalpa are the more durable untreated posts, but they are not obtainable in all parts of the country. Most areas have other woods that are suitable for posts if treatment is given with a good wood preservative. Of course, even the most durable wood posts will last even longer if treated with a preservative; but again, for the man whose wallet isn't always bulging, practical economy must be a prime consideration. Those of you who live in mesquite country already know that mesquite will last a long time in the ground, in spite of what some of the experts contend.

The United States Forest Products Laboratory lists their findings on the durability of various woods used as fence posts as follows:

Woods that will *probably* remain in service longer than 15 years—*black locust, Osage orange.*

Woods that *may* last from 7 to 15 years—*catalpa, white oak, red mulberry, sassafras, black walnut, bald cypress, white cedar, red cedar, redwood.*

Woods that *may* last from 3 to 7 years—*ash, aspen, basswood, beech, birch, box elder, butternut, cottonwood, elm, hackberry, hickory, honey locust, maple, red oak, sweetgum, sycamore, willow, balsam fir, Douglas fir, hemlock (eastern), larch (western), pine, spruce, tamarack.*

In hard, stiff soil, posts usually decay first just below the top of the ground. Posts that are in constantly damp soil seem to last longest. Rotting is fastest at the ground level in soils with a widely varying moisture content. In sandy soils, posts generally rot above the ground first. The U.S. Department of Agriculture questions the practical value of seasoning posts before they are put into the ground unless they are to be treated with a preservative. *Peeling is recommended.* Bark harbors boring insects and traps moisture, which hastens decay. The season of the year when wood is cut is *not* known to have any effect on its decay resistance.

While some fencing experts insist on sloping or tapering the tops of fence posts, the U.S. Department of Agriculture contends there is *no* evidence to indicate sloping adds to the life of a post. That's a new one on me . . . I've heard all my life that a post should be sloped at the top, but if U.S.D.A. doesn't know, who does?

As I said before, preservative treatment of wood posts definitely will add to their life, and whether or not you have

yours treated depends entirely on your circumstances and the kind of wood available for your posts. In your particular case, it may be false economy not to spend the additional money required to preserve your posts. But, a word of advice . . . if you do decide to have your posts treated, have it done right. You can buy pressure-treated posts in standard sizes almost anywhere in the country from authorized dealers for the manufacturer who supplies them.

SPACING POSTS

The life of your fence and the maintenance costs are closely related to the size and spacing of the fence posts. Some of the best fences have a post spacing of about 12 feet, and thousands of miles of range fences are built with posts spaced at one rod intervals. But, because we are dealing with fencing for horses, more for smaller areas than huge pastures, we'll look at spacing from this angle.

The most practical spacing for horses in smaller fenced areas using woven wire is eight feet between posts. Brace posts should be spaced at distances equal to the length of line posts used, for economy of material and labor, for this spacing eliminates the need for special horizontal braces . . . regular line posts can be used without trimming more than several inches from the ends to square them up for good fits. (See Fig. 4.) We'll cover the subject of brace posts and braces more thoroughly a little later.

On unlevel ground, spacing needs to vary with the type of terrain. Fig. 3 shows how spacing needs to be adapted to both hills and depressions in the fence

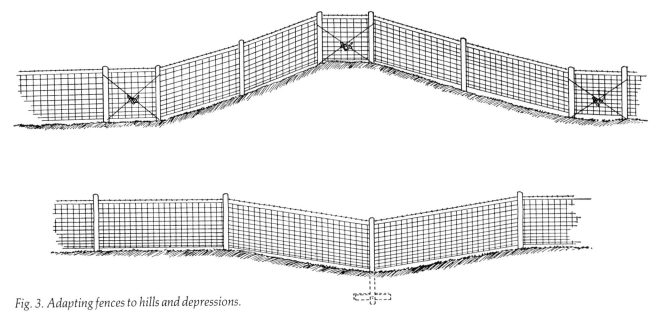

Fig. 3. Adapting fences to hills and depressions.

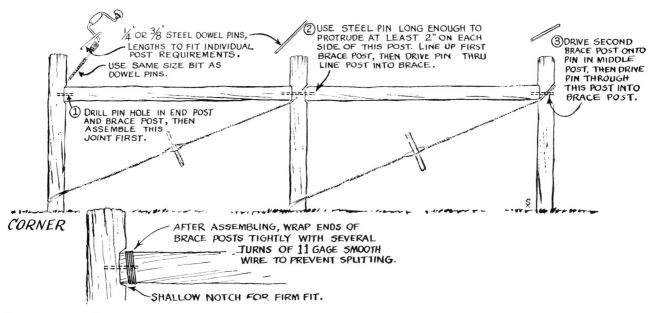

Fig. 4. Brace post details.

CONSTRUCTION

Like building a house, a barn, or a piece of furniture, good workmanship is an important factor in determining the life and service of a fence. A fence built carelessly or loosely will be expensive to keep up, and will give you no end of headaches and annoyance.

After your fence line has been located, the ground should be cleared of all stones, brush, and trash. When the corners are located, a line of sighting stakes may be erected or a line stretched. The locations of the post holes are then established along this line and marked with short stakes where exact spacing is necessary.

If your place is located where the soil is loose, chances are you'll use a post-hole auger. If your holes will be in heavy clay or hard, tight ground you'll be using a bar and digger. Wherever you dig, remember that most of the time, when the going is hard, a soaking with a little water will make your job a lot easier.

If your ground is not too stony, you may be able to hire a tractor equipped with a powered auger. And it will pay you to remember that one of these tractor-powered rigs can put down about 20 holes in the same time you're sweating over one.

line. You'll need to use a little of your own judgment in spacing posts when you run on to conditions like these. Remember, though, it's cheaper in the long run to set an extra post than to have to keep repairing a section of fence with too much space between posts.

Very often the appearance of a fence is spoiled by posts that are set out of line or at different heights or spacing. The results in looks will sure pay you to cut off the tops of any posts that are uneven. A gauge mark on a tamping bar will help you adjust the depth of your post holes as you dig them so the tops of the posts will be even when you're through setting them. And a good tamping bar is as necessary to setting a post right as the digging. A one-inch diameter steel bar, pointed on one end to aid in digging, and with a flat head welded or formed on the other end, is a mighty useful tool.

A word of advice on setting your posts. Don't use rocks to fill up the hole . . . throw them aside. It's impossible to tamp the fill as tightly around rocks as you can by filling with nothing more than dirt. And a rock-set post will loosen up almost every time. If you have to pull it and reset it, you'll teach yourself in a hurry not to use rocks. Believe me, a rock-filled hole is nasty to dig out the second time. Some people advocate using water to dampen the ground as you tamp it, but I've found that I can set a post much tighter by using the dirt just as I dug it from the hole. When you're tamping, add just a small amount of fill at a time, for you can't tamp a large amount correctly.

Just a word on the depth of holes. While rain conditions and types of soil vary widely across the nation, you can use a standard depth to set your posts 'most anywhere and have a good, tight job. I strongly recommend that corner posts, as well as first and second brace

posts, be set 42 inches into the ground. If your soil is sandy, it would be wise to set corner posts in cement. Line posts should be set 30 inches. Fig. 2 shows the depths for different post locations, and also shows the minimum diameters of posts for specific locations. Diameters shown on this drawing are small-end diameters, which is the standard way of sizing posts wherever you may buy them. For example, a four-inch post means that its diameter at the small end is four inches; it may have a diameter of six inches or more on the butt end. And, it may sound silly to even mention this, but the large end always goes into the post hole.

The foundations of a fence are its end and corner posts. Failure of these posts, and they very often do fail, means that practically the whole fence has to be rebuilt. When a line post fails, it can be removed and replaced without too much trouble. Therefore, it stands to reason that special care must be taken in the design and construction of end and corner-post assemblies. While there are many types of braces and bracing assemblies, for the types of fencing discussed here we can narrow down to one or two types of braces. These have been tried and proven in every part of the country. Their design is sound, and there are few problems encountered in building them.

The most commonly used type, and this type has been proven superior to any other similar design, is that shown in Fig. 4. Fig. 5 shows the use of this type bracing assembly in various locations in a typical fence. While no attempt was made to draw the braces in Fig. 5 to scale,

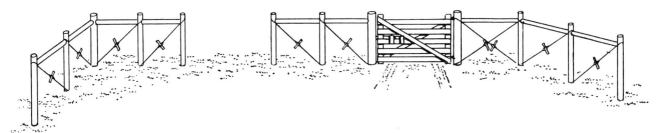

Fig. 5. The most commonly used type of bracing assembly is shown here in various locations in a typical fence.

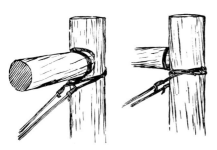

Fig. 6. A method of fastening tie or brace wires in a brace assembly. Both front and back views before the brace wire is twisted are shown here.

the drawing does show that this type brace is used in fence corners, adjacent to gate posts, and anywhere else in the fence where extra strength is needed, such as next to end posts where the fence terminates against a building, or other large structure.

Fig. 4 is complete as far as instructions on how to assemble the braces with steel dowel pins, and wrapping the ends of the braces after assembly to prevent splitting out. The brace wires are attached after the post-and-brace assembly has been completed, and Fig. 6 shows how they are fastened to the posts. Tie or brace wires between each brace post should be four strands of nine-gauge galvanized smooth wire. The quickest way to attach these wires is to use double strands, as shown in the drawing. Be sure to staple these wires securely so there'll be no slipping after you start to take the slack out of them by twisting with a lever. And, incidentally, leave the lever in place when you've twisted the wire as tight as you think it should be. You'll be using scrap pieces of wood or small limbs, and you may want to adjust the tension later. Fig. 7 shows the brace wires being twisted with the lever. Fig. 8 shows a common and inexpensive wire splicing tool that will certainly save your fingers when it comes to fastening the brace wires to the posts. This tool will come in handy as long as your fence is standing . . . for painless maintenance.

Fig. 9 shows a single-span brace assem-

bly with deadman anchors for wire braces. While this is a really strong brace, it takes much longer to construct than the simple double-span brace assembly discussed above. If you're like I am, that pick-and-shovel business is *work*, and while there's no question that any fence-building project entails plenty of *hard work*, there's little sense in doing anything the hard way when an easier way is just as good.

UNROLLING AND STRETCHING

Assuming that your posts are all set, and brace assemblies are completed, with brace wires twisted tight, now's the time to start attaching your woven-wire fencing to the posts. Whenever possible, have your wire on the same side of the posts your horses will be on. The reason for this should be obvious . . . horses

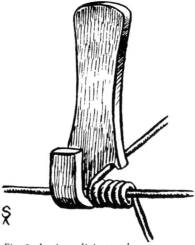

Fig. 8. A wire splicing tool.

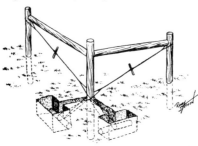

Fig. 9. Corner construction using dead-man anchors for wire braces.

Fig. 7. Twisting the brace wire.

leaning on a fence with the wire on the outside of the posts would soon have the staples jerked out and the fence in bad shape. Be sure you have the right kind of staples for the kind of posts you have. If you'll use one-and-a-half inch galvanized staples, regardless of the posts, you should be plenty safe. Shorter staples have a tendency to work loose or pull out. For greater holding power, set the staple diagonally so that each point enters a separate grain of the wood. Staples should be driven snugly but not so deep as to bury the wire in the post. (See Fig. 10.)

First set the roll of wire on end about one rod from the corner or end post. Unroll enough wire to reach to the post and make a wrap around it. Remove two or three stay wires, depending upon the circumference of the post, and place the next stay wire about three inches from the post. Start with the center line wire and wrap the end of each line wire around the post and back on to the line wire, keeping the stay wire parallel to the post. About five or six wraps around the line wire, using a splicing tool, will hold satisfactorily. (See Fig. 11.) Now unroll the fencing along the post row, keeping the bottom wire close to the posts.

Stretching should not be started until the ground around the posts has had a chance to set. Be sure that your stretcher is a strong one . . . capable of exerting enough pull to really *stretch* wire on the posts. It takes a much bigger and better stretcher to stretch woven wire than you need to stretch single strands of barbed wire. Also, be sure your clamps are dependable . . . you won't want them to slip and injure anyone or damage the wire.

You really need a double-jack stretcher for the wide woven wire, and a good clamp bar . . . one that won't let the wire slip when extreme tensions are put on. If you don't have a stretcher and clamp, I'm sure you'll be able to rent one at your ranch and farm supply store or a tool rental shop.

The entire fence should be propped up against the posts with temporary stakes before stretching starts. The stakes should be set under the top wire and leaned slightly out and away from the direction of pull so they will continue to support the fence as it is tightened. When the fence must be stretched over a ridge, two stakes should be used to support the fence and keep it from crowding down on the ground.

During the stretching operation, the whole length of the fence should be frequently inspected to make sure it is not snagged at any point. If your fencing is the type that includes line curves, the

fence is usually considered properly stretched when the tension curves on the line wires have been about half straightened out and when the fence is springy to the touch along the fence line. (See Fig. 12.) Overstretching the fence can be more harmful than understretching. If the tension curves are straightened out too much there will be no means of keeping the fence tight as temperature changes make it expand and contract.

Before the fencing is cut at the end where the stretcher is attached, the fence should be fastened to the posts on the ridges and then in each of the low places. The hinge joints on woven wire permit the wire to be pulled down into place in the low places without damaging the stay wires.

When the fence is completely adjusted, the line wires can be fastened one at a time—starting at the top. This way will be much easier than trying to pull the entire fence into line at one time, if it has to be lowered any appreciable distance. If the stretcher is left in place and the end of the roll or wire left uncut until the fence is in place on the ridges and all the low places, it is possible to tighten or loosen the tension on the fence, as may be needed.

Before cutting the end of the fencing, measure the distance around the post and allow at least six inches for the wrap around the line wire. It's a heck of a lot

Fig. 10. Staples should be driven snugly, but not so deep as to bury the wire in the post.

easier to cut a little extra wire off than to have to splice a couple of inches on. The last two stay wires should be removed before the line wires are attached to the post.

The smooth or barbed top wire is attached after the woven wire is stretched and stapled. Two men can unroll a reel of barbed wire by passing a rod through the center of the roll and letting it unreel as they walk down the fence line. One end of the barbed wire is attached to the end post or gate post before the wire is unrolled. You can stretch this single strand of barbed wire with an ordinary block and tackle stretcher and a barbed wire clamp. If you don't have a clamp, make a loop in the end of the wire and slip the hook of the stretcher through the loop.

Wires should not be fastened directly to trees along the fence line. If a tree is in the fence line, spikes may be driven into the tree and the fence wired to the spikes. Or, you can nail a two-inch board to the

Fig. 11. Attaching wires to a corner or a gate post.

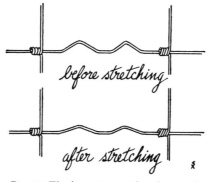

Fig. 12. The fence is considered properly stretched when the tension curves on the line wires have been about half straightened out and when the fence is springy to the touch along the fence line.

Fig. 13. Always put the wire on the outside of the posts on the curve so that it pulls against the posts.

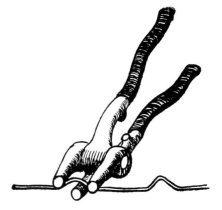

Fig. 14. Crimping tool.

tree and fasten the fence to the board.

Do not stretch wire around a corner which changes the direction of the fence line more than 45 degrees. Instead, cut it and wire it to the post . . . then stretch the rest of the fencing from that point.

If you need to place your fence line along a curve, be sure the curve is a smooth one. Always put the wire on the outside of the posts on the curve so that it pulls against the posts. (See Fig. 13.) A contour fence should be stretched only one-half to two-thirds as tightly as a straight line fence. The sharper the curve, the less tension should be applied. When stretching along a curve, go along it several times and release the fencing wherever it may have caught on the posts. On sharp curves it may be necessary to stretch at 10-rod intervals; otherwise, 20-rod intervals should prove satisfactory.

Remember . . . while stretching any woven-wire fencing, keep those stay wires as nearly vertical as possible, and never pull the top or bottom of the fence very far ahead of the other.

LIGHTNING PROTECTION

Much livestock is killed by lightning carried along a fence. In areas subject to frequent thunderstorms, it's a good idea to ground a wire fence at least every 50 rods. Grounding is especially important in fence corners where horses and cattle have a tendency to gather. A three-eighths to one-half-inch diameter rod or steel pipe, about 10 feet long, can be driven deep enough into the ground to reach permanent moisture. Fasten fence-line wires and the top strand of barbed wire securely to the rod with 11-gauge galvanized wire.

MAINTENANCE

If your fence is to have a long and useful life, you'll need to inspect it periodically, and make any necessary repairs as soon as damage or deterioration is noticed. It will help a lot to keep your fence row cleared of brush and weeds.

Be sure to keep your fence wires properly stretched. If a section of wire becomes slack, a pair of crimpers like the tool shown in Fig. 14 will allow you to add tension curves as needed, or to increase the tension in the old tension curves.

You'll need to check staples pretty often to make sure the fence is always securely fastened to the posts. And, for Pete's sake, whenever you see a broken wire, splice it right then and there. It's surprising how a single broken wire can lead to a whole section of ruined fence in a space of time you wouldn't believe possible.

Be sure to keep your eye on your end, corner, and brace posts. If you see a slack brace wire, take a few turns with the twisting lever. If you didn't do quite as good a job on one of these posts to start with, you'll be way ahead of the game if you'll jerk the defective post out of the ground and reset it.

A LOT OF COLTS are started and kept from pitching by using a good snubbing horse to lead them through the first few saddlings. This is a good method *if* you have a snubbing horse that's heavy enough and completely foolproof, and *if* you have a snubber who's done it before and knows exactly when to take or give slack and who isn't afraid of the fireworks that often occur with this process. It is a method that I wouldn't recommend for amateur horsemen. I've had a hard hoof in the face and in the belly several times when the colt tried to climb in the saddle with me—and I had just an inch or so too much slack. It's a good method, but believe me, you've got to know what you're doing and be suitably mounted for this job.

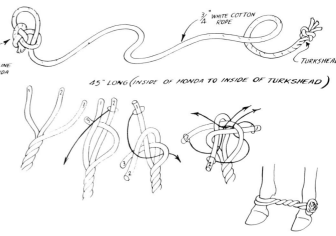

HERE'S A PAIR of hobbles you may enjoy making. You'll need a 7-foot length of 3/4-inch, three-strand white cotton rope. In one end, tie a Turk's head. Just follow the steps I've shown here. Now, 45 inches from the inside of the Turk's head, tie a honda knot, a bowline, or a bowline honda. Whichever you choose to use, make sure the loop of the honda is a tight fit on the bulky part of the Turk's head. I've shown the bowline honda here, which is the least desirable of the three, but the easiest for the amateur to make. I'd advise a regular honda—braided or tied—or a bowline loop. To use this rig as hobbles, double the completed length, take two wraps around one foot at the middle of the rope, twist between the feet several times until you have just enough left for a double wrap and button, and secure the other foot.

ROPES AND KNOTS   3

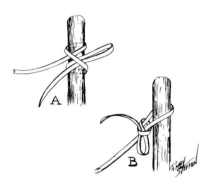

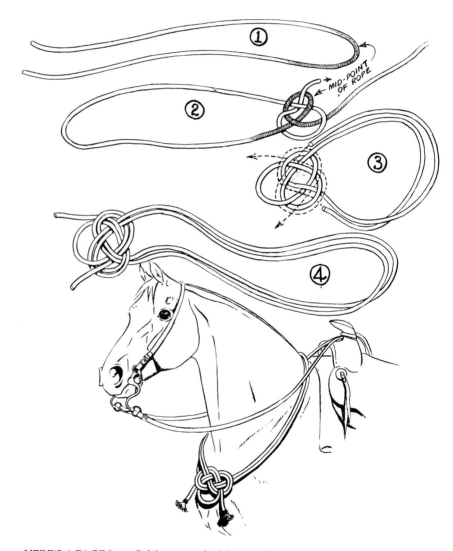

MANY'S the good rein that's been broken just because a hard knot was tied in it when hitching a saddle horse to a hitch rack, fence, or other solid mooring. A good law to enforce on yourself is, as the hoss-tradin' preacher says, "Don't ever tie up your hoss with a knot you can't jerk open!" These two knots I've shown here are used all over the cow country, and are even quicker to tie than most hard knots. Illustration A is nothing more than a simple clove hitch, with the end bent back for a quick untie. Illustration B is a conventional overhand slip knot with the end run back so a pull unties it in a single motion. Use these knots—you never can tell when your being able to untie a horse in an instant will save injury to your horse, or a person.

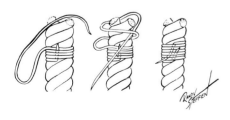

HERE'S A neat and easy way to whip the end of a rope to keep it from fraying. A dab of glue or varnish over the small cord after it's completed will keep it intact for the life of the rope.

HERE'S A PAGE from California's colorful past. This is the Alamar knot the old-time California vaquero tied in a hair rope to drape around his horse's neck for special occasions. It takes about ten feet of rope to do this one, maybe a little more or less for your horse, but you can use some common rope to determine size before cutting a fancy two-color mohair mecate to suitable length. Or, you can make three or four winds around the horse's neck and use all 20 or 22 feet to do it. After passing the end of the rope through the shaded portion that shows the mid-point of the rope, adjust the loop formed by carefully pushing and pulling the end through the shaded portion until the loop is closed up as shown in step 3. It's a simple matter to finish the knot by following the original turns with each end as shown by the dotted lines in step 3. The ends of the rope should be whipped and tasseled as a finishing touch.

31

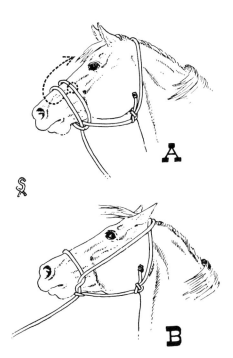

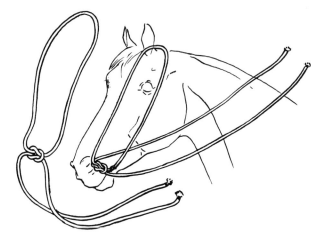

HERE'S another way to make a rope halter cheaply and effectively. First, tie a loop around your horse's neck, using the non-slip bowline. Then, two half hitches thrown around the nose and arranged as in illustration A result in the neat halter shown in illustration B.

THE OLD SQUARE knot is the basis for this emergency bridle. A piece of light rope similar to a cotton clothesline is looped over the poll and tied in a square knot inside the mouth. Be sure the knot is tied *over* the tongue. The ends form the reins.

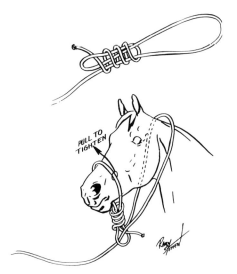

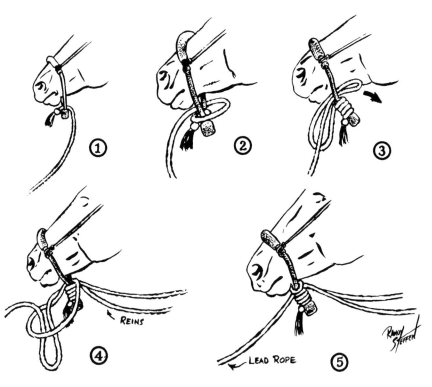

HERE'S A touch of the wild west tamed down a hair for modern horsemen. A reader in Montana uses an old saddle rope tied in a modified hangman's noose to rig a practical halter for his horse. The knot doesn't need more than four or five turns to make a good halter and is tied as shown. The halter is formed by passing the running end behind the horse's ears, then through the lower loop of the knot before it's drawn up tight. This one can be adjusted quickly to fit any size horse, although one that pulls back will have his nose pinched pretty hard!

A FRIEND FROM Abilene, Tex., asked me if I knew how to tie a *mecate* (hair rope reins) on a hackamore. Seems as though not very many horsemen in this part of the country are familiar with the California hackamore, and since that may be true of many parts of the country, these drawings show how to make the *mecate* reins and lead rope the California way. This is the way Ed Connell, author of *Hackamore Reinsman,* taught me. To tie it you'll need a hair rope (other flexible rope about $5/8$-inch in diameter will do if you don't have a hair or mohair rope) about 22 to 24 feet long, with a round Turk's head and tassel in one end.

Follow these drawings step by step, adjusting your reins for proper length when you hit step 3, and you'll wind up with a workable set of reins and lead rope combined. You can coil the lead rope and tie it on the near fork of your saddle where it'll be out of the way until you want to use it. Make as many wraps around the lower part of the hackamore bosal as you need to make it fit right, but don't make it too tight. The first principle of the hackamore is to afford relief from pressure when the reins are slacked off, so you'll want your bosal loose enough to drop away from the jaw when you slack your reins.

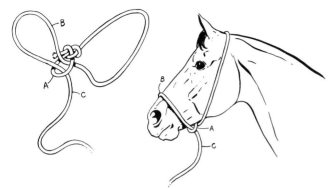

THIS IS an easily-made halter from a length of almost any kind of rope. It's one that you can slip the nose piece down over the horse's nose when you're ready to turn him loose. This is a real handy one to keep in mind for an emergency.

EVERY ONCE in a while, some of us run across a horse that will rear up every time we go to mount him and nudge him in the ribs with a boot toe as we climb aboard. Besides being an annoying habit, it's dangerous. There's not too much a rider can do when he's halfway between the ground and the saddle; a jerk on the reins as punishment might even send the horse over on his back, and on top of the rider. Chances are, after you're in the saddle, he'll settle down. If he's punished, then he won't know what it's all about. And if you step back down on the ground to discipline him, he'll have quit by then and still won't know what his punishment is for. So here's an old trick, one I remember using several years ago on a Thoroughbred polo pony that had this bad habit.

Tie a stout rope on the noseband or cavesson of your bridle, run it between the horse's front legs, through a metal ring tied to the center of your cinch, and then to a leather strap buckled securely around the horse's right hind ankle (between the joint and the foot). Tie the rope in both places with slip hitches that can be jerked loose in an emergency. Now when ol' outlaw rears up he'll pull his hind leg out from under himself and settle down in a hurry. It won't take but a treatment or two from this rope rig to make him see that rearing isn't a very profitable stunt. And what's best, he'll be punishing himself at exactly the right moment, when he can't help but associate the punishment with rearing.

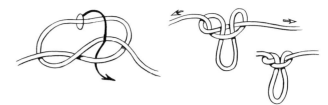

AN OLD FRIEND showed me this real simple-to-tie picket-line knot that the old horse cavalry and artillery used. It's very easy to tie at any position along the picket line. It will not slip, and it's easy to untie, even after a horse has set back on it.

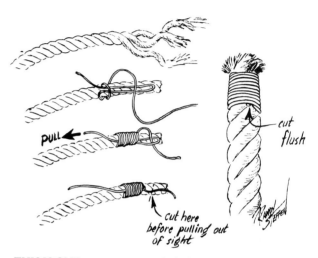

THIS IS ONE common way to lash the end of a rope to keep it from fraying. While the sketch shows the wraps starting from the rear of the rope, the most common way to lash is the reverse; that is, to place the loop at the rear and start your wraps from the front end. Either way you do it will result in a neat end to a rope that would otherwise fray.

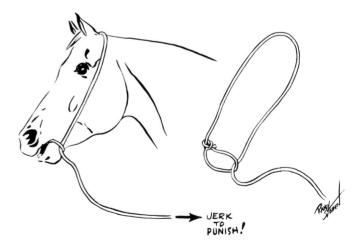

THIS VARIATION of the war bridle comes from a California reader. The loop around the jaw is tied with a snug fit, then the running end is passed up over the poll and brought through the jaw loop on the near side. When you are handling a horse's feet, sharply jerk the end of the war bridle each time he tries to take the foot away from you. It's a method of punishment that works well with green horses, but must be used with sense and caution.

33

WE HAVE a subscriber in Michigan who raises Arabians, and she has been an enthusiastic reader of these hints. She's an accomplished horsewoman and she submitted this method of tying a horse that I have never seen before. In my opinion, it's a mighty practical idea. She takes a stout, three-strand rope, makes a loop just the right size to fit over the horse's head as I've shown in my drawing, but not long enough to slip down over the nose. She makes a long splice in the rope for a permanent loop. When she's ready to tie a horse to the hitch rack, she slips the loop up through the halter and over the ears, as shown, then snugs it down and ties the long end to the hitch rack or ring.

This is much stouter than tying with a lead rope snapped to the halter, and should save a lot of halter breakage on pull-backs. She cautions that when you remove the rope, use care to see that the loop doesn't slip over the halter nosepiece and down under the jaw, for a pull-back at this moment could easily break the halter, or skin up the horse's nose.

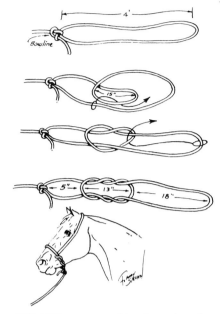

WE ARE passing on this adaptation of the old Spanish halter. The drawings show just how it is made, step by step. An advantage is that this halter is cheap and anyone can afford to keep several around the corrals.

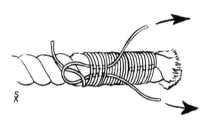

THE OTHER day I watched an old-timer making up some rope halters. He was using a little different twist in whipping the raw ends of the rope, so I figured it would be a good one to show here. His way is simple enough, and completely hides the ends of the whipping cord. Makes a real neat job, too.

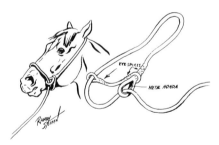

HERE'S A rope halter a friend is using to halter break colts. A ³/₄-inch rope has a metal honda braided into one end, and another short piece has a loop braided at each end, so there's about six inches between the cheeks of the halter, as shown. This will adjust to any size horse or foal, and can be made up in a few minutes. The best part about this is the fact that it won't bind tight on an animal. It slips free when pressure is released.

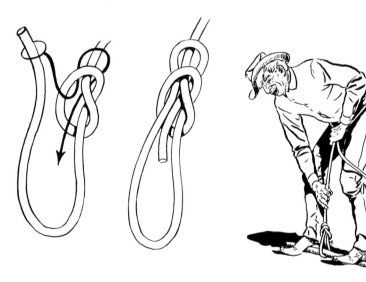

WHEN I FIRST bought a little ranch we had near Auburn, Calif., I met a grand old man, then in his late 70s or early 80s, who was still breaking colts, riding an occasional bucker, and acting as a pickup man and hazer at all the rodeos within a 50-mile radius or farther. Charley is gone now but this "center-fire" honda, as he called it, is one that I had never seen before. As he claimed, it's a good one, better for long catches than the conventional tied honda, for it uses a little more rope and is heavier. The drawing at the right shows how Charley pulled it up tight, after first wetting the knot. The hitch around the hips lets you throw a lot of beef into a pull when you straighten your legs, and standing on the stick through the honda keeps that end in place. After the end is pulled down tight, the end coming through the center is cut off so it won't interfere with the running end of the rope as it slips through the honda.

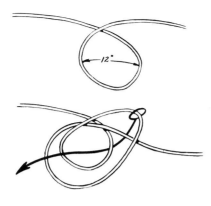

ONE OF our readers in Missouri wrote that she had concocted this emergency halter and lead. Actually, she had stumbled across an ancient type of war bridle that has been in common use by horsemen for hundreds of years; but it is a good one to know, so we are passing it on to you. She ties a small loop in one end of her rope, using a non-slip knot (I show a bowline), then threads the free end of the rope through this small loop to form a larger loop. This is fitted on the horse's head as I show, and it will make him come along nicely. Of course, with this rig, as well as with any other severe outfit that goes in the mouth, the user must use a lot of sense to keep from tearing up ol' Paint's mouth, for even a slight girl can exert tremendous leverage on the sensitive parts of the mouth with this outfit.

HERE'S another version of the packer's knot. A Canadian reader who spent quite a hitch in mountain warfare training sent us this mountaineer middleman's knot which he used in climbing those rough Canadian crags. He suggests that this knot can be adapted to leading a pack string, or as a real good picket-line knot. Like the old packer's knot, this one needs no loose ends, won't slip, and can be untied with ease.

AN OLD Sandhills rancher who runs a 22-section spread near Sutherland, Neb., and who is still a mighty slick hand with a rope, comes up with a hint that's being used by hard-and-fast ropers in some parts of the country where steer ropers are plentiful. A heavy chain link, of the right size to take two sections of your rope, is rigged like I've shown in the drawing to form a horn knot. Use a Matthew Walker or other end knot to keep it from slipping through the link, and you'll have a horn knot that's simple and quick to make, and will hold anything your rope or your pony will. These chain links can be bought in any size to fit any rope, from the light maguey to the heavy steer roper's nylon.

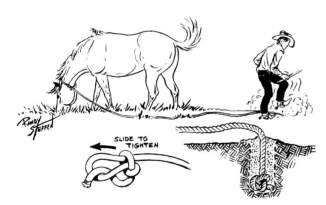

NEXT TIME you want to stake your horse out and there's no brush, buildings, or stake pin to tie to, use this little Texas trick and I'll guarantee it'll hold if your stake rope's 20 feet or more in length. Tie the kind of simple knot I've shown in the end of your stake rope, just to make a bulky end on it, then dig a hole in the ground about eight inches deep, and large enough in diameter to squeeze the knot down into. Then, with your boot heel, stomp the thunder out of the hole, packing it as tight as you comfortably can and your old pony'll be there hours later when you're ready to saddle up again. There's a horse-trading preacher in Texas who will give you five-to-one that you can't pull a knot like this out of the ground—even if the other end is tied hard and fast to your saddle horn. That's on a lariat 25 feet long or more.

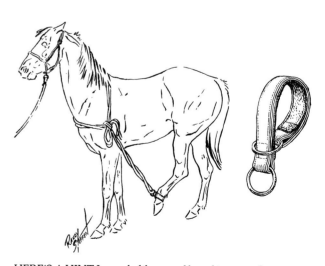

HERE'S A HINT I sure do like myself, and it comes from a Canadian reader. He tells me he has used this foot strap since 1917. This idea will save burned heels on ol' ponies that fight a Scotch hobble. It's made by sewing in a large steel ring at each end of a 2- or 3-ply leather strap, about 1½-inches wide, and 9 inches long, finished. Of course, you'll have to put the end of the strap through the one ring before the second one is sewed in place. My friend further padded this rig by sewing a heavy layer of felt on the inside. Yes, sir! I'm all for this'n.

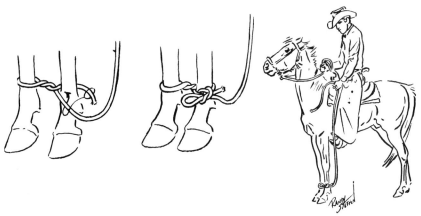

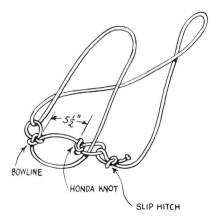

A READER CAME up with this suggestion for saddling and mounting horses that won't stand, or those ornery ones that try to swallow their heads before you get that off stirrup. He uses a 1/2-inch or larger soft cotton rope about eight or ten feet long, ties a twist hobble just above the ankles like I've shown, and carries the free end of the slip hitch to the saddle with him. When he's got a deep seat he can tug lightly on the rope, free the slip hitch, and by pulling gently toward the rear of the horse, release the rest of the hobble so it falls to the ground. Be sure to allow no more free end of the rope than is absolutely necessary to make the slip hitch. Any excess length here will make the job of shaking the hobbles free a tough one.

THIS ROPE bridle is very effective. When the reins are pulled, the rope under the jaw tightens, exerting pressure on the jawbone nerves and on the poll nerves at the same time. It is made from a 22-foot length of rope, and is tied as I've shown in the drawing, using standard knots that everyone should be able to tie without much difficulty.

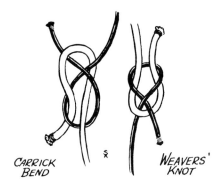

AS RELIABLE as the square knot is, there are times when this reputable old standby won't get the job done. This is always true when you're tying two ropes of different sizes together; then you'll want to use either one of the two knots I've drawn here. You should be able to tie them by looking at the drawing if you're not already familiar with them, as the knots are sometimes used to tie a leader to a fish line.

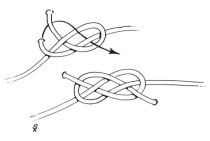

HERE'S AN old knot, familiar to many, that comes in handy so often. Its chief use is to tie two big, heavy, stiff ropes together, and it is ideal for tying two stiff saddle ropes together to make an emergency fence or picket line without putting a permanent kink in the ropes.

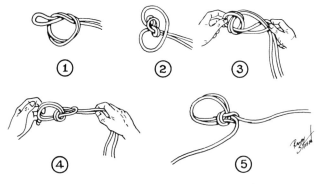

HERE'S AN OLD cow country knot that some cowboys use when heeling calves at branding time. A long rope, generally 30 to 40 feet, is used, with a honda at each end. This knot is tied in the middle and fastened to the saddle horn. Each end of the rope is coiled and fastened to the fork of the saddle so the roper has two ropes to work his calves with. The Indian-fighting cavalry also used this knot to improvise picket lines on bivouac. One of these knots was tied every six or eight feet along the picket line, and the lead ropes of the troop horses were tied into the loops with an ordinary slip hitch. If you ever need a picket line on club rides, remember this one.

HERE'S A WAY you can drag firewood, or anything else, behind your horse without wearing out your good saddle rope. Use a piece of stout rope and tie it to the log or other object with a half hitch and a "twisteroo" like I've drawn, and fasten the horn-loop end of your saddle rope to the free end of the other rope with either a carrick bend or a weaver's knot. Then drag 'er to your heart's content with no worry about rocks or the hard ground eating up your good rope.

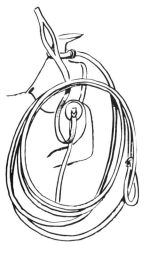

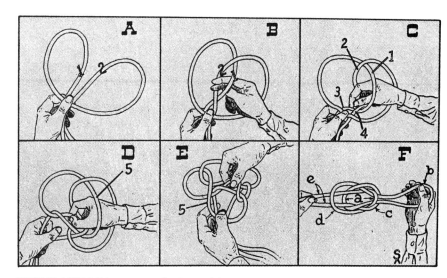

THIS IS AN EASY way to tie the Spanish hackamore heel knot, used with a fiador on the California hackamore. While I've drawn these diagrams with a single strand, you tie it exactly the same way with your rope doubled. This is the way the Navy used to teach their men to tie the "jug knot," for these two knots are exactly the same. In the days of the old sailing ships, jugs of one kind or another were hoisted aboard ship by slipping the neck of the jug through the center of the knot ("a" in step F) and pulling it up the side. If you follow the steps closely, you'll be able to master the knot after a short time.

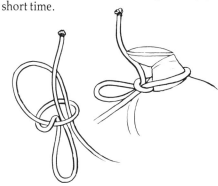

A READER in California tells us that he uses this quick-release horn knot when roping calves. "It'll hold anything your horse can hold," he says, and it can be released fast in an emergency. He cautions anyone who uses this to leave plenty of free end so it can be grabbed fast in a tight situation.

A GOOD many years ago, an old-timer in Maverick County, Tex., was riding with me on a horse gather. Without saying a word, when we got off to stretch our legs, he reached over and cut the rope strap off the fork of my saddle with his pocket knife. He then slit the end of a saddle string at the bow, after measuring it to the horse, and fastened my rope to the saddle as I've shown here. I'd heard of riders getting bucked off and hanging a spur in their saddle rope and, while I've never seen this happen, it sends shivers down my spine when I do think about it.

With the rope string slit this way, it'll break when a man's weight is thrown on it, whereas a stout strap and buckle would hold and could be the death of a man. There are other ways to use a slit strap for holding the rope against the fork of the saddle, but this is one of the best and holds the rope where it doesn't chafe the saddle or your leg.

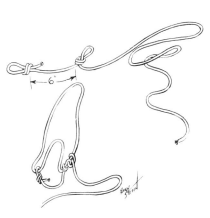

THIS ROPE halter is one of the simplest and most practical homemade halters I've ever seen and I've run across a lot of them. It can be made from just any piece of rope in a matter of a few seconds, and won't slip off the animal's head when he's staked out. A simple overhand knot secures the lead part of the rope, and prevents the halter from changing size and loosening.

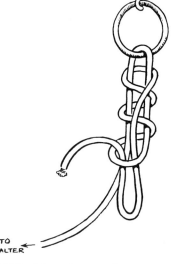

TO HALTER

HERE'S A knot that's used to tie up a horse or cow that's bad about slobbering. An old-timer writes from Fair Oaks, Calif., that he has been tying up stock from Montana to Yuma for a good many years and that this hitch will not jam no matter how wet an animal gets it. And naturally, it won't slip.

37

HERE'S one of the simplest makeshift bridles you'll ever find, and with it you can control the liveliest horse you can mount bareback. The drawing explains it; all I need to say is that a small-diameter rope works best, from a quarter to a half inch. But, take it easy on the horse's mouth—you can get mighty severe with this rig.

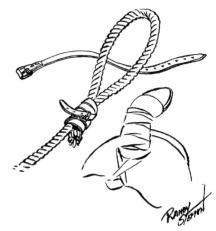

ANOTHER good one for the working cowboy and the arena roper comes from a working cowboy who uses this leather strap to make a quick-release horn knot. He writes, "For a hard-and-fast knot that I use in contest roping and for doctoring steers on the range, I use a 1/2- or 5/8-inch-wide leather strap about a foot long with a good buckle on one end. By wrapping it around the doubled horn end of my rope, I have a horn knot that I can undo by merely yanking the tongue out of the buckle in case of a storm, like when my saddle turned last summer."

This beats fishing for a knife to cut yourself loose from something more than you dare keep tied to—and maybe saves a good rope, plus your neck.

2-half hitches   Bowline knot

THIS ROPE HALTER is easy to tie whenever you need to lead a horse and you don't have a ready-made halter at hand. First, tie a bowline to form a fairly snug loop around the neck, up close to the throat. Then, using the free end, throw two half-hitches around the nose; take the loop of the hitch closest to the horse's eyes, pull it toward the nose and under the second half-hitch, and then place it over the poll, back of the ears. Work the rope around until it fits well, and lead him off. It won't tighten down when tied right, and will be comfortable to your horse.

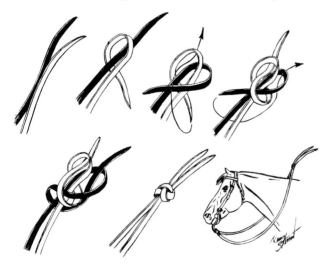

MANY HORSEMEN like to tie their split reins in a knot to keep them from coming off their saddle or horse's neck when they dismount. Most of them use a simple overhand knot that doesn't look too good no matter who ties it. Here's a two-strand Turk's head and diagrams showing how to tie it step by step, that will make tied bridle reins look mighty neat. And it's simple to tie—just try it.

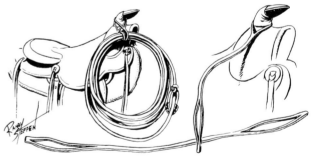

MANY A COWBOY has hung his spur in the coils of his saddle rope when a colt proved more than he could stick to. You can bet your best pair of Sunday boots you'll never find a rider who has had this experience fastening his rope to the saddle with the regular rope strap most saddles are fitted with. This drawing shows the most common method of hanging a saddle rope in all parts of the cow country. Use a thin piece of whang leather, slotted at both ends to fit over the horn, and long enough to make several wraps around the coil. It's thin enough to break if a foot or spur hangs in the rope, and prevents the rider from being dragged. For safety's sake, put one on your saddle today.

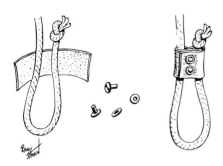

HERE'S another horn loop that's easy to make. Maybe you're like me, you don't think much of it at first glance. I'll admit I didn't either. A number of years ago, I ordered a new catch rope from a friend of mine in Cisco, Texas. When I went into his shop to pick it up, I found he'd made this type of horn loop on one end, and a conventional honda with a wear leather on the other. The honda was swell, but, although I didn't say anything to my friend, I didn't much like the horn loop. It was too bulky, I thought. Besides, a few years before, I'd learned to dally rope in Nevada and was used to a little *casca-bob* on the end of my rope, and no horn loop at all. But I did a lot of corral roping with that rope, and came to like it fine as long as I was horseback. Maybe you'll like it, too. It's easy to make.

FOR THOSE HORSEMEN who like to let a horse or pony graze at the end of a rope while they're doing a little relaxing, too, here's a way to keep the lead rope from getting snarled up in the horse's feet. Tie a scrap piece of rope as shown, securing it to the horse's mane to keep it from slipping out of place; then run the lead rope between the horse and the rope, and you'll have it made. This is not to be used for staking a horse—only when the end of the rope is being held by someone.

HERE'S A useful rope hitch. As long as a steady pull is exerted on it there'll be absolutely no slip. A flip of the slack frees it so a man doesn't have to get off his horse. This same hitch can be used to tie a horse's leg up to his tail, or to head and tail a bunch of led horses or pack animals.

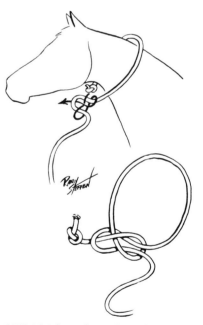

HERE'S A knot that's almost like the familiar sheet bend, so effective for tying two ropes of different sizes together, but not quite like it. A Canadian reader writes that he stumbled across this one years ago and has been using it ever since. He uses it (instead of a bowline) to tie up a horse and claims it's easy to untie even after the horse sets back on it. The knot in the end is necessary, although a neat crown knot would look better than the simple overhand I've shown. It's an easy one to tie.

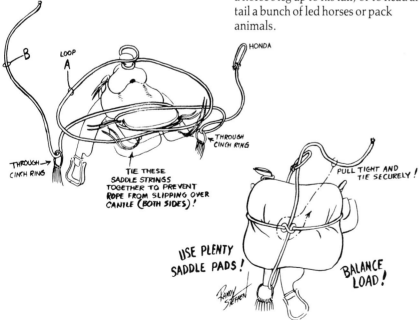

B

LOOP A

HONDA

THROUGH CINCH RING

THROUGH CINCH RING

TIE THESE SADDLE STRINGS TOGETHER TO PREVENT ROPE FROM SLIPPING OVER CANTLE (BOTH SIDES)!

USE PLENTY SADDLE PADS!

PULL TIGHT AND TIE SECURELY!

BALANCE LOAD!

A MAN HUNTING by himself on horseback without a pack animal often has a tough time packing out his meat if he's lucky enough to bag a big one. Here's a way to pack a riding saddle as effectively as a regular sawbuck pack saddle. This, and many more practical tips on the art of packing, are to be found in Joe Back's wonderful little book, *Horses, Hitches, and Rocky Trails.*

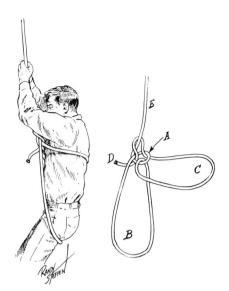

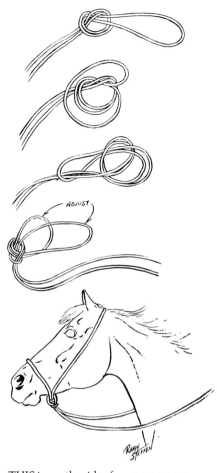

THIS variation of the bowline will allow you to hoist even an unconscious man up a canyon wall without any danger of his falling out of the rig. In the Navy we called this a French bowline. It's formed in the same manner as the regular bowline, except that the end (D), instead of going around the standing part (E) at once, is given a turn about the bight of the goose neck (A) and then the knot is finished off in the regular way. This leaves two loops which are loosely connected to the goose neck. The loops are made so a man can sit in one (B) while the other (C) goes under his armpits, the knot being in front of his chest. The weight of the man tightens the armpit loop, keeping him securely in the rig even if he's unconscious. Every horseman who rides over remote and dangerous mountain trails should master this variation of the bowline. It may save a life one day.

HERE'S A rope buckle that's as old as the hills. Almost every packer in the country makes good use of it every time he loads an animal. Some use it with a bowline-on-a-bight; others won't have any part of it without an eye splice in one end of the rope. Whichever way you use it, it's a most useful knot. The one on the right is a double-locked rope buckle, as secure as any knot a packer might use, yet easy to adjust or undo.

HERE I've shown a method of tying up your lead rope so it'll be out of the way, but can still be undone in a hurry. Pass the running end through the fork of the saddle and tie around the horn, using a slip hitch knot.

THIS is another idea for an emergency hackamore and a good one. It takes about ten feet of rope to make, and is done by tying a bowline-on-a-bight loosely, then adjusting the two final loops so that one fits over the muzzle, and the other over the ears. The knot under the jaw will not slip, but will allow good control. This one shouldn't take over a minute to make, start to finish.

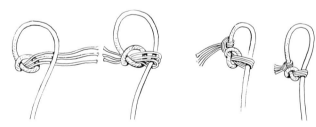

I'VE HAD quite a few people ask me how to make a horn loop in a saddle rope. Here's a method that I learned many years ago. The steps are self-explanatory. Be sure, when the knot is ready to pull down tight, that the knot is well dampened—then pull it up tight and let it dry completely in the shade. When it's dry, cut the ends off within an inch of the knot for a horn loop that will slip freely, and hold a mighty big load. Be sure to allow enough freedom in the stranded loop to allow the rope to slide freely—a horn loop that binds on itself is no better than a hard knot when you have to turn loose in a hurry.

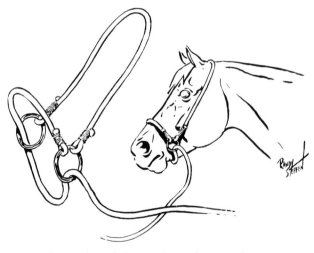

THIS ROPE and ring halter can be made up in a few minutes, and is a good one to tie up a horse, for it will squeeze down if he pulls back, and slack off as soon as he steps up.

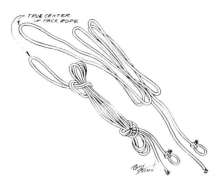

THIS IS one method of tying up a pack rope when it's not in use. If you follow this method, the true center of the pack rope is always right at hand, at the top, and the two ends are at the bottom where they can be flipped out easily. This kind of tie will save time and handling in throwing any kind of a hitch on a pack.

A FRIEND who is an authority on the old cavalry has helped me many times with research on my books about the horse soldier. The last time I visited with him he showed me this picket-line hitch that was used by our cavalry. I show two ways to tie it here—with and without a quick-release loop. As always, I recommend that you never tie up a horse with a hard knot of any kind.

ONE OF my cutting horse friends showed me this method of keeping the ends of his ropes from coming undone. After tying a Matthew Walker knot or a Turk's head in the end, he dips the knot in glue or shellac and sets the rope aside to dry for a couple of hours.

WHEN the rope you're using is too short for its job and you have to tie two ropes together and pass them through a rigging ring, a grommet, or an eye of some kind, here's a much better way to fasten them together than tying a knot. This reeving of two lines together, as they say in the Navy, presents far less bulk than any knot. It's properly termed a reeving-line bend.

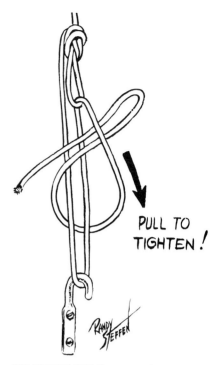

PULL TO TIGHTEN!

ALMOST EVERY horseman has occasion to tie down a load of some kind. Whether it's on a pack horse or a pickup, it needs to be tied tightly and securely. Here's a modified trucker's hitch that will do the job. An overhand knot with a loop forms a sort of pulley through which the loose end of the rope can be pulled to tighten a lashing. A simple overhand hitch, with a loop so the knot can be jerked loose in a hurry, secures this hitch well. Practice it a few times, then see how often you'll use it.

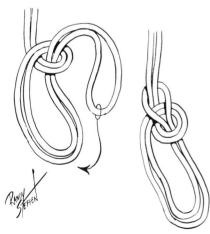

THERE have been several times when I've had to use a loop made with a bowline for lifting heavy weights which could have snapped a single strand of rope. This bowline-on-bight knot allows you to use your rope doubled and is easy to tie. Comes in right handy around a pack string, or anywhere ropes and horses are used.

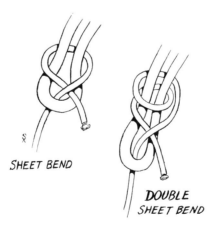

SHEET BEND

DOUBLE SHEET BEND

THE SHEET bend has a real fine reputation among seamen, packers, and horsemen in general as being a reliable knot for tying the ends of two ropes of different sizes together, and one that won't bind on itself and be difficult to open. As good as the sheet bend is, the double sheet bend is even more reliable and just as easy to tie.

THIEF KNOT— NO GOOD!   SQUARE KNOT

GOOD!

SOME TIME ago, in a 4-H class on horses that I was helping out with, a little girl kept telling me her square knot pulled right out. It took me a few minutes to figure out what she'd done wrong, for at first glance, her knot sure looked like a square knot. Then I noticed that the ends of the rope were on the opposite sides of the knot instead of on the same side, and that is what seamen call the *thief* knot. It is far worse than a granny knot and it won't hold a thing. Compare it with the square knot shown and see if you can figure how to tie it. Bet it will take you a few minutes.

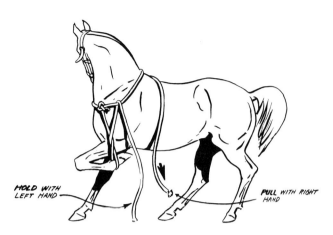

HOLD WITH LEFT HAND

PULL WITH RIGHT HAND

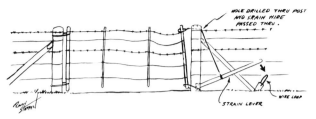

HOLE DRILLED THRU POST AND STRAIN WIRE PASSED THRU.

STRAIN LEVER

WIRE LOOP

WE GOT a kind of big ha-ha from a reader who was referring to a method of throwing a horse that we described in which some of the throwing ropes were placed on the hind feet of the bronc. Her hilarity stemmed from thinking that if a bronc was gentle enough so you could reach down and slip some fetters on his heels, he more than likely wouldn't need throwing. Well, the method I described was to be used with a bronc chute and you know, it is possible that I forgot to mention the chute! Anyway, here's how she does it.

She ties a fairly loose loop around the neck, deep at the shoulder, using a bowline knot. Then she slips the running end of that rope up through this "collar," leaving a loop at the end. Then she slips the loop over a front foot at the pastern, making a twist or two in the loop before slipping it over the foot. By pulling on the running end with her left hand, she can lift that foot clear off the ground and bend the leg until the hoof touches the elbow; it takes little effort to hold it in that position.

Now, by pulling on the lead shank that's snapped to the halter ring and passed over the back right at the withers, she can pull the head around far enough to where it takes just a slight tug to topple ol' hoss right down on his side. His feet will be out to the right and his head in just the right position to fall on, so you can keep him down as long as you like. And, as she says, he doesn't go down with a thud; he just eases down with no scare, no bruises. It's a sure-enough good method and one that's been used all over the cow country for better than a hundred years.

WE GET LETTERS from around the world from readers who enjoy these little tips. One of our contributors in Australia writes that he has used many of these hints on his outfit, and he has passed on to us a few of his own ideas. This is one type of gate latch used on Australian cattle stations (ranches), and while it's some different from anything I've ever seen in our own cow country, it sure looks good to me. The strain lever shown here exerts enough force on the wire gate to pull it up really tight when the wire loop is slipped over the end. Notice that the big post is mortised out for the butt of the strain lever to fit into.

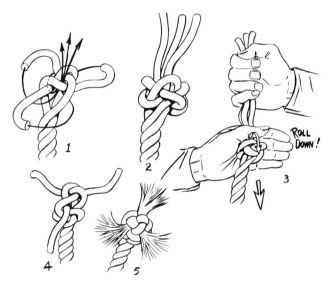

ROLL DOWN!

1 2 3 4 5

HERE'S A bulky end-knot for a rope that takes the place of the more common Turk's head. I don't know what this one is called but it is a good one. After unwinding the strands as shown, make the first step in the knot per Fig. 1; the arrows in Fig. 1 show where to thread each end to come out as shown in Fig. 2. Now hold the knot and ends as shown in Fig. 3, and skin the knot down so the top half winds up on the bottom; then pull the ends tight. Now go back to Fig. 1, and make the same tie—as shown in Fig. 4. You can now fray the ends as I've shown, or if you're using nylon, cut them short and sear them.

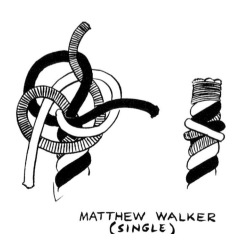

MATTHEW WALKER (SINGLE)

MATTHEW WALKER (DOUBLE)

WHILE THE Matthew Walker knot has been shown before, I've had so many requests from readers to illustrate both the single and double that I'm including them both here. I've tried to draw these diagrams as clearly as possible. Believe me, it's not nearly as hard to tie the knots as it is to draw them.

That Old Cotton Rope

NEXT TIME one of your ponies starts acting up and gets hard to control, think of that old cotton rope before losing your temper. That pony has you outweighed and outmuscled, but the cotton rope has proved to be one of the best "equalizers" known to the horse handler. A little know-how in its use and application can quickly bring the unruly horse around to your way of thinking, and be a great saver of your time, strength, and patience.

Fig. 1. A great many ranches, especially those in the Northwest, break their horses after they have reached four years of

Fig. 1

Fig. 2a

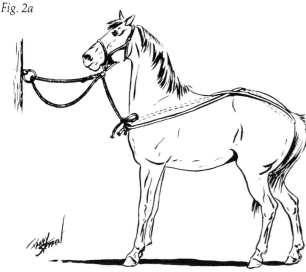

Fig. 2b

age . . . and by that time a range pony has become stout enough to be dangerous to mess with. Since both ends of the horse must be broke, the heels as well as the head, it's often necessary to employ some safety measure in gentling the heels, to keep your head from being kicked into the next county. The old reliable method, used by horsemen on every continent, is the poling method—using a long pole to accustom the green bronc to handling every part of his body.

First lay the bronc down, using the easy method described in the Fig. 2a copy. When he's quit struggling to get up, use a long stick or pole to rub his hind legs and hindquarters from the safety of the far end, as shown in Fig. 1. Don't use the war bridle any more than is absolutely necessary . . . and then do so with a sharp jerk to punish the horse when he tries to kick during the poling process. Just one or two treatments of this medicine will make him gentle about his hind parts without your risking a foot in the face.

Fig. 2a. The serious horseman sometimes finds it necessary to lay a horse down to doctor him, or for some other important reason. Unless he knows a method that will allow him to overcome the horse's greater strength, someone or something's liable to be hurt. And those of you who have valuable horses sure don't want to take a chance on injuring them.

The method illustrated here is an old one, and one of the easiest on man and horse this writer has ever used. The drawing shows the necessary equipment—a length of stout, large-diameter *cotton rope* (hard twist hemp will burn the tender skin under the tail, cotton rope will not), and a 10- or 15-foot length of smaller cotton rope, to form a sort of war bridle as shown. Cotton clothesline that has had all the sizing washed out of it will do nicely for the war bridle.

Now for the doing. Use a short piece of rope and take two half hitches around the forefoot, as shown, on the side you want to be down. Tie this foot rope with a slip knot, for safety's sake in case you have to turn him loose in a hurry, to the large cotton rope that's been looped around the belly, then crossed through an old harness ring, and passed under the tail. This tie will prevent your horse from fighting that tied-up foot so much, for he punishes himself at the root of the tail when he does, and that's a tender spot.

Make your war bridle by tying a loop around the neck, up close to the throatlatch as shown, using a bowline. Pass the running end down through the mouth, so the free end comes out the side that will be up when the horse lays down. Now pass the free end through the harness ring at the withers, and bring it forward, where the cowboy stands in the drawing. Now you're ready to lay him down . . . but remember to be easy!

Start to pull easy, allowing him to struggle a short time before increasing the pull. In a short time he'll lie down easily of his own accord, and holding him there is a simple matter of keeping pressure on the war bridle rope—just enough pressure to keep him from trying to struggle to his feet.

Fig. 2b. This is a way to halter break big stout colts, and grown broodmares that have never been handled, without a lot of fuss and sweat. It's a quick way, too, and much easier on the horse than merely tying him by the head to a tree or post. Here again, be sure to use a large-diameter cotton rope under his tail.

You'll notice on the drawing that the cotton rope is crossed on the rump, and tied in front of the breast. Now take a good stout lead rope with a snap in the end, snap it in the halter ring, run the free end through a stout ring in the hitch post, or around the tree or post that will do the anchoring—then back through the halter ring, and down to the large cotton rope, where you'll tie

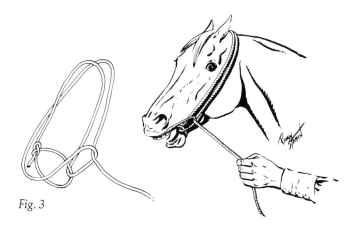

Fig. 3

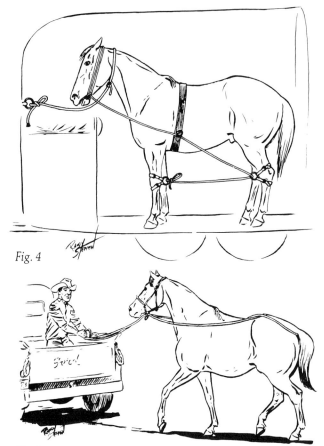

Fig. 4

it securely with a slip hitch, again for safety's sake.

Be sure the rope is around the post high enough to prevent any possibility of the horse getting his front feet over the rope. It won't take but a comparatively short time for the horse to convince himself that fighting the rope is foolishness—his tail will tell him that in a hurry! Tie him this way for an hour or more at a time for several days, then by just the halter alone for a day or two, and you'll have a horse that will never be a halter puller.

Fig. 3. This is a type of war bridle that has several names that I know of. Among them are the Comanche bridle, Bonaparte bridle, and Napoleon halter. While it can be cruel if used roughly, it can also be used humanely by anyone with a fair share of common sense to achieve more results in horse training quicker than most any other method. Its only purpose is re-straint and punishment when breaking the horse, and is used by standing at or near the shoulder and jerking lightly when the animal resists or does something wrong. Cotton clothesline that has had the sizing soaked out of it should be used. Notice the business end of this bridle is looped over the gums of the upper teeth. We'll show this rig in use doing specific jobs in other parts of this series of drawings.

Fig. 4. If your horse kicks, stomps, and paws in the trailer or stall, here's a way to make him cure himself of this habit—and not get hurt doing it. The drawing shows how to rig the sur-cingle and the straps around the front leg and the hock. The straps should be stout enough to prevent breaking from the first kick . . . but after that, wrapping twine would probably do just as well. If your animal is a kicker, you won't need the straps on the front leg . . . but if he paws, rig him just as shown here. The

rings at both hock and front leg should be at least three-inch ones. Old cinch rings can't be beat!

Fig. 5. Here's the same old cotton rope crossed under the tail again, only this time we're using it to break a horse to lead well behind a pickup, or another horse, without pulling back. Don't know about you, but I've had my arms ache like a toothache from leading pullers or just plain lazy horses from another horse—and this rig always cured that vice quicker than the time it takes to put it on. You can sure persuade a reluctant one to jump in a trailer with this rig, too.

Fig. 6. Some time ago at a small rodeo and livestock show

Fig. 6

Fig. 7

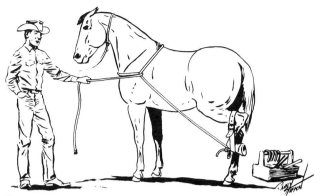

Fig. 8

Fig. 9

here in Texas, a bunch of prize hogs broke loose as they were being transferred from one barn to another, and made a mad dash for a line of ropers' horses that were tied to one section of the arena fence. As the porkers squealed their way right behind the horses, all but one flew back against his reins or lead rope, broke free, and stampeded away. The horse that stayed was as scared as any of the others, but he respected his reins more than he feared the hogs and stayed put, never taking up all the slack.

After this incident, I talked with the owner of the horse that stayed and picked up a darned handy training tip. My illustration pretty well explains it. Again the old cotton rope under the tail, but this time both ends are brought up through the halter ring and tied to the tree or post that will serve as the anchor. Now for the secret of the whole thing. Notice the light rope that's tied to the halter ring and to the post? It's a little shorter than the cotton rope, and it's been nearly cut in two at about the middle, so it will break easy. Now the trick is to get in front of the horse, roll a barrel toward him and yell like a Comanche, or shoot a gun in the air. Do anything to booger him back hard enough to break that light rope and let him come up hard against that cotton rope under his tail. About two doses of this medicine will break the worst halter puller. Even with a horse permanently cured of this habit, it's never a good idea to tie your horse up with the reins. Always use a tie rope of some kind that is a good deal stouter than leather reins.

Fig. 7. Some horses have a cranky disposition, or an unusually sensitive skin, or just don't like to stand still, and so are hard to control while grooming. The Bonaparte bridle, described in Fig. 3 and shown on the horse's head here, will enable you to cure one of this habit in a short time. When he dances away from you, or turns around and tries to bite, jerk on the lead, but just hard enough to make him stand still.

Fig. 8. When it comes to shoeing their hind feet, some horses are real devils. If yours is this way, and your blacksmith doesn't already know this trick, use it and show him you know a little something about horses yourself. The strap on the hock and ankle should be wide enough to keep from cutting, and the rope is tied around the ankle below the fetlock. The hitch around the neck makes it easy for you to hold the foot in position while your farrier trims the foot and sets the shoe. Of course, you can use the Bonaparte bridle to control the horse here, too . . . and with good results.

Fig. 9. Fence-jumping horses, once they get the habit, are mighty hard to keep in any kind of an enclosure they can see over. Here's a simple enough rig that will allow them to walk and graze freely, but which will literally set them down on their backside when they try to jump a fence. Notice the ropes under the belly go from near front leg to off hind leg, and from off front leg to near hind leg . . . being crossed as they go through the surcingle.

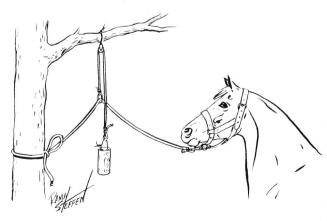

HERE'S A GIMMICK from a lady who uses this on her frequent camping trips. She says her horse, who ordinarily runs in his own pasture, is reluctant to lie down when tied to a tree on these camping trips. Now she ties him to a tree with a length of cotton rope; then arranges her pulley-and-weight gimmick so that the weight of the sand-filled can keeps the slack out of the rope to enable the horse to lie down without being afraid of becoming tangled in the tie rope. She fastens the can to the clothesline with a piece of baling wire. The other end of the clothesline is tied to a metal ring, through which the tie rope slides freely. She says this works fine on a horse that won't panic with a rope dangling near his head.

4 AROUND RANCH AND HOME

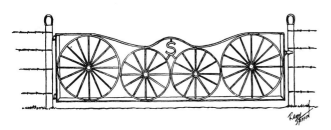

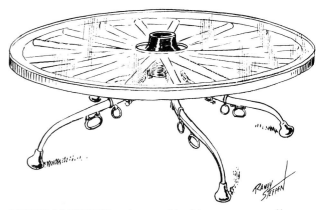

THIS IS AN iron gate that's both useful and attractive on a place where there are horse-minded folks. Passed one like this on my way to Austin, Tex., and I stopped on my way back to make a quick sketch. The side and bottom members are 1¹/₂-inch angle iron, welded with a 45-degree angle joint. The piece that's curved to fit the contour of the wheels across the top is a ⁵/₈-inch steel rod, welded to the top of each wheel. And the wheels are old iron ones rescued from obsolete farm equipment. The wheels are welded to each other and the frame members of the gate at each point of contact. The brand in the top center is formed from welded pieces of ⁵/₈-inch rod. A coat of bright aluminum or white paint makes a gate that will really glisten. The one I saw had iron posts as shown, with a horseshoe welded at the top on either side. This is a husky gate that's extremely easy and inexpensive to make.

HERE'S AS CLEVER and as good-looking a western coffee table as I've ever had the pleasure of seeing. The reader who sent me this one used an old buggy wheel, sanded it well, stained it, then applied several coats of varnish. Four metal buggy hames make the legs. The maker said he sawed the rings from the hames, but I show them still attached. You can do whatever suits your fancy. The hames are welded to the hub, and the hub and hames were given several coats of flat black enamel. The brass knobs on the ends of the hames help protect the floor or rug, and when they're polished, add a bit of equine glamour that is hard to beat.

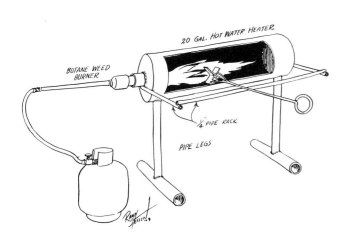

HERE'S A MIGHTY useful branding iron heater you can make if you are handy with welding tools. The one I saw was made from an old 20-gallon water tank, some scrap pipe, and a butane weed burner. The device can be carried easily to chute or pasture.

IN SPITE OF the publicity about abandoned refrigerators, they still can be mighty useful on a working ranch. Placed by the corrals and chutes, an old fridge can provide a clean storage place for vaccines, syringes, and the other medical supplies used at branding and dehorning time. It would be just as handy around a horse barn.

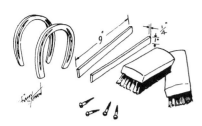

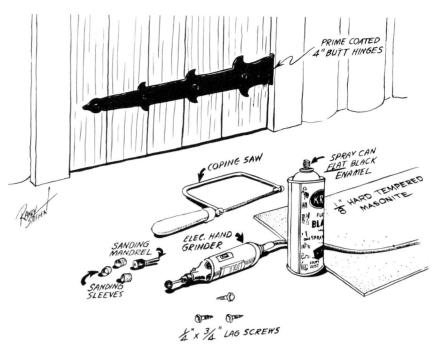

HERE'S A good-luck symbol, a gadget the lady of the house will be grateful for, and a mighty handy outfit to keep the mud slicked off your boots. You can make it easy enough with the help of your local welder. The flat pieces of iron or steel need to be welded to the two No. 2 or No. 3 horseshoes, after the heels have been bent over and drilled as shown in the drawing. Then it's a simple matter to fasten two good stiff-bristled brushes to the horseshoes with a screwdriver and four slim wood screws. You may have to drill holes in each of the nail slots in the horseshoes to get your screws through. The holes in the heels allow you to fasten the boot scraper and cleaner firmly to the porch floor.

IN THE process of building a new studio, I saved some money and still got an old-time air by making some fake hinges of masonite. First, I drew a design on heavy paper, exact size, and traced it onto a sheet of 1/8-inch masonite. The masonite was cut with a power jigsaw (or use a coping saw), and 1/4-inch holes were drilled for the lag screws. A 1/2-inch burring tool in an electric hand grinder gave the masonite a hand-hammered appearance, after which the hinge was sanded and the edges rounded. A penciled outline of the hinge was made on the door, contact cement spread inside the outline and on the back of the hinge, which was painted with a flat black, and the affair glued in place and then fastened with the lag screws.

WATERING LIVESTOCK in northern climates during the winter is a constant battle with Mother Nature for most cowmen and horse owners. Here's a practical solution that has proved itself over a period of years for a reader in Michigan—and that is really cold country. He tells us the steel water tank forms ice on the inside, but when the water is turned on and left running for ten or fifteen minutes, the higher temperature of the water will melt the ice enough so it can be removed in a single chunk. The drainage details shown here—the hole in the elbow, the drainage sump, and the air pinhole in the freeze-proof valve by the house are all vital to the proper operation of this system. I believe this is worth some effort to build if you live where the water lines freeze in the winter months.

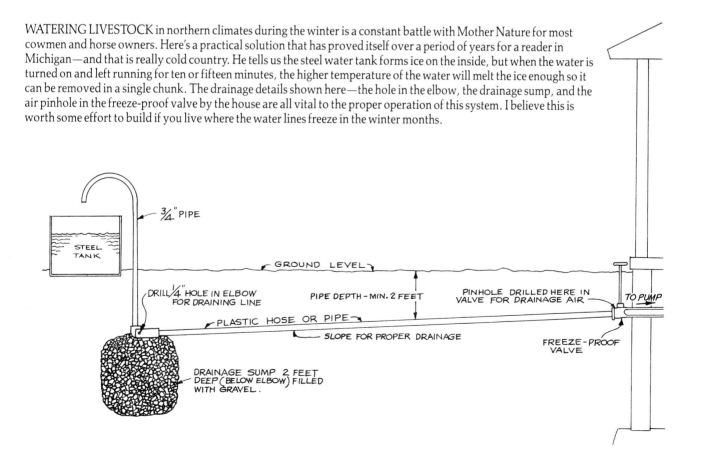

A GOOD, easy-to-make boot scraper is a handy thing to have around any place where there are horses and the dirt that goes with a horse lot. This one is made by welding a 1¹/₂-inch-wide piece of steel to the inside of a large horseshoe whose sides have been straightened to afford sufficient width for a muddy boot to slide between. The shoe and plate are then welded to a 6x8-inch, or heavier, boiler plate, which is drilled so it can be screwed to the porch steps or floor.

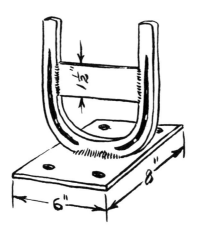

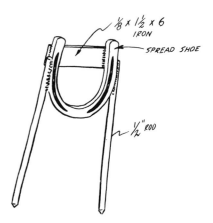

HERE IS still another design for a boot scraper, and the beauty of this one is that it can be easily changed from one place to another. The shoe will have to be spread to accommodate the boot, and the scraper and side prongs welded into place. I suggest that the side prongs be at least ¹/₂-inch steel rods so they won't bend, and they should be no shorter than 16 inches.

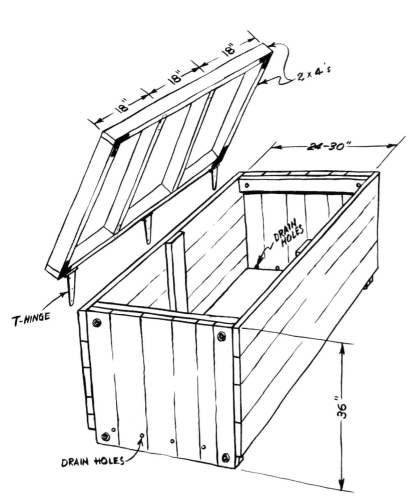

AN OLD FRIEND of mine used to live on the Carl Raswan Ranch near Albuquerque. He ran a bunch of dude horses there and had feeding problems that he solved neatly with this compartment hay bin. Made from 2x4s and rough one-inch lumber, it has a hinged top divided into 18-inch sections that provide individual feeding spaces for the horses. Drain holes drilled at the bottom allow rain water to run out. The bottom is raised up the height of a 2x4 off the ground. You can make one or more any size you want to accommodate as many horses as you have. Looks like a real practical feeder to me. My friend says it sure saves hay and keeps 'em from tossing it on the ground.

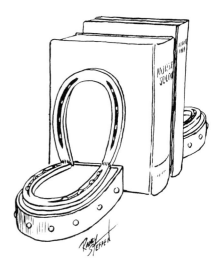

THIS PAIR of book ends was a gift from a friend in California, and I'm real proud of them. My guess is that a number of readers will want to make a pair just like 'em, so here's how. Two pairs of shoes are welded together as shown. Then give them a coat of flat black enamel with a spray can before nailing them to the band-sawed two-inch blocks with horseshoe nails. A strip of leather around each block is glued on, then studded with brass tacks. Green felt glued to the bottoms of the blocks makes them scratchproof.

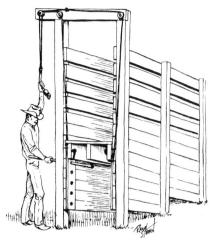

HERE'S AN OUTFIT that takes a little time and effort to build, but I'll guarantee you'll get more pure fun out of using it than anything you've tried in a long time. I show a pit filled with sawdust under this flying barrel bronc, but I've seen it used over a swimming pool with mighty good results. You'll need a 55-gallon metal drum, some iron rods with loops or eyes bent on the ends (of course, one eye will have to be formed after the rods are stuck through the drum) and some stout rope fastened to eyebolts at the tops of the four stout posts you'll set firmly in the ground. I've seen several with varying distances between the posts. The greater the distance between posts, the greater the arc of movement of the bronc. Use your own judgment, but I'd suggest a distance not greater than 14 feet between the side posts, and about 10 feet between the end posts. Two stout men are required on the ropes to set the barrel to pitching. And believe me, it takes a mighty good bronc rider to last more than a few high jumps on this *ersatz* bucker.

IF YOU are handy with tools, you could probably make this permanent loading chute from my sketch. It's from a U.S. Department of Agriculture design sheet and it is adjustable for truck or trailer heights from 12 to 42 inches. The cleated ramp rests on a 2-inch pipe and can be raised or lowered by the cable arrangement shown.

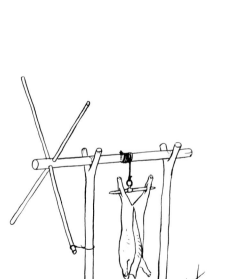

I SAW these book ends in California, and they were made from the shoes of the owner's Arabian stallion. He had chrome plated the shoes, but a coat of flat black paint will make them look real good, too. The felt is glued to the bottom of the sheet metal plate after it is fastened to the bottom of the block. A coat or two of varnish, or a rubbed wax finish on the wood block before nailing the shoe in place, makes a nice touch. Trace around the outside of each shoe to make the patterns for the wood mounting blocks.

EVEN IF you never dress out beef on your place, this Australian way of handling a beef carcass should interest you. Made from forked poles and a stout, smooth pole, this winch would make a dandy in a deer camp, as well as on anyone's ranch. This method is used on stations in the Northern Territory of Australia.

IF YOU like western horses, and have a set of corrals to keep your saddle animals in, or have a driveway you'd like to decorate with a western theme, this corral gate arch motif can't be beat for simplicity, economy, and effect. The vertical posts, and the cross pole in this drawing, are made of utility company poles. These poles are hard to beat for this sort of thing—they are creosoted, rustic in appearance, and usually as sturdy as anything you could obtain. The cow skull hung over the gateway is a carry-over from the early days, when the ranchers copied the skull decoration from the Plains Indians, to whom the buffalo skull was powerful medicine. Many ranches in the Southwest have corral gates that are crowned with a sun-bleached cow skull. I have three or four on my place.

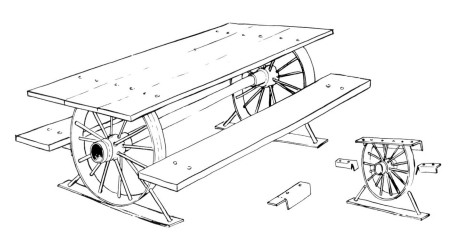

THIS PAIR of andirons is not only easy to make, but is as horsey as a bucket of oats. They are made from a couple of lengths of light mine rail, with a pair of horseshoes welded to each as shown. Finish by painting them with a coat of stove-black enamel. These andirons will keep the logs against the back of the fireplace and would take a hundred years to burn through.

A CLOSE FRIEND who lives in Auburn, Calif., builds a lot of unique projects in the large shop behind his house. This redwood picnic table with benches is one of his latest, and is a mighty good-looking set, believe me. The sketches show how he attached the redwood planks to the wheels. A little welding is necessary, but is well worth the trouble.

THIS IDEA will come in handy if you need an inexpensive, moisture-proof base on which to stack baled hay. The tires, preferably of the same size, can usually be had for the asking at service stations.

I SAW A lamp similar to the one I've shown here in an office at the Buffalo Bill Museum in Cody, Wyoming. The lamp I saw was made with a buffalo skull, and it was mighty attractive. Since buffalo skulls are a little hard to come by these days, and darned expensive when you try to buy one, I've shown this one with an old range cow skull. You can use a piece of dried desert cholla for the upright shade standard, or a piece of gnarled driftwood, manzanita, or whatever's handy. Drill or burn a hole through it for the cord, mount a socket and shade base on the top, use a piece of plywood with sand and rock embedded in plaster of Paris for the base, and your lamp is complete. The brands on the shade can be painted on with an artist's brush and burnt sienna oil pigment from a tube, cut down with paint thinner. If you do a good job, they'll look almost like they're burned on with an iron.

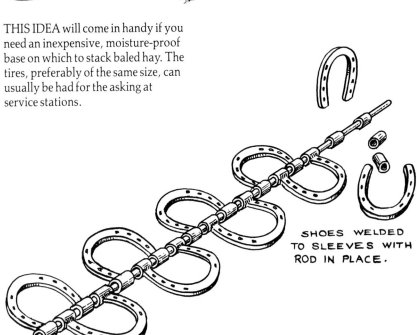

SHOES WELDED TO SLEEVES WITH ROD IN PLACE.

THIS IS a piano-type hinge a reader in Arizona made up to keep a large barn door from sagging. He used short nipples of $1/2$-inch pipe, a $1/2$-inch steel rod, and a bunch of old horseshoes that were straightened out on the forge before welding. He advises anyone building this type of hinge to assemble the nipples on the rod before welding so there's no misalignment possible. The shoes are fastened to the door frame with horseshoe nails, which are clinched on the back. This same type of hinge would look good in many places.

THIS ONE comes from a reader in Michigan where the wind and snow send temperatures way down. Folks in that country have trouble keeping their stock-watering pumps thawed out in winter, especially the old hand pumps. Here's how our friend in Michigan solves the problem. He rigs a fiber barrel, and a 100-watt light bulb on an extension cord. He places a small kettle of priming water inside the barrel, too. All he has to do on the coldest morning is lift off the barrel, maybe prime the pump, and he's set to water his stock.

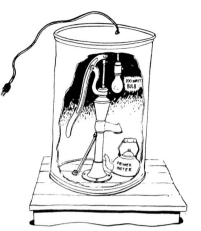

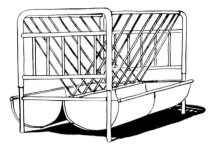

THIS USEFUL hay feeder can be made very economically from a couple of old metal bedsteads, some scrap pipe and rods, and a few dollars worth of welding if your outfit doesn't sport its own welding equipment. Four oil drum halves, with drain holes, complete the feeder.

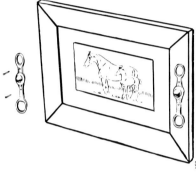

I DID A watercolor sketch of a mare and colt for a friend's birthday. He is a whiz with hand and power tools in making things from wood. He made a frame for the sketch and, as a finishing touch, took an old aluminum bit, sawed the cheeks off the mouthpiece, drilled a couple of tiny holes in each cheekpiece, and mounted them on the frame with small brass brads. It sure made that frame look good, and was about as appropriate for a horse picture as anything I've ever seen.

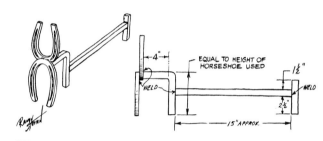

HERE'S AN EASY way to make a set of fire dogs, or andirons, whichever you prefer to call them. Use ¾-inch, or heavier, square bars for the body of the andirons, and form by heating in a forge, or with a welding torch. Weld the parts together at each joint, and finish by filing and giving a coat or two of flat black paint.

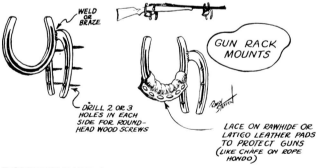

GUN RACK MOUNTS

WELD OR BRAZE

DRILL 2 OR 3 HOLES IN EACH SIDE FOR ROUND-HEAD WOOD SCREWS

LACE ON RAWHIDE OR LATIGO LEATHER PADS TO PROTECT GUNS (LIKE CHAFE ON ROPE HONDO)

DON'T DISCARD those worn shoes you pull off your horse's feet. If they're not too badly gone, there are a number of useful and ornamental gadgets you can make for your home as well as for the stable. Of course, you can use new shoes if you and your pocketbook prefer. Have your local welder braze, or weld, two shoes together like I've shown in this sketch—after you've cleaned them up and straightened them, of course. Then, drill out three of the nail holes so a No. 8 round-head wood screw will slip through them. Fastened to the wall, these horseshoe racks make fine coat and hat hangers, bridle racks, and, with a leather pad laced in place, they'll make mighty showy gun racks. A coat of flat black paint adds the final glamour that will make them an attractive addition to your home or barn.

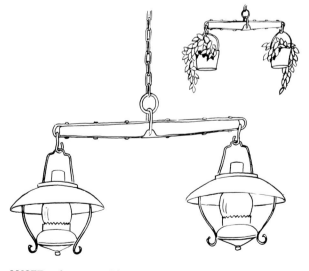

I USED to know an old-time blacksmith in Sacramento, Calif., who rigged up some nice-looking items from old horse and wagon equipment and a few pieces of scrap iron. In his house he had a pair of kerosene lamps, like the ones I show here, hanging from an old weather-beaten singletree. And on his side porch, he had several potted plants hanging in similar fashion. I'll tell you, they looked real good!

THE IDEAS shown on these pages need no explanation. They are representative of ways our readers have modified treasures from the past to perform useful functions around the ranch or home. These illustrations will guide you or suggest other designs that can be adapted to your own treasures and limited only by your imagination.

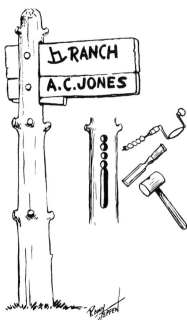

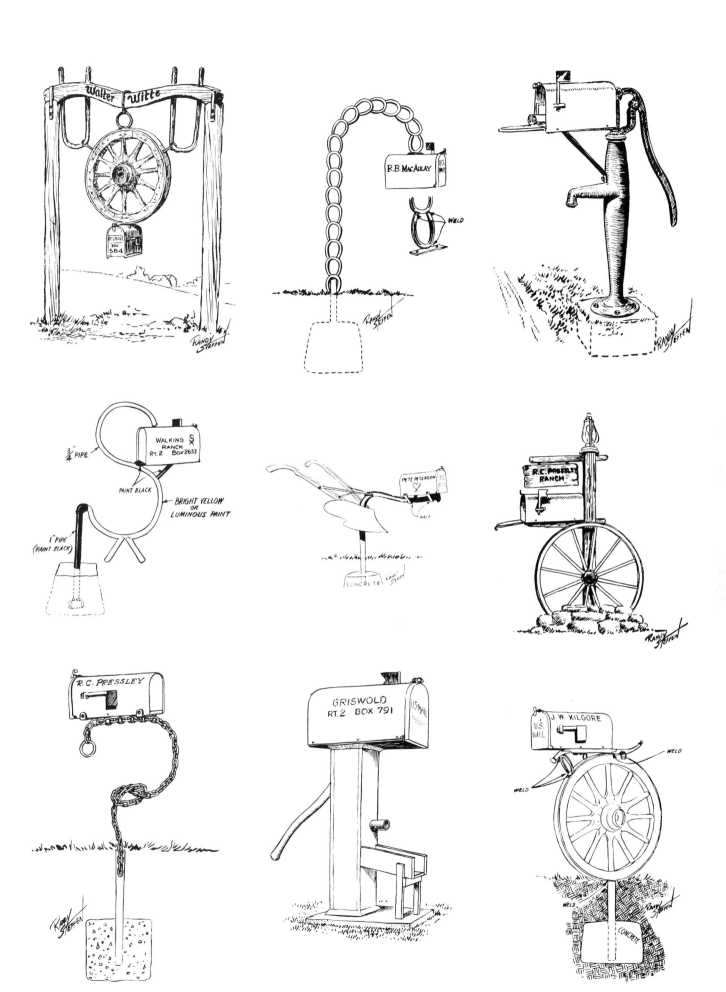

53

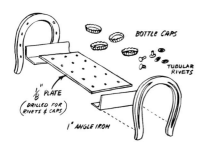

THIS IS a boot scraper you can make from simple materials and a little drilling and welding. I've shown the component parts—some angle iron, a handful of bottle caps, some rivets, a piece of 1/8-inch plate, and a pair of horseshoes. Rivet the caps to the plate, weld the plate to the angle iron, then weld the horseshoes to the angle iron as shown. Another way to place the bottle caps would be to stagger the rows.

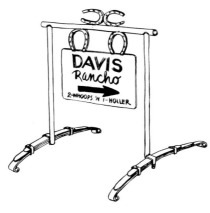

THIS IS a handy design for a portable sign. You'll need a couple of car springs, a piece of flat iron long enough to weld to the springs as a standard (as shown), four horseshoes, and a piece of fairly heavy-gauge sheet metal for the sign itself. Weld it all up for a sign that will stay put wherever you set it.

SOME OF our readers seem to lie awake at night dreaming up all these ideas. This one comes from a friend in California, and it's a horseshoe door knocker made from shoes with heel calks. The only work required on a pair fresh from the keg is drilling a hole through each heel calk, fastening them together with wire or leather strings, as shown, and a coat of black paint. The knocker is fastened to the door with horseshoe nails.

HERE'S A small, portable hay rack and feed trough that can be hung on a corral fence almost anywhere. It's made from half of a 20-gallon steel drum and small diameter rods, welded as shown. It is light enough to move from one location to another with little effort.

THERE'S BEEN many a time when I've hunted for a gate in a big Texas pasture. I'd have given a lot for a series of signs on the fence telling me where to find the gate. So here's a suggestion for you ranchers who have big pastures. Hang a small metal sign every eighth of a mile or so, showing in which direction the gate is and about how far from the sign.

HERE'S A design for a gun rack that any horseman would be proud of. The maker used a pair of hames from an old harness, and cleaned up the wood with paint and varnish remover so it was good and slick. After everything was assembled, he painted all the metal parts black. The iron straps that hold the hames together can be welded to the metal binding strip on each hame; or, they can be fastened to the wooden part with wood screws, from the back. The horseshoes are fastened to the edges of the hames with two wood screws in each shoe after the holes have been drilled out to the proper size. Before placing guns in the rack, it is a good idea to pad the inner surface of the shoes with leather or felt.

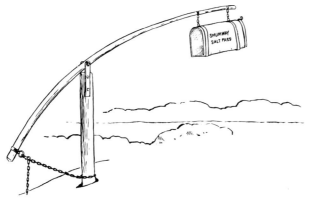

THE WIND BLOWS and the snow drifts deep in the northern plains country. A reader who lives outside Salt Pass, Wyo., rigged up this mail box adjuster so his rural mailman could find the mail box no matter how deep the snow got.

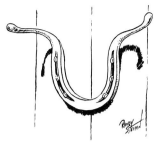

HERE'S A good coat rack that you or your horseshoer can easily make. You'll have to put a new shoe in the forge until it is red, then beat it into the shape I've shown here. The ends are rounded so they won't tear any garments hung on them. You will note that the ends are bent forward so there is plenty of clearance between the rack and the wall. A coat of flat black paint before it's nailed to the wall with horseshoe nails puts the finishing touch to it.

THIS ONE'S handy for those folks who put out blocks of salt in their pastures. Use a cinder half-block for a base, then run a piece of 3/4-inch pipe or suitable rod through the opening and into the ground. About three or four inches of pipe should protrude above the cinder block. Set the salt blocks over the pipe. Your horses won't be tipping it over, and it will stay clean and off the wet ground.

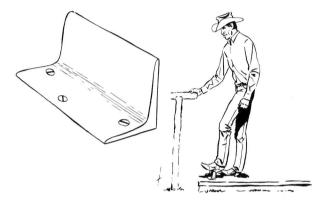

A RANCH in winter and spring can be a mighty muddy place. I don't know of any ranch wives who don't get madder than a wet hen when their husbands or kids or one of the hands drags gobs of mud into the kitchen. The simple angle iron scraper I've shown can be rigged at a strategic spot outside the house.

THIS IS A design for a permanent ranch directional sign. Cut the arrows from 16-gauge sheet iron, file the rough edges, coat with some good outside paint, allowing about an inch of pipe to stick up above the top of the arrow so you can pound it into the ground without damaging the arrow. A sign like this will last a long time, requiring only occasional repainting to keep it fresh and attractive looking.

SOME TIME ago, I spied an entrance sign at a ranch in northern California that was made like the one I show here. It was as good-looking a sign as I've ever seen, and while it takes a little skill with metal and metal-working tools and a welding outfit to make it up, it is sure worth the effort. Made from 1/8-inch x 1-inch iron strap to form the letters and the base, it's mounted on a pipe set in concrete. The horseshoe is an added touch that I stuck on.

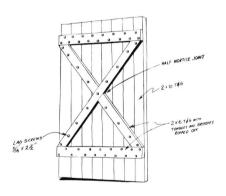

A MASSIVE-appearing door, attractive for any western setting, is made of 2x6 tongue-and-groove Douglas fir. The cross braces had the tongues and grooves ripped off, as did the edges of the door. Lag screws, 5/16-inch by 2 1/2-inch, were used to hold all members of the door together. The cross-braced side was hung on the inside of the studio, and the plain side outward. Dutch doors for use in box stalls can be made up the same way.

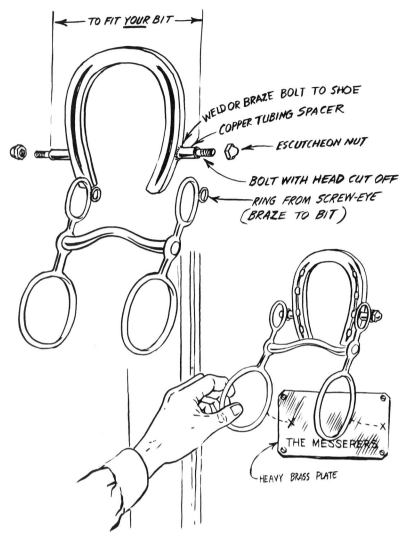

TO FIT *YOUR* BIT

WELD OR BRAZE BOLT TO SHOE
COPPER TUBING SPACER
ESCUTCHEON NUT
BOLT WITH HEAD CUT OFF
RING FROM SCREW-EYE
(BRAZE TO BIT)

THE MESSERERS
HEAVY BRASS PLATE

HERE'S A table designed from an iron wheel. The wheel was slicked off good with sandpaper and painted a brilliant red. The three chain legs, each link of which is welded to the next one so the legs are rigid, were welded to the wheel hub. These legs were painted black. Small clips were welded to the edge of the rim to hold the glass top in place. A friend cut the top piece of plate glass two inches bigger in diameter than the wheel to complete the coffee table. The wheel, I'm told, is the rear one from an old corn planter—the one that covers the corn after the kernel is dropped in the hole. But most any iron wheel will do.

HERE'S A real good-looking door knocker you can make with a horseshoe, an old bit, a piece of heavy brass with your name engraved on it, and a few dollars worth of welding. Most any jeweler can do the engraving on the brass plate.

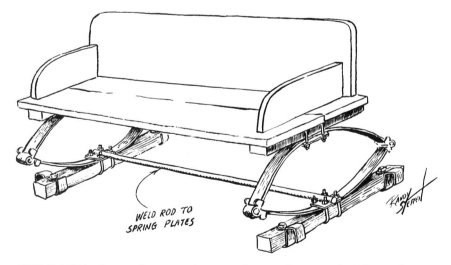

WELD ROD TO SPRING PLATES

RANDY STEFFEN

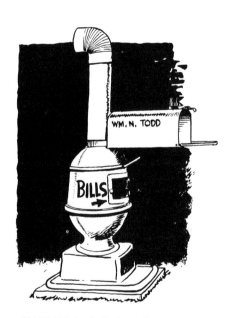

WM. N. TODD
BILLS

THIS IS AN idea for a really western lawn seat. It comes from a reader in Iowa who recommends that you weld a rod between the two springs, in order to make the seat rigid. Paint or varnish the seat to suit yourself. The best place to weld the rod is to the U-bolt plate, as I've shown. It would be best to remove this piece before welding to prevent scorching the wood.

AN OLD friend of mine who was stationed at the U.S. Military Academy at West Point showed me a photograph of this mail box that's on his daddy's ranch in Texas. The separate compartment for bills is a humorous touch.

HERE'S HOW to make a napkin holder from an old stirrup. The stirrup has the bolt and wooden spreader removed, and has been sanded down well and given a few coats of varnish. Treated this way, it makes a mighty attractive addition to the table setting in a cowboy household.

A GOOD-looking mail holder can be made from a piece of horn; simply cut slots in a polished cow horn, using a hacksaw. Two blades make the slot just the right width to hold the average letter or bill.

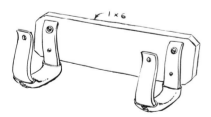

STILL ANOTHER use for old stirrups is this excellent gun rack. The maker removed the bolts from a pair of leather-treaded stirrups, fastened them to a polished and waxed piece of mahogany with round-head wood screws and washers to keep the screw heads from going through the bolt holes, and wound up with a real good-looking gun rack that cradles his favorite deer rifle on the wall of his living room.

CAST PLASTIC LETTERS

½" MASONITE

¾" PLYWOOD

½" PLYWOOD FRAMES

THIS IS a sketch of a sign a California wood-carver designed and made for a friend. The drawing at the right shows how the pieces of plywood and masonite go together to form a simple sandwich. The center piece of ¾-inch plywood is cut to the shape of the horse's head. All pieces were glued together with weldwood glue, and held in clamps overnight. Then the letters, cast out of plastic and bought at a graphic arts supply store, were glued in place, and the whole thing painted. Sure does look good! Those cast letters come in a pretty big variety of styles and sizes, and are ideal for making signs of all kinds, for both indoors and outdoors.

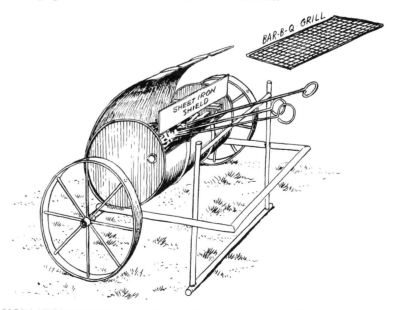

BAR-B-Q GRILL

SHEET IRON SHIELD

HOW ABOUT THIS for a combination branding pot and barbecue? The wheels make it easy to move when there's a shift of the wind, and the addition of the grill makes the perking of coffee or grilling of ribs a cinch when chow time rolls around. It is made from old iron implement wheels, scrap pipe, and angle iron, and a 55-gallon drum with the side cut open and rolled back. Sand placed in the bottom of the drum will prevent it from burning out.

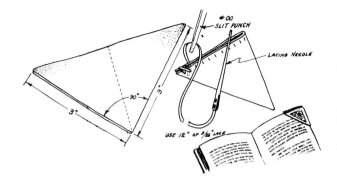

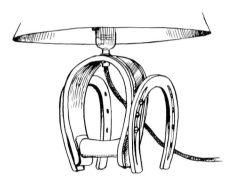

I'VE SKETCHED a real neat leather bookmarker that won't mar the pages of a good book. Use light tooling calf hide if you want to fancy it up with some tooling. If not, then any light leather or even plastic will do. A neat job of lacing will certainly add to its appearance. Of course, you can make it any size that suits your fancy, and it'll work just as well.

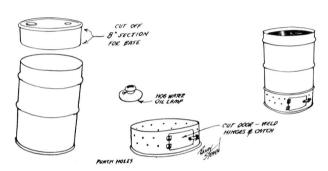

A FEW YEARS ago, a reader from the cold country asked for some method of keeping a water trough from freezing without using electricity. Here's a practical answer for that problem from an anonymous Iowan. He cuts an 8-inch end section from a 55-gallon drum, turns it over for a base, punches a series of small holes in the sides for air, cuts and installs an access door and latch, places a hog-water oil lamp on the bottom, sets the other part of the drum on top of all this, and lets the temperature drop where it may. One filling of this lamp will cause it to burn about 18 hours.

HERE IS a design for a real western lamp that uses standard lamp parts available from any electrical supply house. The base is made from a pair of horseshoes fastened to a wooden stirrup with wood screws just long enough to hold without going clear through the stirrup. It is necessary to drill out the nail holes in the shoes so the screws will fit properly.
A nice western-style shade completes the lamp. It will sit on a flat surface or can be hung over the headboard of a bed.

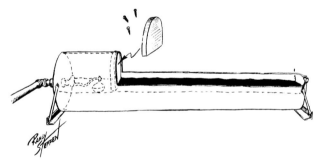

A SELF-FILLING water trough is a handy thing in warm country where freezing temperatures won't complicate things. I've fussed with many kinds in an effort to save time in taking adequate care of my horses, and this seems to be the best idea of this kind I've run across. I made mine from an old 20-gallon hot water heater tank. I had a friend with a welding torch cut the top part of the tank away as shown, then installed an inexpensive float valve at the covered end, screwed a half-round piece of marine plywood to the tank at the opening to keep the horses from messing with the valve, welded a rod and angle iron stand at each end, hooked it up to a water line, and I have the handiest gadget in the country. Try it, but make sure that you spend a little time and effort with a file on the sharp edges of the tanks so your animals won't cut themselves.

A READER in Pennsylvania evidently has a horse outfit for he has come up with a mighty fine way of making ranch signs that look as though the letters have been burned in with a hot branding iron. He uses 2-inch thick pine for his signs, draws the design for the lettering, then uses chisels and gouges to carve the letters in the wood. When this part is finished, he pours lighter fluid in the carved letters and lights it. The result is a charred edge on the letters that makes them look mighty good.

HORSE GEAR 5

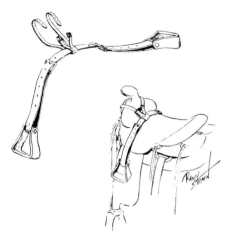

BEFORE my little Bonnie Jo was big enough for a saddle of her own, she was riding gentle horses, and the stirrup problem was a tough one to solve safely. I did tuck her little boots into tied saddle strings a time or two, after making sure her boots were loose enough to pull free of her feet if her boots should get hung in the strings; but that always worried me, so I dreamed up this kiddie-stirrup leather gadget I've drawn here.

Anyone who can work even a little bit with leather can make one in a hurry, using only a single leather strap 2 inches wide by 48 inches long, a smaller piece of leather 18 inches by 2 inches, two 2-inch tongue buckles and two 1-inch tongue buckles. Be sure to use small child's stirrups, preferably with hoods so little feet can't get hung. Attach the two large buckles as shown to the wide strap, cut the small piece with double tongues, as shown, attach the two small buckles to the stubby end, and sew in the center of the large strap as shown. The small straps are passed through the saddle fork, as shown, and buckled securely.

This rig can be adjusted to fit almost any size child, and will be perfectly safe and comfortable. I don't show hoods on the stirrups in my drawing for the sake of clarity; but please don't let your kids use any stirrup that isn't fitted with a hood—it's too dangerous.

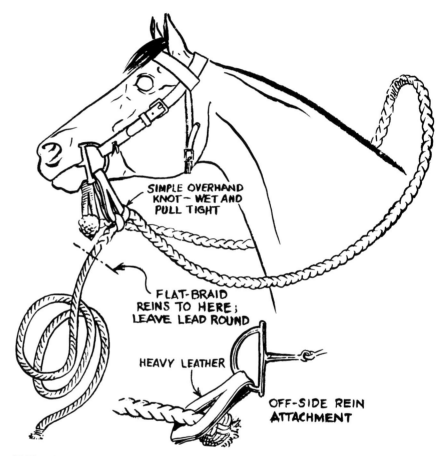

SIMPLE OVERHAND KNOT — WET AND PULL TIGHT

FLAT-BRAID REINS TO HERE; LEAVE LEAD ROUND

HEAVY LEATHER

OFF-SIDE REIN ATTACHMENT

I NOTICED THIS SNAFFLE bit arrangement in Nevada. I'd seen rigs similar to this fairly often, so I made a sketch of the bridle and rein arrangement. I think it's mighty practical since it does make a tie rope available in case the old pony jumps out from under you. If the lead rope is tucked under your belt, as it should be when you're riding a colt, you'd have a chance to grab it on the way to the ground and save yourself a long walk home.

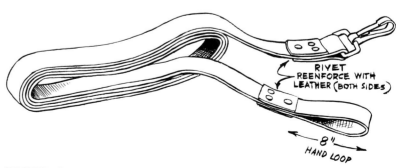

RIVET REENFORCE WITH LEATHER (BOTH SIDES)

8" HAND LOOP

WHILE MOST any rope will serve as a longe line, here's the way I made up a good, light, strong one from a surplus web strap and a heavy snap.

THIS IS a non-slip latigo hitch and it's easy to follow. It's tied almost the same as the regular one, except the end of the latigo goes under the first strand, as I've shown, instead of over all the strands as in the regular hitch. It's easy to undo, too.

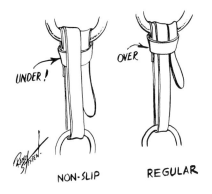

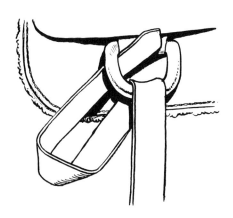

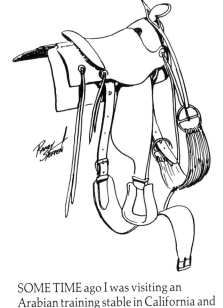

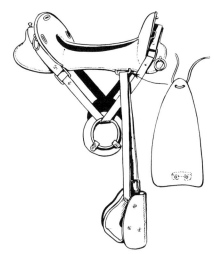

IF YOU ride a McClellan saddle and the stirrup leathers occasionally pinch your legs, here's a way to remedy the problem. Make a paper pattern for a pair of fenders, and cut them from a fairly heavy piece of leather. Punch two holes at the top for tying to the stirrup leather staples, rivet a small leather strap at the bottom, and hang them on your saddle.

SOME TIME ago I was visiting an Arabian training stable in California and that's where I came across this clever tip that anyone can benefit from. The idea is to keep the cinch ring and flank girth from slamming into the horse's front legs when the saddle is heaved into place. The rider had cut a slit in one of the saddle strings on the front jockey (off side), had slipped the slit string through the cinch ring, and the whole works was hung over the saddle horn. When the saddle is in place, the string is slipped off the horn and the rigging slides gently into place. This is a worthwhile stunt for all of us to use, and one that our horses will really appreciate.

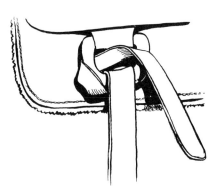

HERE'S ONE OF the greatest cinch-tie methods I've ever run across. It comes from a reader who lives in Illinois but who did some cowboying in Wyoming-Montana country some years ago. He writes that he rode a single-rigged saddle and that one time he was hung up on a horse that bucked him off. After that, he always fastened his cinch this way, telling anyone nearby to jerk the loose end if that should happen again. A word of caution: this works best with a flat ring, and *only* when the skirt of the saddle comes *below* the rigging ring. And the latigo must be a good wide one. Otherwise there is a chance that it could slip. I can vouch for the fact that this works; I've given it a good try since learning about this one.

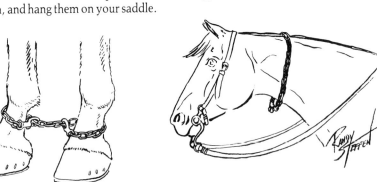

IF YOUR HORSE is already well hobble-broke, this inexpensive hobble will prove mighty handy to use and to carry. If he's not hobble-broke, DON'T USE A CHAIN HOBBLE, for he'll cut the dickens out of his legs the first time he goes to fighting them. This is the type of hobble we used in Nevada when we were catching mustangs for the Department of the Interior; but all of our horses were well used to being hobbled for hours at a time, and didn't fight them. When not in use, they're handy to snap around your horse's neck to use as a neck line while roping, and they're just a little more effective used this way than a rope is. We made ours by using a length of welded chain that would fit around the horse's neck where the neck rope usually hangs, then fastened a snap at each end with cold-shot links obtainable at any hardware store. Make sure your chain links are big enough for your snaps to slip into.

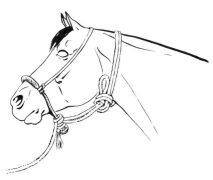

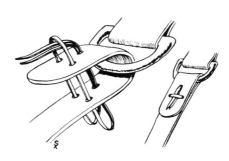

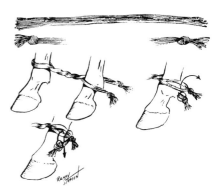

WHEN A hackamore man uses a thin pencil bosal, he seldom uses a fiador, so if he ties up to something solid it wouldn't take much to pop the light headstall usually used with the pencil bosal. By tying the reins around the neck with a bowline knot, all the strain of a pullback is on the reins and the lead rope, and not on the headstall.

SEVERAL readers have asked to be shown how to lace a new latigo into place on their saddles. In the drawing, I show a three-hole latigo lacing. It's easy to do, strong, and makes a neat job. This same type of lacing can be used in many other instances.

HERE IS a real good handy hint from a Canadian reader. He tells us that an old bronc stomper who worked for his family years ago taught him how to make these hobbles and he's been using them ever since. The old-timer used binder twine but, since that's relatively scarce these days, baler twine will do just as well. To make these hobbles, you cut eight or ten pieces of twine three feet long, lay them together and tie a simple overhand knot in each end. All you have to do to put 'em on is flip one end around the off foreleg and get the two ends even, then twist them together between the legs and bring the ends, one on each side of the near foreleg, toward you. To fasten them, you split the strands in your left hand and push the knot in your right hand through, then up and over and through again in the same place. Now give the two knots a half counter-clockwise turn. To take them off, you give the two knots a half clockwise turn and the knots come out very easily.

THIS no-hands twitch allows you to twist the attention-getter on the horse you are clipping or shoeing, and continue with your work without requiring an assistant to hold the twitch.

A READER sends this idea from New Zealand. He's seen blacksmiths in New Zealand use this type of twitch while shoeing horses. Looks as though a piece of cotton sash cord would be just the ticket for this twitch. After the correct tension has been put on the lip by twisting, the end of the shoe is slipped through the halter ring, where it holds the tension until removed. There is no doubt that this type of twitch will prove handy for many of you.

IT WOULD be hard to beat this nose-band for use with a tie-down on a head-slinging horse. Made by covering a length of bicycle chain with leather and wrapping the ends with wire, it's extremely flexible and strong enough for the worst horse. Be sure the seam where the leather covering is stitched is on top so it won't chafe the horse's nose.

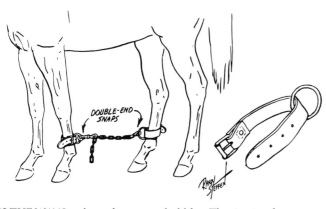

HERE'S THE WAY I make and use cross-hobbles. They're simple to put together this way and adjustable to any size horse. If you're going to use these on a wild one which will fight, I'd suggest lining the ankle straps with felt or woolskin to keep from peeling too much hide.

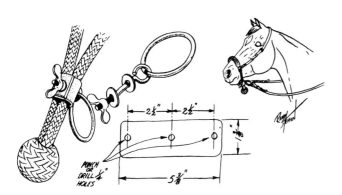

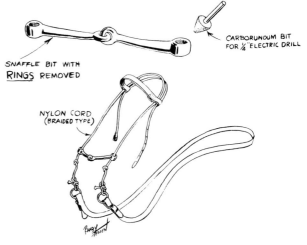

HERE'S A bosal-adjusting device to be used with leather reins instead of a hair or mohair *mecate*. Cut a heavy piece of leather in the dimensions shown, punch or drill three $1/4$-inch holes in it, then rig it between the branches of the bosal with a $1/4$-inch eyebolt, a $1\,1/4$-inch metal ring, a wing-nut, and two $1/4$-inch washers. Adjusting the height of this device acts the same as adding or taking off wraps of a *mecate*, and the ring provides a place to buckle a set of leather reins.

HERE IS an easy way to make an effective gag-bridle from a snaffle bit from which the rings have been removed. It takes a length of braided nylon cord the right diameter to pass easily through the ring holes in the mouthpiece, a pair of rein rings, and a set of leather reins. The brow band and throatlatch can be taken from another bridle. I'd suggest using a carborundum bit shaped like the one in the drawing to smooth the edges of the ring holes in the snaffle mouthpiece. A simple overhand knot *below* the bit will prevent the bar from dropping too low in the horse's mouth. This is a real effective type of bit to use on horses that are bad about pulling. For best results, pull the horse's head to one side or the other when he pulls. Do not pull straight back.

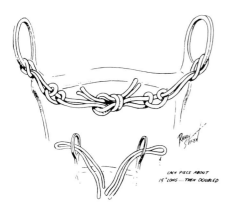

IF YOU have had a curb strap break when you were away from home, you might be interested in this one which can be made of light rope, baling twine, or even one of your saddle strings. Use two pieces of whatever material is handy, equal lengths, double each piece and tie as shown with a couple of hitches and a square knot in the middle.

WHEN RIDING a saddle mule in the mountains, don't leave your crupper or breeching hanging on a hook at home. That saddle just won't stay back there where it belongs. Brother mule's back isn't built to carry a saddle without a holdfast at his nether end. If you do get caught short, you can improvise by using your flank cinch as a crupper to keep the saddle off the mule's ears.

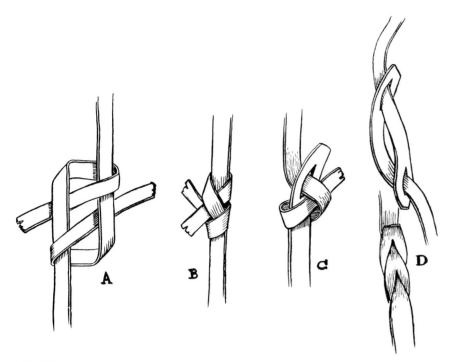

THERE ARE THREE ways to repair broken reins or straps, temporarily. A saddle-making friend of mine in California uses these methods to make neat and flat repairs in a hurry. A shows how the "grass knot" is started and B shows how it appears when snugged up. C is called a "buckle knot" and is used at times by packers with an eye splice in a rope. D is what my friend calls the "Mexican special," and it is well-known throughout the cow and horse country.

THIS plaited collar with a handhold makes bareback riding easier and less hazardous for youngsters. A young lady in Lander, Wyo., tells me that they do a lot of bareback riding and some of her friends had a tough time staying aboard; so, this three-strand braided collar came into existence. A handhold is braided at the top. They use baling twine or leather to plait the collar but it needs to be bulky enough to prevent cutting off the horse's wind and strong enough to support the rider's weight.

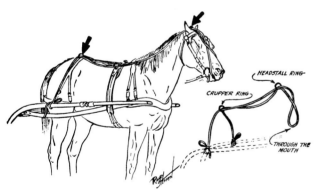

WHILE I REALIZE that there aren't too many horses driven to buggies in single harness in this age of the automobile, there are a few horsemen who keep an old buggy around the place to use occasionally for pleasure or parades. A horse that's just hitched every once in a while may get an uncontrollable urge to kick up his heels pretty high just to hear the crash and see the pieces fly. Needless to say, this stunt is funny to the horse, maybe, but to no one else. Here's the way my granddad rigged a kick-rope; he always contended that the conventional rump kick-rope was just so much waste of time and rope—and I'm inclined to agree. I know this rig will work, I've used it myself, and I've seen him use it a hundred times. The good part about this rig is that the horse punishes himself the instant he raises his hindquarters in kicking. A few times is all he'll need. Use your own judgment about slack in the rope; allow enough so he'll be comfortable when he behaves, pulling or standing. In effect, this outfit is the same thing as a loose over-check, but it will hit him swiftly and severely when he cuts loose with his heels.

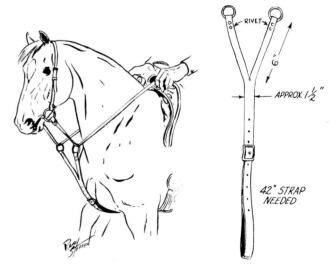

A RUNNING MARTINGALE is one piece of equipment that many horse trainers find extremely valuable in schooling a young horse in the bridle. It's easy enough to make one from a leather strap about 42 inches long and about 1½ inches wide. Two strong 1½-inch rings are riveted to the two split ends, and a 1½-inch Conway buckle is rigged in the body of the martingale to provide plenty of adjustment. Be sure to punch a hole in the strap with a sharp leather punch where the slit is to end. This'll prevent the leather from tearing past the split when an unusually strong pressure is put on it. (*Editor's note:* The martingale shown is adjusted much too short. It should be adjusted so it applies pressure only when the head gets too high. Constant pressure creates a tough mouth. Adjust the rings so they extend to just below the area in front of the withers.)

63

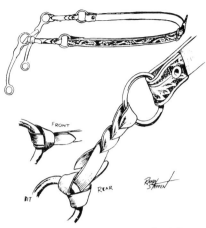

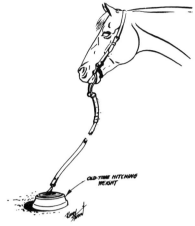

WHEN first bitting a green colt, every precaution should be taken to make him as comfortable as possible. Many colts will mouth the snaffle so vigorously at first that they'll get their tongue over the bar without your knowing it, and then they'll naturally fight any pressure you put on the bit. This rig keeps the bit well up in the mouth and prevents the colt from slipping his tongue over the bar. All you'll need will be a thin leather string long enough to go through the mouth with the bit and tie on the top of the nose. A light piece of string attaches the fore-top to the leather string and holds it up in place.

ONE OF our troopers stationed in West Germany sent in this idea for a dress bridle fashioned from a one-inch tooled leather belt and buckle and a couple of pieces of latigo string. The belt is cut in the middle and the ends riveted around the rings. A combination of Spanish lacing and a cinch tie holds the rings to the bit. The length of the latigo strings will depend upon the length of the belt and the size of your horse.

SOMETIME ago I saw quite a discussion in a national magazine on what was the proper name for those old iron weights the old-timers used to hitch their horses to when they stopped to pick up a load of groceries in town. I remember them well as "hitching weights" and they are so labeled in some 19th century hardware catalogs I have in my reference library. I was surprised a few months ago to see a half-dozen horses standing around the outside of a roping arena, each hitched by the snap on the end of their roping rein to one of these hitching weights. It's interesting to know that they came in 10-, 15-, 20-, 25-, and 30-pound sizes, at least from the Shaw-Batcher Company catalog, Sacramento, 1906.

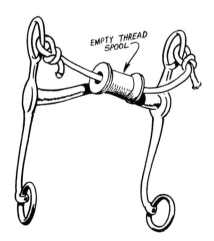

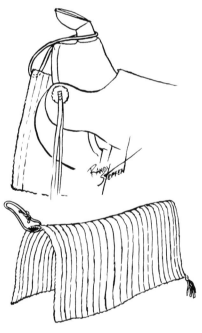

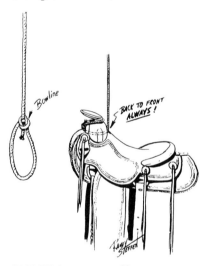

ONE OF our readers in Seattle has had several experiences with horses that were insensitive to the bits. Rather than put a more severe bit in their mouths and taking a chance on injuring the bars, she rigged up this twist on an Argentine breaking bit. She removed the regular leather curb strap, and in its place tied a piece of light, strong rope run through an ordinary thread spool. The spool causes pressure on the sensitive jaw nerves, and is more effective than a leather or chain curb.

THIS TIP is from a reader in Kansas who punches a hole in the front of his saddle blanket, threads a piece of leather string through it, and ties it so the loop formed is long enough to hook over the saddle horn when the blanket and saddle are in place on the horse's back. He says this sure keeps the blanket from sliding off in rough country, especially on a high-withered pony that you don't have to cinch up tight to keep your saddle in place.

ONE OF the easiest and best ways to store a saddle temporarily without getting the skirts and side jockeys all out of shape is to hang it from the ceiling, as shown in this sketch. Tie a loop in the rope, using a bowline, and always push the loop through the fork from back to front, and then up over the horn. Doing it this way will make the bulk of the saddle balance in more nearly an even position.

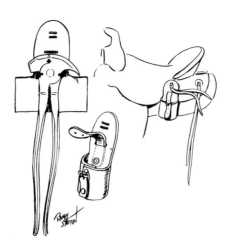

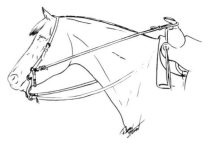

MOST HORSEMEN are familiar with this way of doing up a latigo, but I show it here for the beginners that might not know this method of keeping the latigo off the ground or floor and out of the dirt. When you are ready to saddle up, a pull on the end snaps the latigo out to its full length.

HERE'S AN easy way to make a saddle holster for a fencing tool. I saw one just like it some time ago in California and made a sketch of it. Made from a piece of leather with the strap and buckle riveted in place, the finished holster is mounted on the near side with the saddle strings as shown. If you make it a snug fit, the fencing tool can't fall out.

A READER in Cheyenne used this little stunt to deal with horses that just like to buck. It's a check rein, made from a piece of small-diameter strong rope with a harness snap tied at one end, and a stationary loop tied in the other end to slip over the saddle horn. He advises snapping one end of the check rein in the headstall ring of the bit, and after adjusting it so it's fairly tight, slipping the loop over the horn. He says, and his logic is sound, that his device gives the horse less chance to buck, and makes it easier on the rider by giving him more confidence when he's topping a spoiled one. You might try this one on yours if he's inclined to try to bury his head in the ground when you ride him.

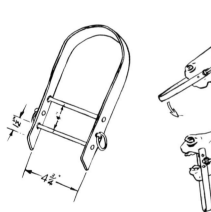

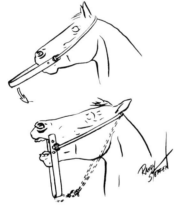

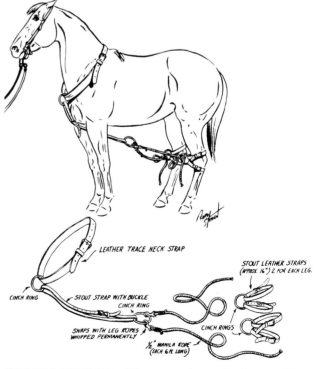

LEATHER TRACE NECK STRAP

CINCH RING

STOUT STRAP WITH BUCKLE
CINCH RING

SNAPS WITH LEG ROPES
WHIPPED PERMANENTLY

½" MANILA ROPE
(EACH 6 FT. LONG)

STOUT LEATHER STRAPS
(APPROX. 16") 2 FOR EACH LEG.

CINCH RINGS

MAYBE SOME of you have had a tough time finding a ready-made speculum. Here's a design for one that I had made up and used with great success to file down the teeth of an old mare that had been wasting more grain that she'd been eating. The body of the speculum is made from a piece of black iron ⅛-inch thick, 1⅛-inches wide, and 38½-inches long. The two mouth bars are ⅛-inch steel rods, 5-inches long, which are welded into holes drilled in the speculum body after forming. The rods should be spaced as shown in the drawing. The headstall rings should swivel freely, and their bases should be welded or brazed midway between the two mouth bars. The speculum is placed in the horse's mouth just like a bit when bridling, then the end of the body is pushed down so that the two bars lever the mouth open for floating the teeth. Another piece of leather with a wire hook can be used to hold the speculum in position when working without an assistant. The leather goes over the poll, behind the ears, and the wire hook fastens to the bottom of the speculum body.

OWNERS OF GOOD stallions many times take chances with mares of unknown dispositions that could, and often do, lead to injuries, and, in a case or two I've known, death for their stud horses. A pair of reliable breeding hobbles are not at all hard to make and certainly are a lot more effective than using a foot tied up, or a war bridle, or a twitch. Here's a sketch of a pair I made and use on every mare I breed to my good Quarter Horse stallion. They're adjustable enough to fit any size mare you might breed to one horse.

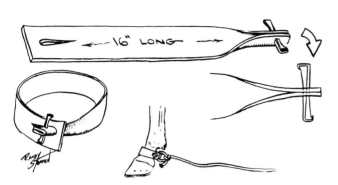

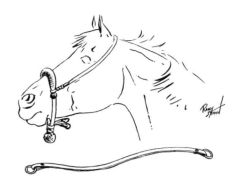

THIS HOBBLE STRAP from Australia is a new one on me. Take a close look at that horseshoe nail button in the end of the rawhide strap. As soon as I heard about this idea, I hurried out to the barn to experiment with some horseshoe nails, and believe me, this clinched arrangement really works. A pair of straps, coiled together with another leather or rawhide strap, will make a good stout pair of hobbles. Or it can be used as a strap around the pastern for tying up either a front or hind foot. I don't know of an easier or more effective way to make such a strap. Try one or a pair!

THIS ONE comes from an old-time Wyoming cowboy. He says, "I like to use a hackamore or bosal as long as possible on a colt, and I never put a bit in his mouth until I have to—purely a matter of personal preference. I start a colt with braided rope reins and work down to small leather ones. And, because I use the same bosal on many horses each day, I devised this method of changing reins quickly. I use a piece of $3/8$-inch latigo about two feet long, rivet a $3/4$-inch ring in each end, and take my wraps on the bosal with this rig, using a series of half hitches. I can snap all sizes of reins in without untying each set."

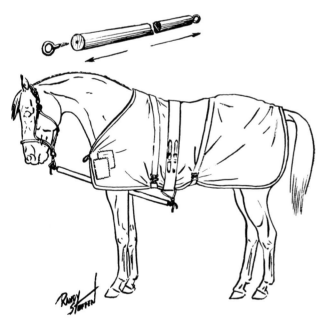

A HORSE that's continually tearing his blanket or stable sheet with his teeth is annoying and destructive. Lots of times the habit is hard to break, using anything short of a muzzle. The hint I've shown here will get quick results. The stick is merely a $3/4$- or 1-inch hardwood dowel, easily obtainable at any lumber yard, with a large screw eye in each end. One end is tied to the halter ring, the other to a surcingle buckled over the blanket or sheet. This arrangement allows the horse plenty of freedom for eating and other normal movement, but he can't get his head around far enough to tear or chew his blanket. But remember to use a breakaway halter for safety's sake.

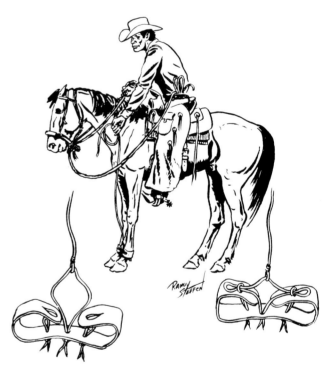

HERE'S AN ODD set of hobbles that are mighty handy for the lone-wolf horse breaker who has to climb aboard snaky broncs during his day's struggle to earn his beef and beans. I saw a Havasupai Indian bronc twister down in the Supai Reservation below Grand Canyon using a pair like I've drawn here, and they really got the job of a second man done for him. They're easy to make if you think you'll be in a position to need 'em any time. Me, I quit the rough ones that require such rigs long ago.

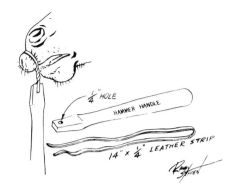

IT'S SURPRISING to learn how many folks who mess around with horses don't know what a twitch is, much less how it is used. I know that most every *Western Horseman* reader is familiar with this oldest of all horse barn tools; but just in case there's a new-comer or two, here's a quick description. The simplest way to make one is by using a hammer handle with a 1/4-inch hole drilled through the end, and a piece of stout leather string about 14 inches long and 1/4-inch wide—latigo or leather boot laces are good. The leather string is passed through the hole in the handle and tied or fastened with a Spanish braid, so there is a loop about six inches long at the end of the handle. The drawing shows how and where it is twisted on the horse's upper lip. This is used not to hurt the horse, but is twisted just tight enough to center all his attention on the twitch and his lip instead of on whatever you may be doing with his feet or any other part of his body. It has the same effect as twisting an ear. Of course, you'll need an assistant to handle the twitch while you take care of the doctoring, shoeing, or whatever else you may be doing to your touchy horse.

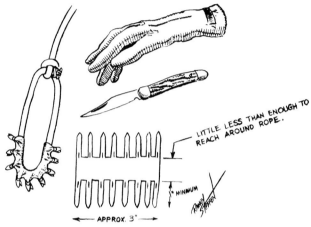

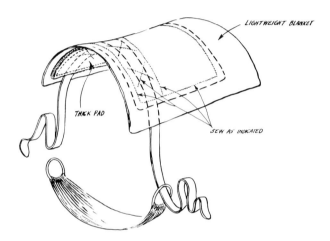

A READER from the state of Washington had the wear leather rip off his rope honda. Being away from the ranch, and not having anything in his saddle pockets but an old pair of gloves, he improvised this highly satisfactory wear leather . . . which he says is still on his rope and giving good service. He used the old simple saddle-string tie to hold the "burner" together.

THIS BAREBACK riding pad is a good idea, and if you really must ride without a saddle, this is about as comfortable a way to do it as I can think of. The latigo is slipped through the pocket between the pad and the blanket, then stitched in place by your local saddlemaker.

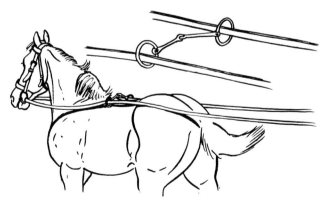

IF YOU DON'T have a driving harness to drive your horse with long lines, then this tip from a reader in Oregon may work for you. Place an old jointed snaffle over the lines and let it rest on your horse's back. The snaffle will help keep the lines up where they belong, and prevent possible tangles around his feet. This sounds like a practical idea. I don't know why you couldn't fasten this same snaffle to a surcingle, or to a latigo tied into a regular saddle cinch that went around the horse's girth like a surcingle. This would keep the bit in place and would act like a set of rings (terrets) on a regular harness saddle.

HERE'S A REMINDER of an old stunt that's as old as the horse and cow business in this country. The contributor of this one hails from Missouri and says, "Almost the oldest and best cowboy trick in the book seems to be forgotten nowadays, especially here in my part of the country. That is the use of the blindfold to saddle an ol' spooky horse, to lift the feet, to load into a spooky truck or trailer, to cross railroad tracks, concrete highway, or a river bridge—or anything else that can booger a pony. It can also be used to keep one from bucking wildly on the first mounting by circling until he starts to stagger before taking it off and mounting. Now, if you don't have a hackamore with a wide, sliding browband, take off that denim jacket, or even your shirt, slip it up over his nose, and tie in place with the sleeves. And a gunny sack makes a good one, too."

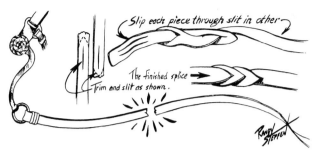

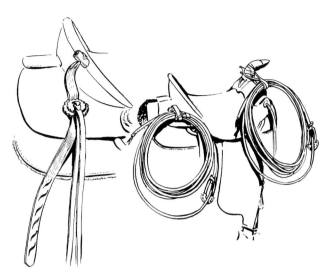

NEXT TIME you break a rein, don't tie a knot in it—make a slit braid splice like the one shown in this drawing, and you'll have a strong, neat-appearing splice until you can replace it with a new rein. First remove the broken rein from the bit, then trim each broken end and slit as shown. Now slip each trimmed end through the slot in the opposite half of rein, and pull tight to form the neat splice you see in the drawing.

WHILE THE DAYS of the mustanger are about passed, a few folks still like to go after the wild ones in some parts of the West. This is one way mustangers carry an extra rope. A light leather strip, usually elk hide or something similar, is made as shown with a rolled leather button at one end. Button holes, shaped the way I've shown, are cut at intervals the length of the strap end. It's very important that the holes are cut this way, so if the rider is thrown and a spur hangs in the coils of rope, the leather will tear quickly and release him. I hate to see the heavy rope straps that most saddles have on the fork. There's little chance of one of these straps breaking and freeing a man who is hung in the coils of his rope.

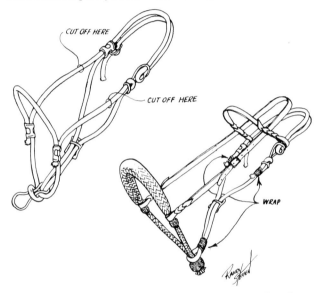

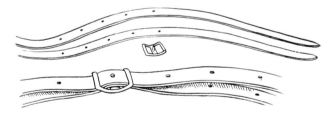

IT ALWAYS gripes me to see a rider ruin a good set of reins by tying a knot in them. A better choice is this simple Conway-loop adjustment for reins that *must* be fastened together. Make sure the holes are spaced exactly from the bit end of the reins so one rein won't turn out shorter than the other.

HERE'S A REAL fine gimmick for the man who has a lot of different colts or horses to work in the hackamore. The contributor of this one makes a simple alteration in a regular cotton Johnson halter and uses it as a quickly adjustable *fiador* instead of the usual sash cord *fiador* on a hackamore. The drawing shows just how and where the alterations are to be made. Simply cut off the cheeks on the sides, and wrap to the throatlatch as shown; remove the noseband completely with its accompanying ring, and fit it to your hackamore headstall as shown in the lower drawing. A few wraps of cord above the bosal heel knot secures it in place, ready for tying the *mecate* reins in place.

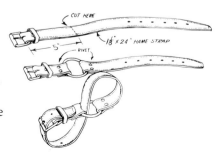

HERE'S the way to make figure-eight, Utah, or Mormon hobbles (whichever they're called in your part of the country). Use a hame strap, the size shown here, or any other suitable leather strap with a buckle on one end. Cut it about five inches from the buckle, rivet a large steel ring in place, and the hobbles are ready to use.

THIS ONE is an adaptation of the Mexican curb. Instead of spending a lot of time plaiting a rawhide button to slip over the curb strap, use a 1/2-inch pipe coupling. It's a little heavier and stays away from the jaw when it's not needed, but it puts the squeeze where it needs to be when you pull on the reins. However, you can't use it in most horse show classes.

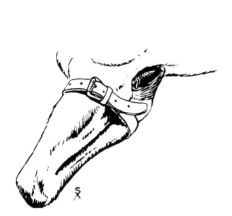

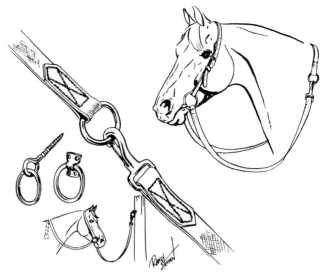

HERE'S HOW to use a belt to tie up a front foot to work on the hind parts of a horse that is prone to kick. This is a good one to remember, but also remember not to leave the belt on for a long period of time. This can cut off the circulation in the leg. Ten minutes is long enough.

A CANADIAN READER suggests that you make your training reins from heavy canvas and save the expense of costly leather reins. She sews a ring and snap into the ends of the reins and fastens a number of tie rings in strategic places around the corrals and barn. If it is necessary for the rider to get off a horse during training, he can tie the animal to the closest tie ring by merely unsnapping the reins and hooking the end to one of the rings.

8-POUND
MUSHROOM ANCHOR

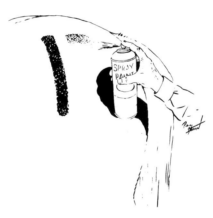

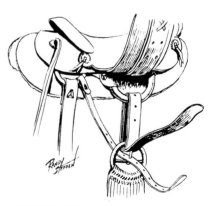

THE OLD-time cast-iron hitching weights are just about impossible to find anymore since they have become collector's items. A suitable hitching weight can be made from an eight-pound fisherman's mushroom anchor that you can buy in boat supply stores. A large ring through the hole at the top makes a fine place to attach the hitching rope or strap that has snaps at each end.

IT'S NECESSARY for some trail rides and other horse events to have the horses numbered very clearly for judging. I found that a spray can of fast-drying red enamel for the light-colored horses, and a can of yellow for the darker ones worked like a charm. I could rest the bottom of the can on the horse's rump and be steady enough to spray a legible number. Owners found that ordinary paint thinner on a rag removed the paint quickly, and a quick flooding of soapy, warm water eliminated any discomfort to the horse. I used this method of marking on 100-mile endurance horses and those painted numbers were just as legible at the end of the hundred miles as they were when they were put on.

JUST AS with humans, horses have different physiques, and one saddle won't fit all horses equally well. If your cinch has a tendency to slide up under one of your horse's elbows, here's the way a lot of good cowboys remedy it without having their saddles re-rigged. A stout strap, a piece of whang leather to lace it on your off-side flank cinch rigging ring, and a few minutes of your time are all that are required to turn this trick. Don't worry about the near side—after you've adjusted the location of the cinch so it won't gall your horse on the off side, the near side will follow suit.

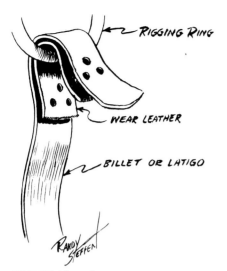

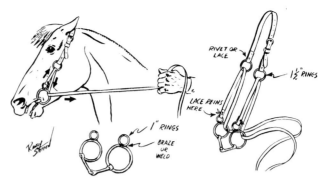

HERE'S A hint that may save you quite a few *pesos* over a period of years. It comes from one of my buckaroo friends and it's a good one. Fact is, after hearing about this I spent about 30 minutes putting latigo leather chafes on all the latigos and billets on the whole family's saddles. These wear leathers may have to be replaced every so often, but that's a heap better and cheaper than having to buy new billets or latigos.

DON'T KNOW if you've ever paid much attention to the rigging used on polo ponies, but, take it from me, some of the best horsemen in the country are those men who train polo ponies and some of those who play the game. Here's a homemade gag bridle that is darned effective on hard-mouthed or cold-jawed horses. Hope you don't have any such animals in your corrals, but if you do, this gag rig will educate them in a hurry, and without further injury to the bars of the mouth. A glance at the drawing will show you how it works, and how it's made. Pulling on the reins pulls the bit (and be sure to use a limber bit or jointed snaffle) up into the corners of the mouth, and not down on the bars where the feeling has been dead for a long time on old cold-jawed ponies. Experiment with it a little after you've made one up, and I'm sure you'll consider it a valuable addition to your equipment.

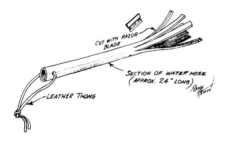

ONE of our readers in Ohio makes her own quirts from two-foot sections of old rubber or plastic garden hose. She slits the end of the hose into narrow lashes with a razor blade, drills a hole in the opposite end for a wrist loop, and ends up with a useful quirt. She says that the longer the lashes are made the harder they sting.

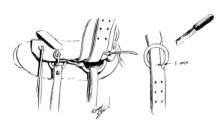

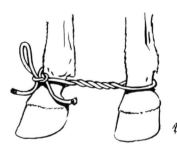

MANY OF us have often wished, when topping a snaky colt, or when doing some really active cow work, that we had just a little more free swing to our stirrups. A friend in Nevada sent in this method of adding about ten inches of additional swing without doing a thing to your saddle except cutting an inch from the stirrup leathers where they come through the rigging rings. He assures me that removing this small piece of leather will in no way weaken the leather.

A BREAST collar is necessary on some horses in rough mountain country, but I've seen many leather keeper straps broken when a horse is allowed to graze with his rigging left on him. Here's a simple way to prevent the keeper from slipping down on the neck where it stands a good chance of being broken when a horse raises his head.

A FRIEND tells us that he learned to use this type of hobble while wrangling. He uses either soft rope or leather, folds it in the middle, hooks the loop around one pastern, then twists until he has about 10 inches of twist, and ties the loose ends around the other pastern, using a regular hitch knot so it can be pulled loose in a hurry. He says that it takes about 2½-feet of rope or leather to tie the hobbles, and that an old rein is ideal.

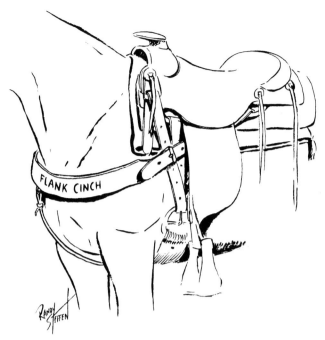

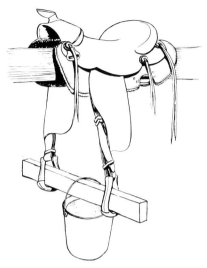

A BREAST COLLAR is mighty useful in the mountain country. If you should get caught in rough country without one, you might try this stunt. Take off the flank cinch and use it as a breast collar. You can tie it down to the front cinch with a piece of cord or leather string to prevent cutting off your horse's wind.

A FRIEND in Nevada writes that this is the way he finds that will really set the stirrups on a new saddle more quickly and positively than any other way he's heard of. He puts a double twist in the leathers after soaking them with a wet sponge. After running a two-by-four through the stirrups, he hangs a bucket of sand on the center of the board. This weight certainly should make the leathers hang straight and true.

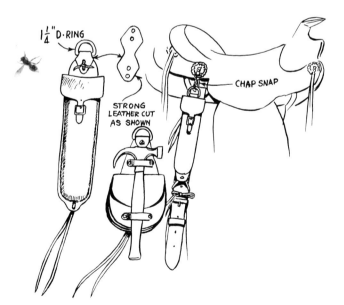

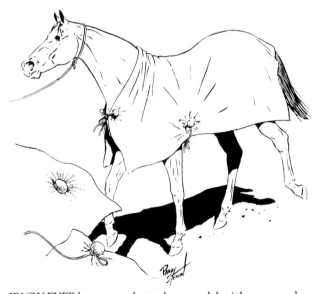

HERE'S A WAY to make a staple and hammer bag, pliers case, and other leather cases for carrying various items. The cases are quickly interchangeable. This one comes from a reader in South Dakota who braids a small chap snap in his off-cantle saddle strings, and arranges a small, stout leather holder for a small D-ring on each side of the cases. He uses one case for fencing tools and another during calving season when he needs his ear-tag pliers. Long tie strings are added to the bottom of each case so it can be tied to the back cinch and held in place.

IF YOU EVER have to cool out a horse and don't have a regular horse blanket or cooling sheet, you can use an ordinary old bed blanket by using this old-time Indian method of fastening tie-strings to it. The Plains Indians used this way of tying down their tipi edges to stakes. Select four small rocks, press them into the blanket cloth, and tie a small cord tightly around the blanket material and rock, as I've shown. With this arrangement, you can fasten a regular blanket on your horse without damaging the blanket.

IF YOU use pack horses or pack mules and let them follow along loose, you might consider using a check rein on them so they can't stop to graze while you're on the move. Otherwise, when they trot to catch up they shake the thunder out of the pack.

NEWCOMERS TO the horse business might like this come-along idea. Most old-timers know how to flip a half-hitch around a horse's nose to make him respect a command to lead. A lead chain works better than a soft rope lead.

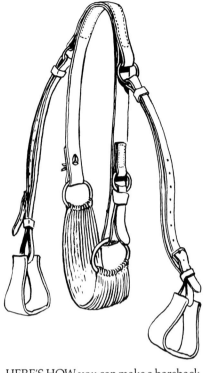

HERE'S HOW you can make a bareback surcingle for yourself or your family. Use a good, heavy, two-inch plain latigo strap for the upper part, attach the off side to the cinch ring as shown, then have your saddlemaker sew the ring billets at the top and on the near side as shown in the drawing. The stirrup leathers should be good, heavy, harness-weight leather, with a buckle and keepers as shown. This rig should be cinched on the horse up fairly close to the withers, and can be used with or without a folded blanket under it. Placed properly, the rider's legs should clear the upper stirrup rings.

HERE'S A handy *morral* or nosebag. A pair of snaps are fastened to the sides of a canvas or leather bag as shown. The nosebag can then be snapped into the halter rings. Be sure to punch adequate drainage holes in the bottom of the bag so your horse can't accidentally fill his *morral* with water and drown in it.

THIS ONE'S from a subscriber in Iowa. He wraps the noseband of an over-size Johnson halter with rawhide strings, then runs a horsehair rope, or a three-strand braided rope through the ring for reins. It makes a pretty economical hackamore, and works real good, too.

FOR HORSES that are tough to handle with a leather or ordinary chain curb, here's a stout curb that should let you handle a bull buffalo with no trouble. It is made from a section of bicycle chain and fastened to the bit with a set of hooks made from heavy steel wire. Links can be removed to adjust this curb to fit any horse. Although it's flexible and smooth, use it with caution and avoid injury to the horse. And remember, you can't use it in the show ring.

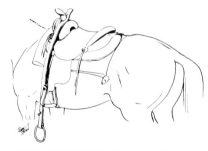

THIS MOUNTING aid is a good one for the little shavers or the little woman, if she's built pretty close to the ground and rides a tall horse. All it requires is a stout leather strap and an old cinch ring for the extra stirrup. After the rider is aboard, the cinch ring drapes over the horn to be completely out of the way.

A LOT of us use chain or half-chain curbs on our horses, and every once in a while a sore jaw turns up from the severe use of the bit. If that happens, one of our readers suggests substituting a sheepskin-lined hackamore bit noseband for the curb chain—at least until the injured tissues are completely healed.

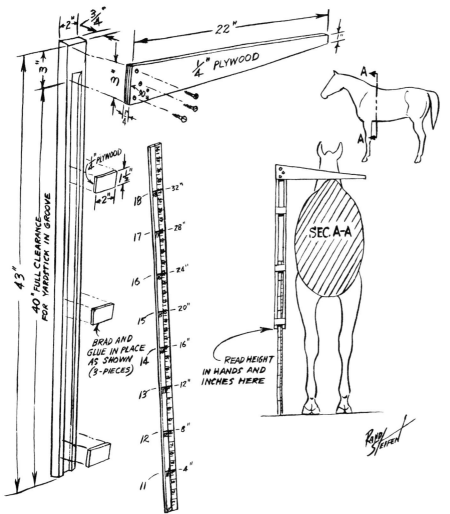

A READER who used to be with the U.S. Forest Service picked up some mighty good hints he was kind enough to pass on to us. I'm sure many of you have known old, wise ponies that could move off with hobbles around their ankles about as fast as they could without them. A hobble-happy bunch quitter in a pack string can cause a lot of delays and sour dispositions in a hurry. A cure for this type of horse is to place the hobbles on the hind feet instead of the front. Our friend says to be sure to have the horse on good grass because he won't travel more than about 100 feet in a night.

A HOMEMADE measuring stick can be made from an ordinary yardstick and a frame. Using paint and a brush or one of those felt-nibbed pens, mark a line on the yardstick every 4 inches, starting at the 4-inch mark. Number these lines, starting with 1 at the 4-inch mark, 2 at the 8-inch mark, up to 8 at the 32-inch mark. The frame consists of a sliding channel, 40 inches long, cut into a piece of pine 3/4 inches thick, 2 inches wide, and exactly 43 inches long. The channel should be the depth of the thickness of the yardstick. This groove can be cut with a dado blade on a bench saw. The top standard is a piece of 1/4-inch plywood, cut as shown and fastened to the top of the frame. The three small plywood keepers are glued and bradded into place, as shown, over the groove of the vertical standard. In use, slide the yardstick into the groove and be sure that the device is held perfectly straight for accurate measurements.

THE RANCH cowboy who works wild stock in rough country at fast speeds must make sure his gear and tack will stay put on his horse. An extra-long latigo stuck through the keeper on the fork of the saddle can be one source of danger to a man on a running horse, if it should slip out and fall low enough to trip the horse. Here's a simple method of eliminating that danger. Punch an extra-large hole in the latigo at just the right place, and thread a saddle string through the hole after the latigo has been slipped through the keeper. This certainly will help prevent the latigo from slipping out.

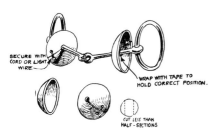

A YOUNG LADY in Denver had a saddle horse with a very fine muzzle, and she couldn't find a snaffle bit that would fit. Here's the solution she came up with.

She cut sections from a tennis ball, as I've shown here, slightly smaller than the full halves would be. She punched a hole in the center of each, then cut a slit from the edge of the section to the center so it could be slipped over the bar of the bit. A few wraps in the right place with plastic tape made a stop on the bar so the ball section would stay in place. Then a small piece of light wire (strong string could be used) fastened the slit part of the sections firmly together on the bar, and she had a bit that fit her horse real well.

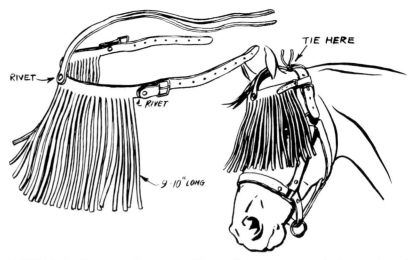

THIS IS the way the Plains Indian rigged a rawhide bridle on his pony. While I don't recommend it for a regular bridle, it is a handy thing to know in an emergency. The two half-hitches in the mouth can be pretty severe, so be careful how you use it. It won't tighten up excessively unless you really lay on the reins—and then it won't relax unless you pile off and loosen the turns. It's best to check this rig periodically so you don't accidentally cut off circulation in the pony's mouth.

FLIES DO devil horses in the summer. Here's a fly net you can make from a piece of leather, three rivets, a pair of small buckles, and a long strip of whang leather. Dimensions will vary from horse to horse. The drawing shows how it should fit, so get your measuring tape out and see just what dimensions you'll need for your horse. For safety's sake, be sure to use a breakaway halter.

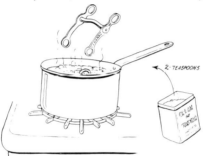

HERE'S ANOTHER good use for a rolled gunny sack. A horsebreaker in Utah ties a rolled sack around a colt's neck when he's to be halter broken; then he ties the breaking rope to the sack and runs the free end through the halter ring. This prevents the poll and neck from getting raw and sore in the halter-breaking process. It's surprising how strong a rolled gunny sack can be.

ALUMINUM BITS can easily be cleaned with this procedure. Scrub first with a brush and soapy water, then boil for ten minutes in a quart of water to which two teaspoons of cream of tartar have been added. The contributor of this idea says if you use an aluminum pan, the bits will look better, too.

HERE'S a simple hay feeder for foals or calves. The rancher who submitted this idea takes an old feed sack, stuffs it full of hay, and hangs it low enough from the rafters to allow the foal or calf to reach it; he then slices a few holes in the sides and pulls wisps of hay through. Foals and calves get the idea in a hurry.

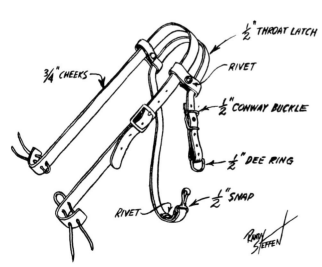

A SIMPLE BRIDLE that can be made from odds and ends of harness leather uses a snap and ring for quick removal.

HERE'S AN IDEA that will let a small child climb aboard a gentle horse that's too high off the ground to mount in a more conventional way. An extra *hooded* stirrup is hung from the regular stirrup on the near side, so that he can virtually climb aboard like climbing a ladder. Caution—to be used only on a reliable horse, and after the horse has become accustomed to the extra dangling stirrup.

74

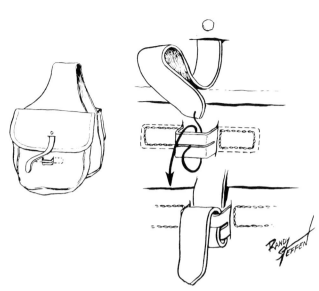

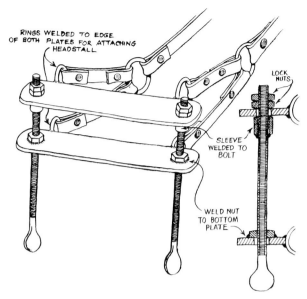

HERE'S A WAY to tie down saddle bag flaps. Made completely from leather, it's hand or machine stitched to the saddle pocket. If you want to replace a metal buckle, this is a good way to do it.

HERE IS STILL another design for a speculum. You'll remember that it is a device placed in a horse's mouth to prop his jaws open while his teeth are being floated (having the sharp points filed off so he can chew his grain and roughage properly). Speculums are sometimes hard to find these days. When one is needed, it's usually needed badly. Here's one that you and your welder can make from common hardware and a couple pieces of 1/8-inch-thick strap iron. The threaded vertical pieces I show are ordinary bolts about eight inches long that have had the heads pounded flat after being heated in the forge. The strap iron bars are fitted with rings and nuts as shown, and a short sleeve is welded to each bolt under the top bar. The assembled speculum will go into a horse's mouth as easily as a bit when the bars are screwed close together, and will open wide enough for any work to be done.

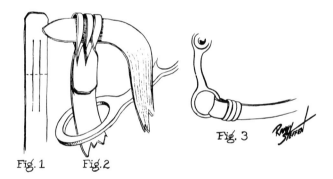

THIS IS a common method used to fasten reins to a bit, but one which has a good many people buffaloed. It's really one of the quickest and simplest ways to attach a pair of reins to a bit, and many reins you'll find in saddle shops will be cut to fasten this way. The bit end of the slotted rein is folded in the middle of the slits, shown by the dotted line in Fig. 1. Then each loop formed is given a single twist while the other end of the rein is passed through the slots, as shown in Fig. 2. When the rein is pulled through carefully, the neat fastening shown in Fig. 3 is the result.

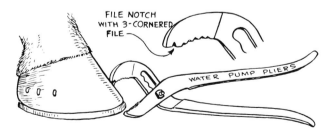

A FRIEND in Colorado sent along this fine tip for farriers and those of you who do your own shoeing. He suggests using a pair of water pump pliers as a clinching tool. If the upper jaw of the pliers slips from the nail end, he says to file a notch as shown with a small three-cornered file. This outfit should do the job well.

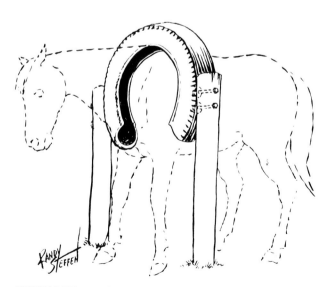

THIS BACK scratcher is made from a rear tractor tire or large truck tire cut as shown, and mounted at a suitable height by means of bolts to a pair of posts. The inside of the tire can be packed with waste or sacking that has been soaked in a pest killer. To refill the tire or replenish with liquid, remove one bolt from each side and swivel the tire upside down.

THIS IS an easy way to make a real good hoof pick from a medium-sized screwdriver. Have your welder or blacksmith heat the screwdriver blade so it will bend without breaking, and then bend over about ³/₄ of an inch of the point at a right angle to the shaft. This one is easy to work with and won't injure the frog as might a sharper pick.

SWIVEL

HALF-SET HOBBLES

AND HERE'S another way to improvise a hoof pick, one that will easily fit in your pocket. Use a hacksaw and file to convert the bottle opener of the type I show by cutting out the section indicated by the dotted lines. This is an easy one to make.

WE HEARD from a reader in Casper, Wyo., who used the clog chain previously described in one of these hints. His clog-chained horses, he claims, soon learn to skip along so the chain misses their feet, and can make pretty fast time in spite of this encumbrance. Not so with the section of tire-sidewall fastened to a strap around the pastern. It will always drag flat as long as the horse stays in a walk, but when he trots or lopes it will flip-flop all over the place, and a horse will step on it with at least one foot before he's gone very many feet. And there's no way he can cut his ankle or leg with this rig, he adds—the rubber will give enough to prevent bruising. This should cure a bunch-quitter in a hurry.

NEXT TIME you give your old pony a bath, tape a section of broom or shovel handle to the handle end of your sweat scraper; then you won't have trouble hanging onto the slippery, soapy thing.

LENGTH OF BROOM OR SHOVEL HANDLE

PLASTIC OR FRICTION TAPE

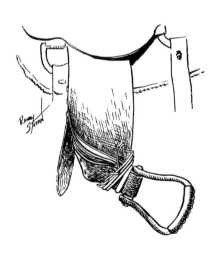

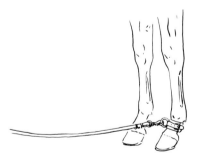

THIS IS the way some of the European cavalry forces used to picket their mounts. And this same method is used in some parts of our West to stake as well as picket. If you try this, be sure your horse is in a soft place the first time or two, and that the ankle strap is padded with woolskin or felt.

A FREQUENT contributor in Missouri adds this idea and comment to our collection of hints. He says, "With so many new saddles flooding the cow country, all squeaking with stiff leathers and stirrups dodging the foot every time you swing a leg over the old pony—here's a tip in setting those new stirrup leathers. Wet the fenders and stirrup generously with Lexol or any liquid saddle soap, then lace to proper length. With stirrup leathers flat, tie a string around the leathers just above the stirrup. Now, sharply fold the leathers back over the fenders and tie in place with string to hold the crease until you're ready to ride. Repeat the process if necessary."

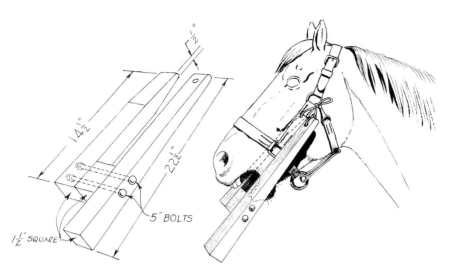

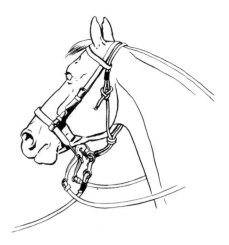

NOT HAVING access to a regular speculum for holding open his horse's mouth, a reader rigged this emergency speculum from three pieces of wood and a couple of five-inch stove bolts. A Quarter Horse he owned had a jaw tooth pulled by his veterinarian and it became necessary to flush and clean the resultant wound every day for a month. This wooden rig, placed in the horse's mouth as shown, enabled him to reach the area for treatment with ease.

HERE'S A way to utilize a tie rope with an Easy-Stop headstall. Rig a throatlatch with 3/8-inch nylon rope, using metal clamps at the two places shown where loops are formed. The knot under the throat is a simple overhand, tied with double strands. The loop through the Easy-Stop hackamore bit is a piece of heavy wire, brazed or welded. The nylon *fiador*, for that's what it actually is, takes all the strain when a tie rope is snapped into it, eliminating broken bridles.

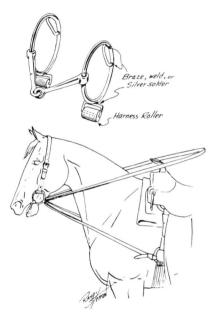

snaffle, and the location of the headstall keepers. Be sure your welder places these alterations on the rings correctly. Use of the draw reins is simple. You can use cotton rope or a piece cut from an old pair of driving lines as long as the material you select for reins will work freely in the rollers. The drawing shows exactly how to rig the draw reins. When using them, remember, keep your hands low and as light as possible.

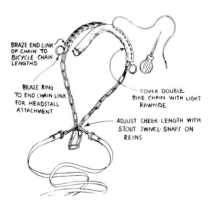

HERE'S A good way to rework a snaffle bit for use with draw reins on that hard-to-hold horse. Your local harness and saddle dealer can probably supply you with the check-rein rollers that are used in this bit. Or, perhaps you can find a pair of these rollers on an old set of harness. Your local handyman or welder can weld or braze the rollers and headstall keepers in place in a few minutes, giving you a mighty useful bit with very little expense and effort on your part.

The drawing shows how the roller should be positioned on the ring of the

WE'VE HAD quite a few different ways to tie up the cinches for easy saddling, and here's still another version; tie both front and flank cinches together with the saddle strings on the fork. This is a good method and easy to jerk loose when the saddle is in place on the horse's back.

A CANADIAN tells us that this hackamore outfit is the best rig he has ever used on a hard-to-control horse. The nosepiece of the hackamore is made of two 9-inch lengths of bicycle chain laid side by side. The end links of a 20-inch length of light chain are brazed to the ends of the bike chains, which keeps them from separating. Small rings are brazed to the links that join the bicycle chain, to accommodate the cheeks of the headstall. Regular leather reins are used, with a good strong swivel snap on each rein. This snap allows the cheeks of the hackamore to be adjusted for each horse. Remember, like all bits and bosals, this one can be abused.

6 STABLE, TACKROOM, AND CORRAL

HERE'S A handy chute for baled hay suggested by a reader in Oklahoma. She obtained a discarded children's slide from a local school playground, cut the legs and feet off it, and fastened it securely to the hay loft edge and to the floor of the barn. The result was a chute that put the bales down to the main floor without breaking the wire or twine.

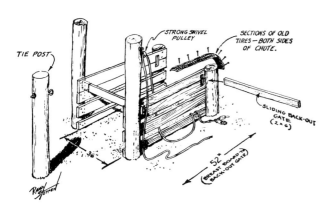

THIS BREEDING stall or chute was suggested by a good friend who was visiting me for a couple of days at my studio in Texas. He had used a similar chute for many years and was very satisfied with the design. My drawing shows the breeding chute built out in the open, but if you have a barn or shed wall located in a convenient place, by all means, build your chute against it, saving construction of one whole side. Posts used must be set deep enough into the ground so they'll literally hold a bull. You know better than I do how deep a post needs to be set into your type of ground to be solid, so the dimensions of the posts mentioned here are above-ground dimensions.

The two tall posts at the head of the chute should be about six feet high. The back ones can be 32 inches, just about the right height to work across when you use this chute for doctoring a horse. Side boards must be good, strong, two-inch lumber so a fractious animal can't tear up your chute. Notice that the two top boards are nailed together with no space between them. These should be 2x8s, and you'll need to notch out each one so the chest board at the front and the sliding tail or back-out gate at the rear will fit between the chute sides and against the posts for maximum strength. The chest board is secured in place with bolts or lag screws, or good-sized nails, but it must be solid enough to stand the combined weight and push of both stallion and mare.

The two lower boards are spaced as shown. Make sure there's just enough room between the bottom board and the next one to get your hands through to fasten the ankle strap around the mare's near hind foot. This one ankle strap, whose rope passes through the pulley set high on the front post, will give the breeder absolute control over the mare, and prevent injury to the stallion. Be sure to pad the low back posts and the upper boards of the sides—there's nothing better or cheaper than sections of old tire casings nailed in place.

The length of this chute can be adjusted to fit various mares. The ideal length should equal the distance from the chest of the mare to the buttocks. Naturally, a chute for Shetlands would be unsuitable for Thoroughbreds. The tie post in front should be located well in front of the mare's head, and should be high enough so an excited animal could not possibly rear up and come down on top of this post. A really stout eyebolt through this post completes the project.

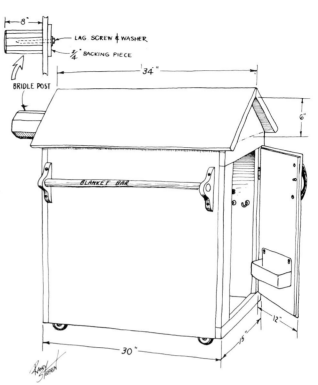

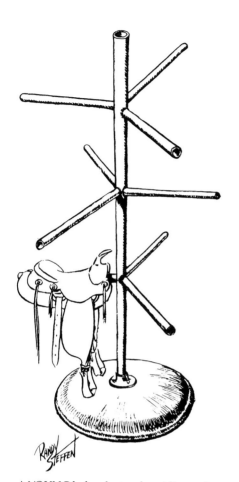

THIS IS a dog house saddle compartment that is neat as well as useful. The designer of this one sketched it out and had a local cabinetmaker build it. But it would be easy for a man handy with carpenter tools to make. All materials for sides, front, back, top, and floor are ³/₄-inch plywood. The door is a lip-type, and the ball-bearing casters on the bottom are fairly large and make it easy to push around, even with the saddle and the other equipment in place. The soap tray, inside the door, is for medicines; the cup hooks will hold brushes, sweat scrapers, and the like; and the blanket bar is for, oddly enough, the saddle blanket. You can let your imagination run wild as far as adding refinements of your own. I'd suggest a chain or steel cable with a padlock through a couple of holes in the roof to keep the saddle from walking off, if this rack is taken to shows, and a hasp with padlock on the door.

A YOUNG lady who teaches riding and jumping at a prominent stable in Sacramento told me about this saddle rack. It's designed to revolve at the base, and will hold nine stock saddles with ease. Made from ordinary black pipe, the rack arms are welded to the vertical pipe. The base needs to be large in diameter and heavy.

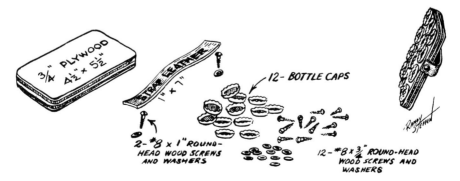

EQUIPMENT FOR the stable or tack room doesn't have to be expensive; here's how to rig a homemade curry comb from a piece of plywood, some bottle caps, screws, washers, and a piece of leather for the handle. It's sure simple to make, and would be real good for chipping dried mud off long-haired horses.

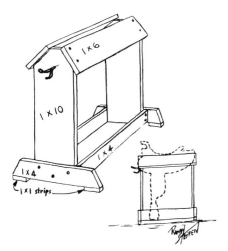

A SMALL hatchet or hand axe is a useful tool to keep hanging in the stable. One swing of this tool will cut baling twine or wire. It does beat untwisting wires or hunting for an elusive pair of pliers or wire cutters. And in cold weather, you won't have to peel off your gloves to break open bales of hay.

RIGGING serviceable, yet economical, saddle racks for the tack room has always involved problems and difficulties. I've seen dozens of really nice saddle racks, but to make them the way they were made would have run into a good many dollars. Having four or five saddles to take care of in our barn, we designed this rack to be made from standard-size lumber with a minimum of effort and cost. You can make it to whatever dimensions will fit your particular stirrup length and skirts. A word of advice: use wood screws throughout to assemble; nails won't give you satisfactory service.

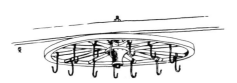

IT'S ALWAYS a problem to find enough storage space for bridles, halters, harness, and other small horse gear. This slick buggy-wheel ceiling-hanger is one solution to the problem. Fasten a light

buggy wheel to a ceiling joist with a large bolt through the hub and through the joist as pictured. A big washer and a nut over the hub allow the tension to be adjusted so the wheel can revolve freely, but without too much wobble. Heavy wire is used for the hooks that are fastened to each spoke. Of course, a coat or two of bright enamel will dress up this western lazy Susan.

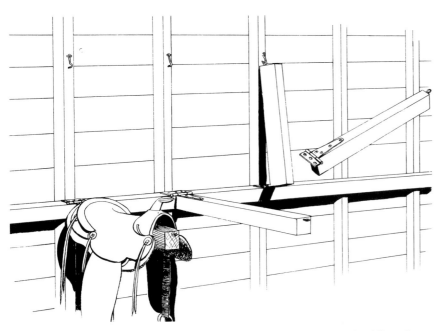

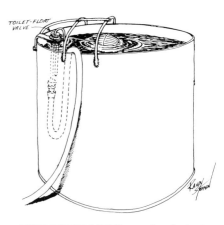

THROUGHOUT the years, I have shown a number of different types of saddle racks; well, here's another—easy to make and it offers several advantages. A 2x4 is nailed to the studs of the tack room wall; then shorter sections of 2x4s or 4x4s are attached to the horizontal stringer using T-hinges. Hooks and eyes placed as shown in the drawing allow the individual racks to be folded up against the wall and locked in place when not needed.

THIS AUTOMATIC watering device is easy to make and should prove useful in most any stable situation. A toilet float valve is mounted on the edge of the trough, with a garden hose attached to the feed connection. The float automatically keeps the water level constant. I've shown a simple iron rod guard welded to the tank to keep playful horses and colts from pushing the float around with their noses. No reason why this shouldn't be a real handy gadget on anybody's horse outfit.

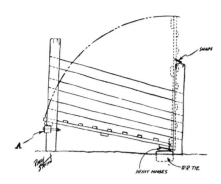

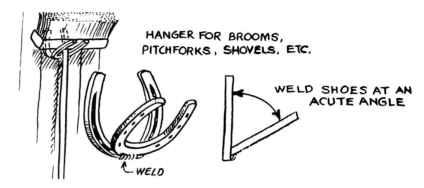

HANGER FOR BROOMS, PITCHFORKS, SHOVELS, ETC.

WELD SHOES AT AN ACUTE ANGLE

WELD

I'VE HAD trouble several times matching a truck bed with the floor of a loading chute when loading out stock; when I built a loading chute of my own last year, I worked out a design that allows me to fit any size pickup or bobtail truck. And, as a little extra touch, the floor folds up to form a solid gate. "A" in the drawing is a 4x4 that supports the floor of the chute when it's down in place, and also forms a platform for shimming up the floor with poles or other pieces of lumber to any height needed to match a truck bed. The back end of the floor is hinged to a section of a railroad crosstie that's buried better than halfway in the ground. Be sure the hinges you use are big, stout strap type, for they bear the full weight of whatever you load through the chute. When I'm finished loading out I raise the floor to a vertical position, and snap it in place with a couple of harness snaps fastened to the sides of the floor. A couple of extra-long staples or big screw eyes fastened to the top of the rear post make the fastening pretty secure. It's a mighty handy arrangement, and I sure do like it.

SOME TIME AGO, my son, Buckshot, suggested a use for some of the old horseshoes we had accumulated around the place. We'd been using large nails in the barn wall to hold brooms, pitchforks, and shovels up out of the way, but the least jar would cause them to fall down, and it was Bucky's job to keep the barn orderly. We had a small electric welder, and made up six or eight holders like I show in this drawing; that put an end to shovels and brooms on the floor and Bucky wore a pleased smirk on his face for a week.

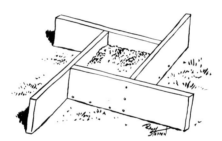

THIS ONE comes from Texas and it's a good idea for anyone who puts out horse minerals. It will just take a few minutes to nail the 1x8s together as shown. A board bottom completes the holder that is hard to tip over, and it will also do a good job of keeping minerals off the ground.

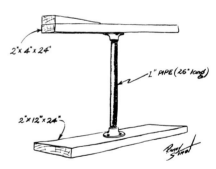

2"x 4"x 24"

1" PIPE (26" long)

2"x 12"x 24"

HERE'S A handy one for any of you who use electric fences to divide up your pastures for rotation grazing. The reader who sent this in molds the concrete bases for his electric fence posts by using an old, round-bottom cooking pan. He inserts the iron rod post after he pours the concrete, and props it while it sets. The insulator at the top is a piece of heavy wire wrapped around the rod, and with a piece of rubber tubing, slipped over the loop that holds the wire. With the round bottom these have, they'll right themselves if they should be pushed over; and it's a simple matter to slip the electric wire through the open part of the insulated loop.

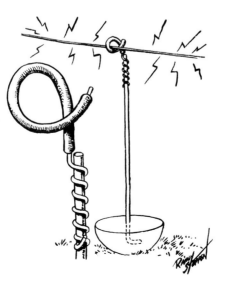

I'VE SHOWN quite a few ways to rig up saddle racks in these hints but without a doubt, here is the handiest portable design I've run across yet. And I believe you'll agree with me after you make and use one a few times. About as simple as ABC to build, all you need are a saw and a screwdriver for tools. The rack requires two pieces of standard-size lumber, as indicated on the drawing, two one-inch pipe floor flanges, a length of one-inch pipe threaded at both ends, and enough wood screws to fasten the flanges to the lumber. A twist of the wrist, and it's together or knocked down for easy storing and hauling in car or trailer. One end is built up, as I've shown, but you may also want to add some padding to your rack.

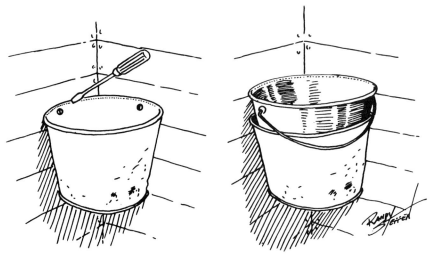

DON'T THROW away that old feed bucket with the hole in the bottom. You can make a dandy feeding rig by hanging it securely in the corner of the stall, at just the right height. Fasten it permanently in place with two good, stout wood screws at the two points where it contacts the walls. Now take your new feed bucket and set it in the one fastened to the wall. It's there to stay until you remove it for cleaning and refilling.

SEVERAL TIMES I've included ways to keep a horse from chewing up the boards in his pen. And if I remember right, I did say that some cures would work on some animals, while some wouldn't. Well, sure enough, who would it be that had a mare that just nothing seemed to work on but ol' Randy himself. My face was real red for awhile, but I came up with the best remedy for cribbers and just plain destructive horses you ever saw; it will absolutely stop those ponies in any man's corral from making like a herd of over-ambitious beavers. As you can see in the drawing, all you need is a sack full of staples, and as much ³/8-inch steel cable as it takes to line the top edge of every board in your lot that might get chewed on. When you've stapled this cable in place, your old cayuse will have to stand on his head to play termite in your corral. Oh yes, many times a local telephone company or utility company will discard this type of cable—it might be yours for the asking.

THIS RUSTIC saddle rack may be just what you need. It uses a 12-inch diameter log for the rail, and 3-inch diameter legs with the ends carved down to fit the holes drilled in the rail. This rack can be made short enough for a single saddle or long enough to accommodate three or four. If care is taken in fitting the legs to the rail, it will be a sturdy rack.

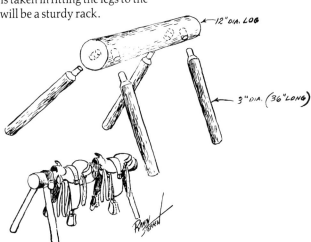

12" DIA. LOG

3" DIA. (36" LONG)

PROP UP REAR OF TANK

THIS TRICK is pretty well known to old-timers but it is worth passing on to the newcomers who may not be familiar with it. Many of us experience trouble with dry hoofs during the hot summer months. This condition is especially prevalent in the western states where summer rains are unusual and relative humidity low. To help prevent dry, brittle hoofs, tilt your watering tank so the overflow spills onto the ground where the horse stands while drinking. The permanent puddle will soothe and soften hard, brittle hoofs, and remedy a good many sore-footed horses. You might consider letting the faucet drip so a small amount of water will continually spill over the edge of the tank. You might also scoop out a shallow depression in the ground around the tank so water will not run off.

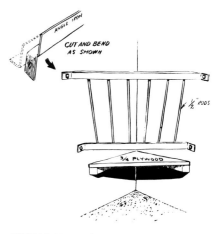

HERE'S another feed box that will hang on the stall door or corral rail. We've shown several designs but this is one of the best. By using 1x6s and 1x4s as shown in the illustration, you'll have a very stout feed box that will take a lot of abuse. The horseshoes, nailed or screwed to the ends of the box, make it easy to hang on a door.

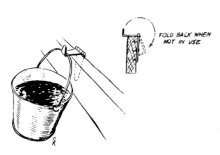

ANY HORSE owner will find this bucket hanger a handy gadget around the stable. It's nothing more than a bent hinge mounted on a corral rail as I've shown in the illustration. Another advantage to this one is that it folds back out of the way when not in use so there is no danger of man or horse snagging on it.

HERE'S AN easily made hay rack I saw in a barn at Cisco, Texas. It's made from two pieces of light angle iron, cut to fit across the corner of a stall. The end portions of the angle irons were bent, after another part had been cut away, and the two strips of angle iron were joined by welding 1/2-inch iron rods behind the iron strips so there would be no projections to injure the horse. A piece of 3/4-inch plywood, cut to fit the corner, was nailed on brace blocks to make a shelf about six inches below the bottom of the rack. This rack keeps hay off the floor and makes it easy to pull out.

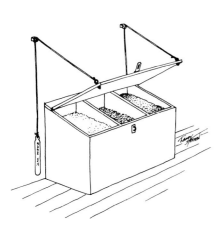

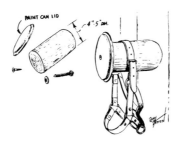

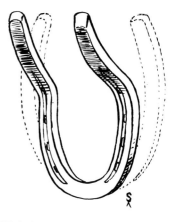

HERE'S A real fine way to keep the lid of a big grain bin from wearing holes in your hat or head. The lid is counterbalanced with window sash weights, so that it stays in place when lifted. You may have to experiment some in placing the eyebolts in the lid so a fairly sensitive balance is achieved. The closer to the front of the lid, the less weight required.

ONE OF our Canadian readers makes bridle and halter racks from sections of peeled log. He uses whatever length he thinks warranted of a 4- to 5-inch diameter log and makes sure the section is sawed squarely on each end. He then fastens it to the wall of the barn with a lag screw and washer, provided he can get at the back side of the wall; if not, he toenails the log to the wall, using some pretty long nails. If you must nail it, drill some undersized holes in the log to keep it from splitting. A paint can lid screwed to the end of the log makes a retainer to keep the gear from sliding off accidentally.

THIS IS one of the handiest all-purpose horseshoe hangers I've ever run across. A veterinarian in Auburn, Calif., has these all over his barn and saddle room. They're made by a local blacksmith from worn-out shoes, and it doesn't take but a few minutes on the forge and anvil to turn them out. A coat of bright red paint, and a few horseshoe nails to fasten them to the wall, make these hangers right attractive.

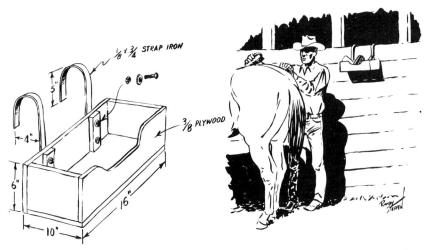

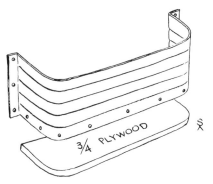

A FRIEND who lives not too far from my place near Auburn, Calif., has a colt that he thinks a lot of. He spends a lot of time grooming that little guy and this grooming caddy is something he dreamed up to make the chore less of a chore. Made of 3/8-inch plywood, with a couple of strap iron brackets screwed to the sides, it fits over a stall door or partition and stays there. Sure prevents a fellow from trying to hold tools under his arm, or stooping down to pick 'em up off the floor.

HERE'S A dandy way to make a real sturdy manger for your stall. Buy a basement window well, the kind that building supply stores and lumber yards handle, cut a piece of 3/4-inch plywood to fit inside the bottom, drill a few holes for fastening the plywood with wood screws, and hang the completed manger on the wall of the stall with six heavy wood screws.

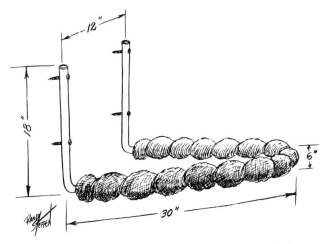

A SIMPLE, yet sturdy saddle rack is made from an eight-foot length of 3/4-inch pipe. The horizontal bars are wrapped with burlap to protect the woolskin lining of the saddle skirts.

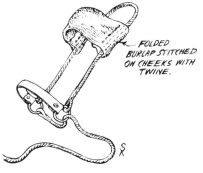

HERE'S A stunt I can remember my dad using when I was a small boy. I know of quite a few people who keep horses in

straight tie stalls, and I know there are some that have a tendency to lay their ears back and take a swipe at their owners when they ease up to untie them. If you have a horse that does this, play it safe. If he's tied the way I've shown, and you pull his head to the stall partition before you enter, his back end will move over to the other side, and your chances of getting a hoof in the belly are far less. Two eyebolts in the left partition, located as shown, will allow you to pass the tie rope through the first one and tie to the second one, leaving enough slack for the horse to eat in comfort.

ONE OF our California readers is quite concerned about the danger of fire, especially where horses are concerned. She suggests every horse owner keep a fire halter hanging near each horse in the barn, so that it could be slipped on the horse quickly in the event of fire. Such a halter would prevent the panic that usually grips a horse in the presence of a large blaze, and would allow a man to lead the animal from danger without fear of the horse running back into the flames. She suggests making the halter from inexpensive clothesline cord, but I show the same arrangement in my drawing of an inexpensive type of halter. The blind is made by folding a section of burlap sack and stitching it in place on the cheeks of the halter. This type of halter can be slipped on a horse faster than most other types—a real timesaver in an emergency.

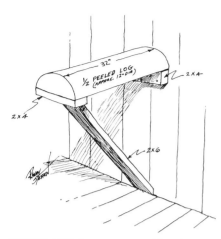

THERE ARE almost as many ideas for saddle racks as there are horsemen. We've included several in this book and the one I show here is about as handy as any of them and a cinch to build. I was visiting an Arabian ranch in California to look at a colt and while nosing around in the tack room, I spotted this saddle rack. The owner had run some 12-inch diameter logs through a saw, cut the half sections into 32-inch lengths, peeled the bark, and let them season well. Then he built the sturdy saddle racks as I have pictured here. The smooth, round log surface lets the woolskin lining of the saddles slide easily into place with no sharp corners to wear away any part of the saddle.

SPEAKING OF saddle racks, here's one I remember seeing at a dude ranch in Nevada. It was made like a hitching rack, but the rail was about 8 or 10 inches in diameter, and the top was adzed off to form a base for the two 1x6 boards nailed down to form a secure rest for the saddles. Iron straps held the rail securely in place in the notched posts. It seems to me this rack was long enough to hold five or six saddles. Some of you may find this one handy around your horse establishment.

I DON'T think there's anything that irritates me more than a horse that chews up every piece of wood he can sink his teeth into. And I have a stallion that does just that. He's not a cribber, but just plain bored to death with standing in his corral while all the other horses have the run of a pasture. I don't mind admitting that I've tried a dozen "sure-fire" ways to treat the wood, or rig wire around the stall and pens, but he kept right on acting like a beaver out of water. Not long after we moved to our place in California, an old-timer came to work for me and he was a sure-enough horseman in every sense of the word. His cure for this bad habit was quick and simple; he took a sack of roofing nails, short but with big heads, and studded the exposed edges of all the corral boards and the exposed boards in the stall that were being chewed to bits. The chewing stopped instantly. My sketch shows how the nails were spaced and staggered. Try it and see for yourself. Another easy way to stop wood chewing: apply metal drywall corner strips to the boards. They are sold at drywall supply stores.

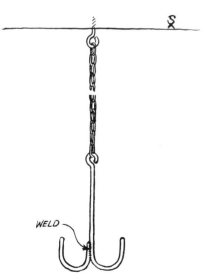

THIS HORSE gear hook is a handy idea; suspended from the ceiling outside each stall, it makes a good place to hang bridles, halters, or any other horse equipment that can be hung. Made from ³/₈-inch iron rod, it can be heated, bent to shape, and welded on the forge—or your welder can whip it out in a hurry.

HERE'S A mouse trap that never needs re-setting. Of course, a man would have to empty the bucket every once in a while, but that shouldn't be too much of a hardship. A baking powder can, strung on a wire fastened to both sides of a pail, is covered with cooking fat, which is then sprinkled with grain, bread crumbs, cheese, or ground meat. The board is a ramp for the hungry little demons to reach the feast on the baking powder can, which revolves when they climb aboard and dumps them into the pail, filled about a third with water.

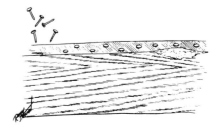

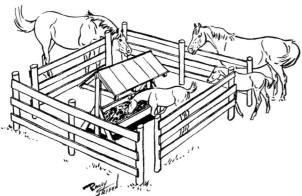

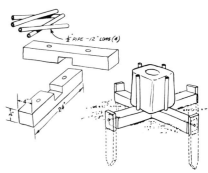

HERE'S A creep feeder for your colts that takes a little more work to make than the calf-type creep, but which is a whole lot safer for horses than the one-rail type. I've seen cranky old mares skin all the hide off their withers trying to follow their foals into a one-rail feeder. This one is made so the openings are just wide enough to pass a colt's slender body, and effectively prod a mare on the shoulders, turning her back without a fight.

A NEIGHBOR who runs a bunch of Shetland mares finds this 4x4 and pipe salt block holder handy. It's simple to make, and costs little to throw four or five of them together. What's more, it holds the salt blocks off the wet ground and keeps the stock from turning them over.

HERE'S another type latch for a stable door. It consists of a large lag screw or bolt, and three heavy screw eyes, arranged on the stall door and frame as shown. It's sure enough stout, and simple to make.

I'VE BEEN asked to show a design for a portable metal hay feeder. While I don't remember running into a portable one, I do remember seeing an extremely simple design in Texas; and I've added a pair of implement wheels to make it easy to move around from corral to corral. It's made from half sections of 55-gallon drums, pipe frame, and 1/2-inch diameter iron rod. The rods hold the hay, and the drums prevent cattle or horses from wasting a lot of it on the ground. A couple of flanges on the bottoms of the front pipe legs will help prevent the legs from sinking into soft ground. Drilling holes in the bottom will let rain water drain out.

HERE'S A design for a feed bunk that's weatherproof with the lid down, and a windbreak for horses or cattle with the lid hooked up. Made of scrap lumber, it makes loading a snap from the alley way in a set of corrals.

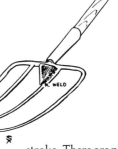

WHEN IT comes to stable design, concrete feed troughs are best, according to one of our readers. But he adds that if you make 'em of wood, use bolts or screws instead of nails. This eliminates *hardware disease* and makes the first cost the last cost.

A MONTANA reader suggests welding a mower blade to one tine of a pitchfork; when winter-feeding cattle or horses, you can cut the twine with one stroke, and pitch off the hay with the same stroke. There are plenty of ranches where hay is still fed with a team and wagon and this idea should be a timesaver for anyone who has to pitch hay off a truck or a wagon.

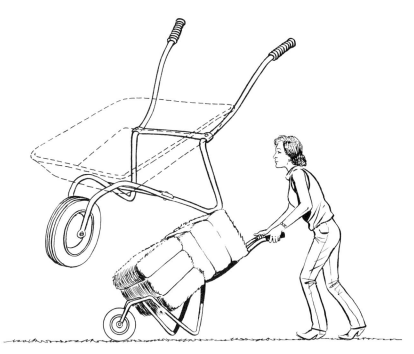

AN OLD wheelbarrow is the basis for this hint. My drawing shows how to modify the wheelbarrow without further explanation. If you have to move a few bales of hay at a time, this is a handy way to do it.

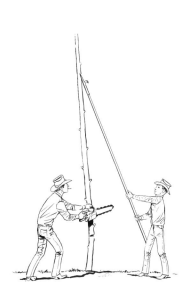

A GREAT many peeled pole corrals are still being built and used in the parts of the West where lodgepole pines are found in abundance. The quickest and best way to harvest a bunch of lodgepole pines is for two men to work together with a small chain saw and a logger's pike pole. While one man cuts down the pine, the other pushes it with the pike in the direction they want it to fall. This action also serves to prevent the tree from binding the saw blade.

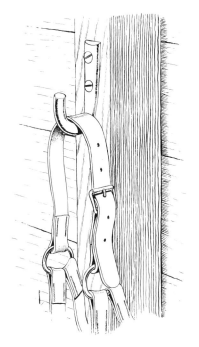

A PICKUP tiedown hook, made of iron and usually galvanized for protection against the weather, makes one of the best and simplest tack room and trailer saddle compartment bridle racks imaginable. They can be fastened to wood walls with wood screws of the proper size, and to metal walls in a trailer with pop rivets.

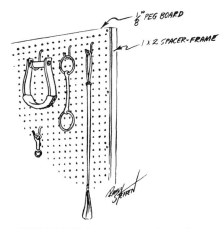

PEG BOARD has many uses in the home and it is ideally suited to the tack room since it provides a convenient way to hang a lot of gear. I've used peg board for a gun rack in my studio for several years, and made my own hooks from short sections of aluminum rod like that used by utility companies. The rod is just the right size for a snug fit in the peg board holes, and can be formed easily with a pair of pliers.

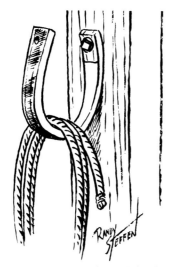

HERE'S another handy hook for the saddle room, made by removing the bolt from an old stirrup, then fastening it to the wall or post with a wood screw, or lag screw and washer. This one is really handy for holding the coils of a saddle rope, and it looks like a good way to use up those old stirrups.

THIS IS A useful and easy-to-make bridle rack. It utilizes a 1x12-inch board of whatever length suits your purpose, with holes cut to fit enough one-pound coffee cans to suit your needs. Then snip, bend, and nail the flanges to the board, nail on a dust cover, and your bridle rack is ready to hang or fasten to the wall.

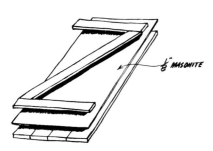

THIS ONE comes from a reader in Minnesota, a country where the winter winds are bitter cold. She suggests sandwiching a sheet of $1/4$-inch masonite between the vertical boards and the diagonal and horizontal braces when making up a door for your horse barn. The masonite will keep the wind from whistling through the cracks that invariably show up between the boards and will help keep your horses comfortable throughout the winter.

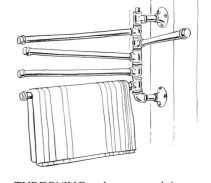

THE DRYING and storage rack for saddle blankets pictured here is a plumber's dream but is mighty practical at that. Each arm is made from a length of pipe, a pipe cap, and a tee. The top brace is a tee, a nipple, and a flange fastened to the wall. The bottom brace is an elbow the same size as the smaller piece of pipe that slides down through all the tees of the arms, and screws into this bottom elbow which in turn is fastened to a nipple and a floor flange. If you have a supply of old pipefittings lying around, this one is for you.

BURN HOLE THRU WITH HEATED NAIL .....!

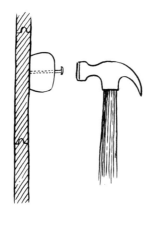

HERE'S ANOTHER bridle and halter rack that's about as quick and easy to make as any I've seen. It is made from the bottom of a plastic soap or detergent container. If the hole is made with a hot nail, the plastic won't split.

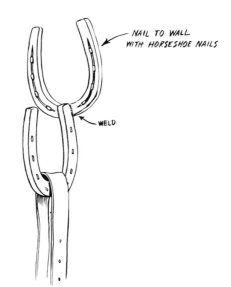

NAIL TO WALL WITH HORSESHOE NAILS

WELD

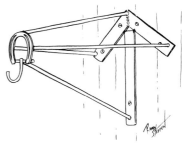

THIS SADDLE rack is made from ½-inch rods, a horseshoe, and some ⅛-inch thick strap iron. A hook for the bridle is welded to the horseshoe.

A FRIEND in California who raises some good Quarter Horses sent in this idea to help out all you folks who own wood-eating horses. In his letter he said, "We always had a colt or two that liked to chew up the corral fences until an old-timer told me to throw a pretty good-sized branch or two in the corral. It really works with our young horses—they chew the branches and leave the fences alone." I threw some post oak branches in my corrals tonight—maybe ol' Maple will play beaver on the branches and quit creating repair jobs for me.

A GOOD friend of mine who has a few horses in the suburban area of Sacramento made up bridle racks like this one for his tack room, and they sure do look good. A coat of flat black enamel from a handy spray can gives them a real polished look that will enhance any man's saddle room.

HERE'S ANOTHER milk-can saddle rack that's good. Four pieces of pipe are welded to the can for legs with the addition of scrap iron braces for support. A horseshoe welded to the back makes a good place to hang a bridle or halter, while the inside of the can will hold any number of items. The lid keeps varmints from disturbing the contents of the milk can.

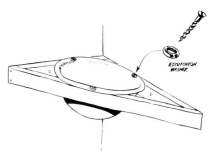

ESCUTCHEON WASHER

A FRIEND fixed up these feeders in his stalls. The large plastic mixing bowls are fastened to the wood corner frames as shown.

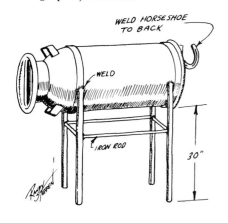

WELD HORSESHOE TO BACK

WELD

IRON ROD

30"

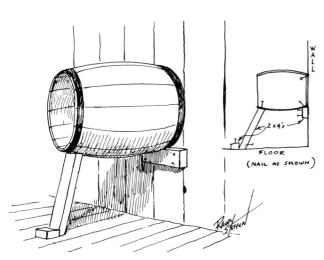

WALL

2 x 4's

FLOOR
(NAIL AS SHOWN)

ANOTHER VERSION of a saddle rack—this time it's made from a nail keg. Some 2x4s and a few nails will complete the job. The inside of the keg makes a handy storage place for curry comb, brush, and other equipment.

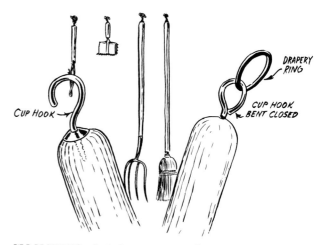

DRAPERY RING

CUP HOOK

CUP HOOK BENT CLOSED

I'LL HAVE TO admit that sometimes I leave things lying around, so that after awhile the barn gets to looking like a boar's nest. Therefore, to keep all pitchforks, brooms, hammers, twitches, currycombs, and anything else that had wooden handles in their proper places, I fixed them as I've shown above.

7 TRAINING AND BREAKING

A RANCHER WHO RUNS commercial Santa Gertrudis cattle near Mammoth, Ariz., sends in this idea, and from the way he writes, I know that he's an old hand at working with spoiled horses. "The best helper I ever had," he writes, "was a small black pack mule. After I had staked out a bronc overnight, I rode him next morning. Then when I turned him in the pasture, I necked him to the mule. Next morning he'd be leading real good and was much easier for me to pull around." I can certainly vouch for this way to break a green horse to lead; I've done the same thing with an old jenny burro. The colt might drag her around for a short time, but come morning, the shoe is on the other foot.

THIS IS A slightly different approach to halter breaking a young colt. Tie a three-inch iron ring in the colt's tail, using an overhand knot of hair. Then tie one end of a 20-foot rope to the ring, bringing the other end up through the halter ring; use both the lead rope and the tail rope to urge the colt ahead. It's surprising how quickly a little fellow will give to this pressure. Sure saves fighting him with just a lead rope. Both ropes can be tied to a post, so the colt can soak for an hour or two and thoroughly learn that he must give to a rope on his head.

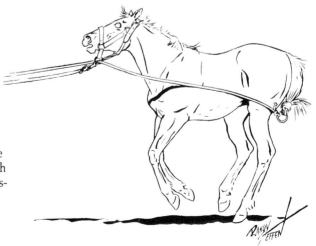

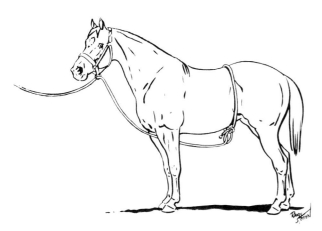

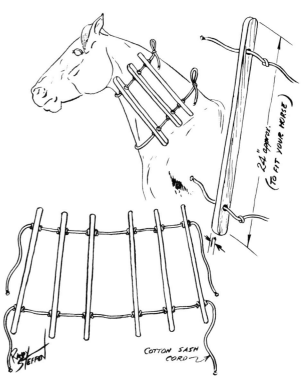

I HAD A LETTER from a reader in Wisconsin who had a mare that was bad about throwing a fit when the cinch was pulled up on her belly. The solution to the problem came when the owner stumbled on to this trick. This is the age-old flank hitch and it's worth showing again. You'll need a stout rope that will hold the horse when he throws a real cattywampus fit. A bowline is used to tie about a six-inch loop in one end. The other end is passed through the loop and drawn up so it forms a loose loop *just ahead of the hip bone.* The free end goes up between the front legs, then up through the halter ring, and on to a stout beam, tree, or post and tied with a slip hitch. When the horse is saddled and the cinch causes it to throw a fit, the loop tightens around the flank and punishes the horse until he steps ahead and gives himself slack. The loop is large enough so it will slack off immediately and relieve the pressure. After three or four goes with this rig at saddling time, the animal should be cured, if he's at all curable.

EVER FIND it hard to heal a wound on your horse's shoulder, leg, or side because he kept gnawing at it? Here's a simple rig that you can make that will sure enough put a stop to this foolishness. The wood staves are simple 1x2s with the ends rounded, and with two $3/8$-inch holes drilled two or three inches from each end. Cotton sash cord, or clothesline, knotted as shown to keep the staves spaced properly, is the only other material needed. Tied at the top of the neck, this device will allow the horse plenty of free movement in the vertical plane, but will effectively prevent him from reaching around to the side to chew on a wound or stable blanket.

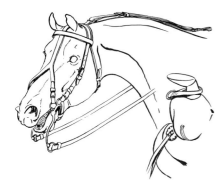

AN EFFECTIVE cure for horses that want to get their heads down and buck is this over-check rig. A small strap with a D-ring slipped over the horn allows the snap at the end of the over-check line to be fastened securely to the horn of the stock saddle. You'll probably recognize this rig as the same type of over-check that's used with harness horses.

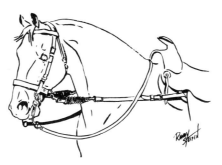

THIS TIE-DOWN has a spring action that should help cure a horse from throwing his head. Using two springs with 15- or 20-pound tension, rig them as shown with leather straps and snaps to the noseband of the bridle. The spring action seems to have more effect than a solid tie-down.

A FAMILY in Maryland bought a horse that was bad about kicking while he was in his stall. They cured this habit by tying him for a few days in a standing stall, and rigging a swinging log right behind his heels as I've shown here. When the horse kicked the log, it swung away and then walloped him right back. It didn't take but a few cycles of this treatment to cure this kicking habit permanently.

91

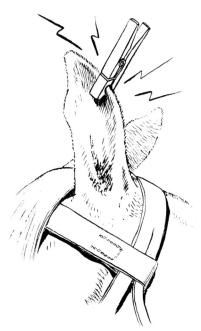

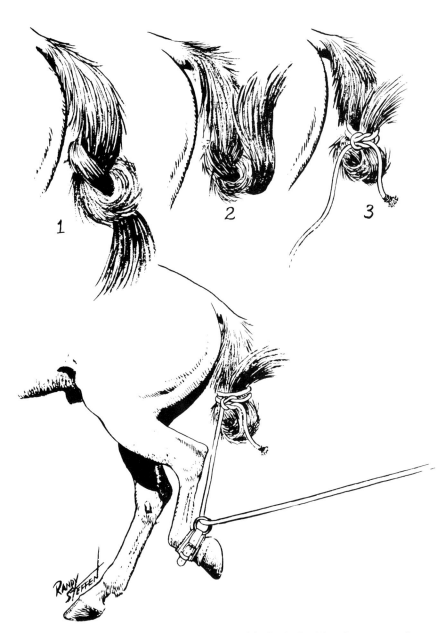

A HORSE that jigs and prances is a pain in the neck, to put it mildly. The cause for most jigging is too few miles and not enough wet saddle blankets, but not always. Try clamping a wooden clothespin to the ear of your jiggin' horse. Sometimes it will work.

HERE'S A bronc-stomper's trick that I'd almost forgotten about, even though I'd used it many times. Take a 10- or 12-foot length of light rope, such as window sash cord; tie a halter snap in one end and snap it to the snaffle bit in the mouth of a salty bronc before you step aboard him. Bring the free end back around the cantle board of the saddle, then stand at his head, with one hand on the shoulder away from the side the rope is snapped to, and pull steadily, making the horse wheel on his hind legs away from you. Do this on one side several times, then unsnap the line and change sides—then pull him around several times from the other side again. You'll be surprised how this takes a lot of the snuffiness out of one before you step up on him.

I TRIED THIS one a few years back when I could take the backbreaking strain of shoeing, and it works. I arranged the tail-knot as I've shown here, tying a simple overhand knot right up against the end of the tail bone so you'll have plenty of hair to work with. Next, bring up the loose end of hair and take a couple of turns with the rope around the whole works at a point above the knot in the tail, and secure the rope with a tight square knot. You'll need to use a leather strap—a good stout one—around the ankle, with a ring attached as shown. It's best to line the leather strap with wool-skin to not chafe the horse's leg. Next, run the free end of the tail rope through the ring and, standing behind the horse, pull the foot up as high as necessary for comfort. You can tie this end to the tail or have an assistant hold it so old Booger won't kick off your head while working on that foot.

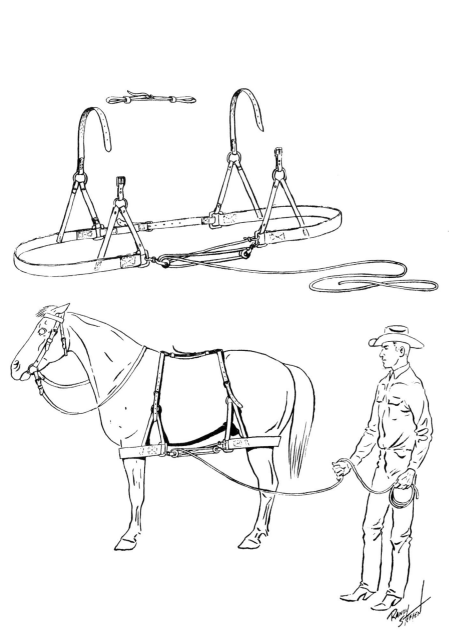

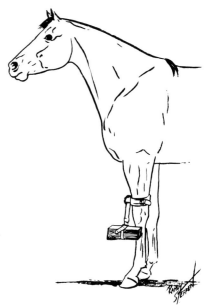

HERE'S another cure for a fairly common stable vice. For a horse that paws constantly in the stable, fasten a leather strap with a ring to one leg, or both, just above the knee; then attach a wood block about ten inches in length and two inches square to the leg strap, so that it hangs low enough on the leg to hit the shin. Every time he paws, the block will strike him on the shin, and he should soon give up this annoying habit.

THIS IS a way to cure a horse that pulls back while tied. Use baling twine to run from the halter ring to the crupper rig under the tail. Two doubled strands will do the trick. By tying overhand knots, as shown here, the rig stays in place. It's tied so some tension is put on the halter ring. The lead rope is snapped into the halter ring and tied to a stout post or tree. When the horse pulls back, tension is put under the tender tail before being placed on the neck strap of the halter—with the result that any sensible horse will step forward and quit punishing himself.

FROM NORTH of our border comes an improvement on the old running W horse-breaking rig. One of our Canadian readers likes to use this device for working on mean horses so he can get in close without getting his head kicked off. Needless to say, this outfit needs to be made up of good stout materials, especially the breast collar, breeching, and adjusting strap on the off side. He suggests doubled and sewn trace leathers, and he recommends that the four heavy rings shown should be squared, as drawn. The front pulley is a double-sheave; the rear one is single.

This rig is best put on the horse in a chute. And, the lower drawing shows how the front and back straps should fit: low enough to draw the legs together, but not low enough to impair natural gaits. The adjusting straps allow the rig to be adjusted to fit almost any size horse. He uses this to teach a horse the meaning of "whoa" and "gid-dap," and after hobbling the horse up short with it, and tying the pull rope with a slip hitch so it won't give, he can get up close and gentle the horse around his legs and the rest of his body.

He also uses this same rig in breaking a horse to harness, putting it over the regular harness; then he can stop a runaway without having to haul on a tender mouth. And, a horse in this rig can't kick over the traces or the pole, nor can he get his front feet over the neck yoke.

AT FIRST GLANCE, some of you may gasp with horror at this drawing. But, look again. That isn't a .30-.30 that ol' boy is blazing away with, it's a BB gun, and he's using it to break a horse from turning his heels when he walks up to place a bridle on the horse. The trainer who told me about this one says when he starts nodding his head at you after two or three shots, you've got him, and a little gentle persuasion on your part will result in his letting you walk up to his head every time. But, just as with any other phase of horse training, you've got to use good judgment. Don't overdo it.

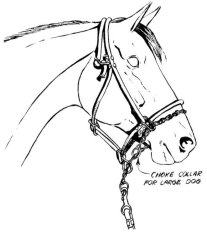

I HEARD about this one from a reader who owned a mare that had become a real problem to handle with a halter and a lead strap until she rigged an old dog choke collar as an additional persuader. With the chain working on the nose and under the chin at the same time, this pulling mare settled down in a hurry to become a model animal. Before this chain device was used, the mare was almost impossible to lead, and pulled back bad when tied up. The wire loops at the sides of the halter, as shown in the drawing, hold the chain in the proper position, and allow the chain to be removed quickly when the need for it no longer exists.

EVER HAVE a colt or a cranky old saddle horse reach around and take a bite out of you when you're cinching him up? If you have, you'll appreciate this little gadget that I saw being used in a sales barn in Texas. The handler had whittled himself a paddle from a cedar shake, shaped as I've shown here, and had stuck some ordinary straight pins through the broad, thin end so they protruded a little more than an eighth of an inch. He was saddling several colts, and one in particular kept reaching around trying to take a

bite. So this fellow rigged this little device to break the habit without having to slap at the colt and scare him. The colt punishes himself when he sticks his nose against the pins, and it won't take long to teach him to stand up there like he should when the cinch is being drawn up.

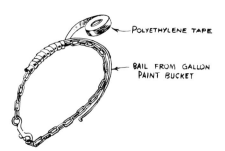

HERE'S A noseband for a tie-down that's severe enough to make a horse aware of it in a hurry, but taped so it can't peel his nose. It's made from a piece of light chain, a bail from a gallon paint can to make it keep its shape on top, and plenty of wraps with polyethylene tape to keep it from chafing.

94

Slip Knot

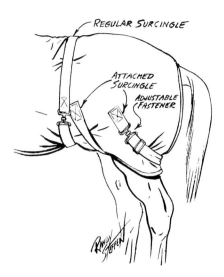

REGULAR SURCINGLE

ATTACHED SURCINGLE

ADJUSTABLE FASTENER

THERE'S NOTHING that irks me more than a horse that rears at any and every excuse. And there's no vice in a horse that is potentially as dangerous. Here's a way, easy on man and horse, that will discourage rearing, and often completely break the habit if used over a long-enough period. And you won't need to pop your horse over the head with a milk bottle, paper sack filled with water, a light bulb, or anything else. Just take a piece of heavy rope, pass it around the swell of his barrel, and tie it at the top with a slip hitch, so you can jerk it free in case of an emergency. You see, in order for a horse to raise his front feet off the ground, he must gather himself behind, expanding his body where the rope is tied, to do so. With the pressure of the rope there, he can't expand himself sufficiently, and his front feet stay on the ground. There are other ways to break this habit, but I doubt if you'll find one that is as harmless, or takes less effort.

HERE'S A solution to a problem that I've never been plagued with . . . mainly because I never blanket my horses except when hauling them during the winter months. But it's evidently a problem with many horses that are blanketed for several days at a time . . . at any rate, it was a problem with a Vermont reader. Her gelding continually wet his stable blanket, and the wet side, being heavier than the other, would hang far down out of place. She cut two extra surcingles from a worn-out blanket, and sewed one on each side, as shown in my drawing. When the attached pieces are passed between the horse's hind legs, above the hocks, and fastened, they will hold the blanket against the inside of the legs and prevent wetting of the blanket.

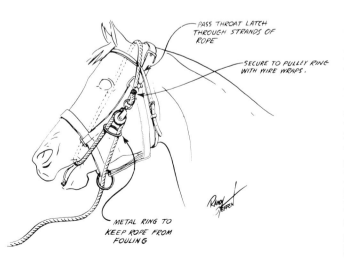

PASS THROAT LATCH THROUGH STRANDS OF ROPE

SECURE TO PULLEY RING WITH WIRE WRAPS.

METAL RING TO KEEP ROPE FROM FOULING

HERE'S A GOOD training hint that works real well for one of our readers in Wisconsin. He writes that this device works so well for him that he wants to pass it on to other readers. He is getting past the age when he relishes a colt breaking in two while he's in the saddle, so he rigged this variation of a war bridle to discourage him from bucking with a saddle before a man ever climbs aboard. The drawing shows how the combination longe line and war bridle is rigged, requiring a 30-foot length of rope not over $5/8$-inch in diameter, a pulley to fit, a fairly large harness ring (about 2-inch inside diameter), and a throatlatch strap. The throatlatch strap is passed through one strand of the rope to keep the whole thing in place, and the harness ring is placed below the pulley to keep the line from fouling in use. The horse should be trained to longe in the regular way before being longed with this rig and a saddle. If he starts to buck, jerk hard on the line and holler at him—he'll stop. Do this every time he lowers his head to pitch and soon he'll be going around with no thought of pitching. Then you should use a gag snaffle when you first start to ride him. It works the same way as this war bridle.

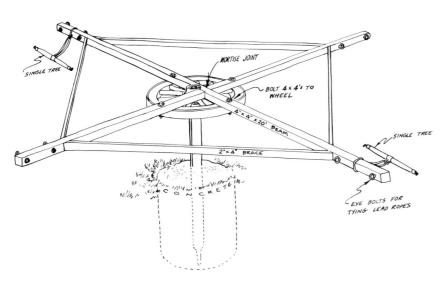

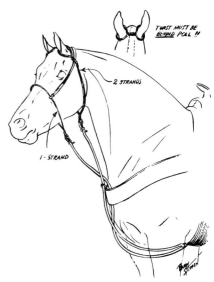

A DISTRICT RANGER in Nevada's Humboldt National Forest submitted this idea. He's horseback a good part of the time and his winter months are occupied with breaking a few colts. This colt wheel helps line the kinks out of the green ones before he ever throws a leg over them. Power for turning the wheel and leading the colts in a circle is provided by hitching two colts to the singletrees attached to two of the 4x4 beams. Even a real spook that's never been harnessed can't go anywhere but around and around, for he's hitched to the singletree behind and his head is tied to the ring ahead of him. The ranger sent some 35mm slides showing six colts hitched to this merry-go-round. He says that a few days of this irons out any kinks that might be in them, and he's yet to have one pitch with him that was started on this rig. The wheel and axle are from an old freight wagon, and the axle is set firmly in a good solid chunk of concrete.

A YOUNG lady in Oregon had a saddle mare that reared and generally threw a fit when she was ridden away from the barn. Realizing the danger in this little trick, she rigged a baling wire tie-down noseband in place of the regular one, and tied the mare's head low enough to keep her from getting it up to rear. She says it didn't take long for the mare to be discouraged from this habit. She was careful to tape all the wire to prevent any injury to her mare.

I EXPECT A good many of you have had trouble longeing horses for the first time—first time for the horse, that is. If he's really halter broke, he'll want to come to you when you cue him to start, and will make you use a whip to get him started around in a circle. A reader uses a long cane pole with a snap on the end to keep the horse away from him during the first one or two longeing lessons, and I'll bet it works real well. He says to use the rope along with the pole just in case the pole should break or slip from your hands.

IF YOU USE a running martingale to help set your horse's head, and have had the rein buckles stick at the rings, here's how you can make a pair of simple guards to prevent it. Use a fairly heavy skirted leather to cut the disks from, make the slot to fit the reins, and insert a small piece of leather lace to hold the disk or washer in place.

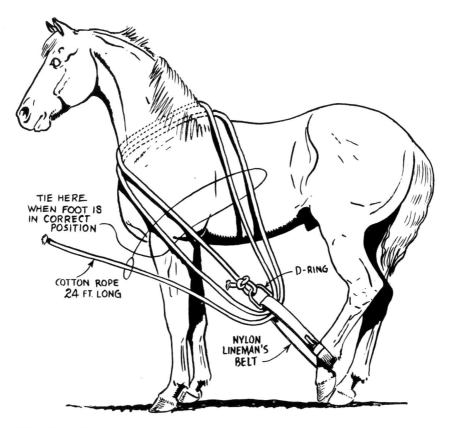

TIE HERE
WHEN FOOT IS
IN CORRECT
POSITION

COTTON ROPE
24 FT. LONG

D-RING

NYLON
LINEMAN'S
BELT

I HEARD FROM an ex-rodeo and wild west show rider who originally hailed from Montana but who now lives in Pennsylvania where he's in the business of breaking colts. He came up with this wrinkle on taking a horse's foot away from him to make him easier to handle. It's an improvement, he says, on the old Scotch hobble. He uses a discarded telephone lineman's belt made of nylon, and runs his cotton rope around the horse's neck and through the D-ring strung on the belt as shown. When the end of the rope is pulled, you can take that foot clear up to his neck if you want to. When the foot's in the desired position, the rope is tied off around the lines coming around the neck, and the horse can do nothing but stand quietly.

WAGON AXLE

CONCRETE

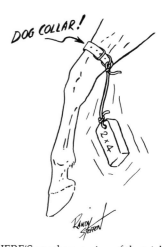

DOG COLLAR!

2x4

A RIG SIMILAR to this one was used years ago to break driving horses, and the same principle is still in use today. It's also mighty handy for breaking and gentling horses. While it looks somewhat complex when you first see it, a study of my drawing will show that it is really quite simple. It's made up of good-sized pipe, wagon wheels, and axles, all welded up as shown. The green horse is hitched to the singletree and he has no choice but to travel in a circle. The two long pipes should be about 25 feet in length.

HERE'S another version of the trick to keep a horse from pawing in his stall. An old dog collar makes a fine leg strap since it already has a ring fastened to it. The 2x4 banging on his leg should get pretty annoying and put a stop to the horse's pawing.

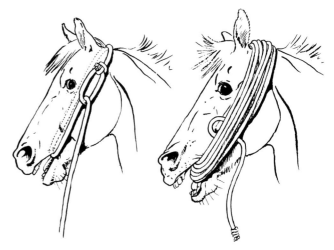

ONE OF THE first things a foal should learn is how to lead and here's another way of getting that lesson across. Remove the wire from a bale of hay without breaking the wire so that it remains a loop. Place this loop of wire over the rump of the foal, tie a short length of light sash cord where the wire is twisted together, and with a gentle pull on the rump wire, urge the baby to move ahead. In nothing flat, the little fellow walks right out.

I HEARD ABOUT this old Indian rope trick many moons ago and had forgotten about it. Recently, I had a problem in trying to make some measurements of the head of a horse we were using for a model from which to do a pony express statue. The horse wanted no part of it until we remembered this gimmick. It's simple as all get-out, and doesn't even start to hurt the horse. But believe me, once it's in place he gives that rope every bit of his attention, and you can do what you please with him without any kind of restraint. Use a regular saddle rope, and pull up fairly snug with the first turn. Then with the remainder, just wrap it around his head, tuck in the loose end, and stand back. He'll just stand there with the most bewildered expression you ever saw on a horse.

AN OLD friend visited me and during the bull session that we had, we talked about riding colts in the slick-fork roping saddles so many riders were using at that time. My friend mentioned that he used the age-old trick of tying his slicker across his saddle when he mounted one that might be hard to sit. This was the old-time bronc rider's stunt when all saddles came without swell forks, and a man had to ride slick and clean unless he cheated a little on the horse with his slicker or a blanket; it gave his legs a little extra purchase when the going got tough.

ONE OF THE BEST ways to break young pack mules from running too close to trees is to wire a heavy limb to the fork of the pack saddle so it sticks out on each side. A few days of grazing timbered pasture will make Mr. Mule mighty careful about getting too close to the trees.

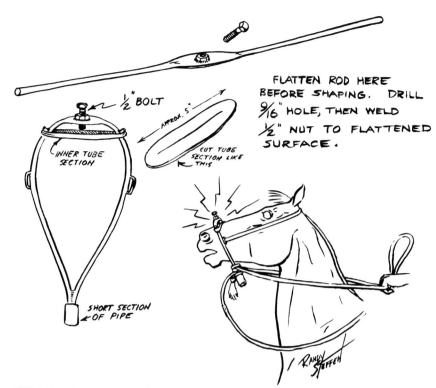

FLATTEN ROD HERE BEFORE SHAPING. DRILL 9/16" HOLE, THEN WELD 1/2" NUT TO FLATTENED SURFACE.

1/2" BOLT

INNER TUBE SECTION

APPROX. 5"

CUT TUBE SECTION LIKE THIS

SHORT SECTION OF PIPE

A RECENT letter from a reader states, "If someone wants me to start a horse neck reining, I slip a small halter ring over the reins so the pressure of the pull on the reins will come from behind the jaw, and won't pull on the bit sideways. My colts have always learned to rein quicker this way." This is a good one; but it's not recommended when first starting a colt. It prevents a lateral pull on the bit—to the left and right—which you definitely need to help steer and control a colt.

HERE IS A SURE 'NUF cowboy gimmick, and it comes from a reader in Houston. He uses this outfit to stop a horse from throwing his head high in the air when he puts on the brakes, and I can see where it would be right effective if not overdone. But a word of caution—this is for the old spoiled horse, not for the colt or green-broke horse. He uses a piece of 5/16-inch or 3/8-inch steel rod, long enough to make the size and shape of the bosal he desires. His first operation is to flatten the rod in the center, so that a 9/16-inch hole can be drilled in the flat part, and a 1/2-inch machine nut can be welded or brazed in place over the hole. Then he bends it to the shape he wants, adds a small section of pipe where the two ends meet, and welds or brazes. This pipe acts as a heel button to keep the reins in place, as well as a weight to drop the bosal when pressure on the reins is released. The small loops on the sides of this steel bosal can be added to afford a place to attach the headstall.

A small tab is welded or brazed to the noseband on each side of the flat place to prevent the rubber inner-tube section from sliding off the rig when it's in use. The principle of this rig is to punish the horse on the top of the nose when he shoots his head up against the pressure of the reins. And the 1/2-inch bolt that's screwed into the nut will sure do just that. The inner-tube section prevents the bolt from touching his nose unless he forces it against the reins with more than usual pressure; then the punishment is automatic. He adds that you can remove the bolt completely after about the second time he hits it, and just threaten him by letting him wear the rig for a few saddles. Be sure the inner-tube section is cut so that sufficient pressure is exerted to keep the bolt from touching the nose except when needed.

HERE'S A different twist in breaking a colt to lead with a burro. Insert a short spring from an iron cot in a two-foot length of chain with a swivel halter snap at each end. To halter break a young colt, snap one end of the chain to the colt's halter and the other end to the halter on a gentle burro. Turn them into a corral for a couple of days and, except for food and water, forget 'em. At the end of that time, ol' burro will have thoroughly broke your colt to lead without any strain on you, and no danger to the colt. I've used this method many times without the spring, but the addition of a spring should make things a whole lot easier on the colt.

A READER in Michigan uses an old wagon wheel and axle set firmly in the ground as an aid in longeing her horse. She ties the longe line to the rim of the wheel, places one hand on the wheel where the line is tied, and walks around the wheel as the horse makes his circle. This arrangement saves strain on her arm in keeping the horse moving in an even, circular path. Be sure the wheel and axle are well lubricated so the wheel turns freely as the horse moves around the circle.

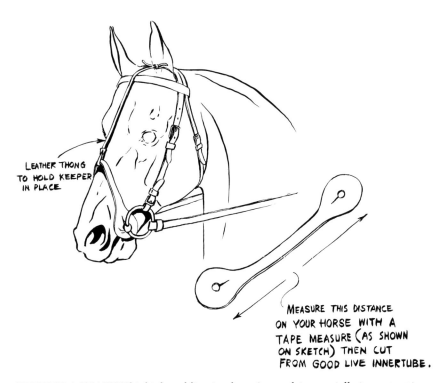

LEATHER THONG
TO HOLD KEEPER
IN PLACE

MEASURE THIS DISTANCE
ON YOUR HORSE WITH A
TAPE MEASURE (AS SHOWN
ON SKETCH) THEN CUT
FROM GOOD LIVE INNERTUBE.

KEEPING A SNAFFLE bit high and firm in a horse's mouth is especially important in early snaffle training. This simple inner-tube keeper is one I remember seeing in use by a trainer in Texas, and it sure works.

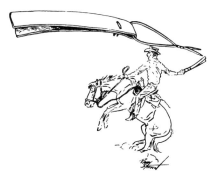

HERE'S A horse breaker's pop quirt that will make a dickens of a lot of noise, but won't actually hurt the colt. Made from a piece of heavy harness leather, it should be at least 2 inches wide and about 18 inches long after it has been doubled. A small piece of lacing through two holes punched in the doubled leather will tie it together at the top, while a leather thong through the loop at the top will make a good place to hold it with two or three fingers. Many times, a colt that starts to bog his head can be scared out of it by slamming him good and hard on the belly with a quirt like this. But it's always a lot better to buffalo the colt with noise than with actual pain; he's not nearly so likely to get mad. And believe me, a horse that's mad is almost impossible to train.

SOME HORSES THAT continually wear blankets or stable sheets in their stalls seem to take great delight in tearing them with their teeth. This rig, made simply enough with a piece of broom handle, a few pieces of whang leather, and a surcingle, will make it impossible for him to reach the blanket with his mouth, yet does not impair him in any other way. This rig also serves well on a horse that gnaws on a wound or sore. He can still lie down, eat from the floor, and stretch, but he can't get his head around to his side.

HERE'S A LITTLE different scald on halter breaking with the old reliable breast hitch. Tie the breast hitch with a bowline, then run the free end through the halter ring and tie to a post, leaving a little less slack than you left in the halter tie rope. When Mr. Hoss throws himself back against that rope, he'll get the fool squeezed out of his chest before the slack's gone out of the halter tie—and he'll bounce back to give himself slack in a hurry. This is a real good way to halter break a horse without the danger of pulling his neck down. Just make sure your post and ropes are bull-stout, and that you've tied slip hitches in both ropes just in case something goes wrong.

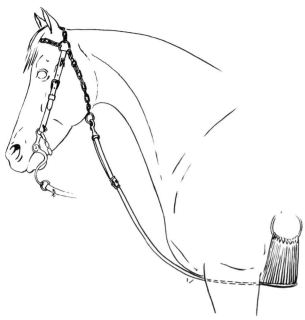

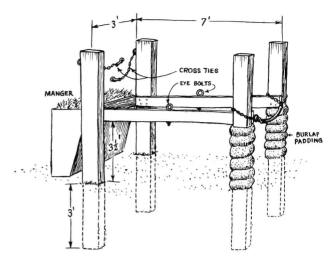

THIS DIFFERENT tie-down rig was submitted by a reader in Colorado. He prefers it to a tie-down noseband, and I'm sure it would be pretty effective in making an old high-headed horse keep his *cabeza* down where it belongs.

A READER IN Bozeman, Mont., writes that he breaks and trains a lot of colts for other people. The bronc stall I show here is one that he built and uses constantly for sacking out, handling, and gentling. It saves him a lot of time and sweat, he says. The drawing shows pretty well how the stall is made, and what materials are used in it. This rig can be used for shoeing bad ones, too. He says the stall has saved many a horse from getting hurt, and I'm sure it saved him from getting hurt many a time as well.

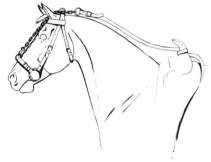

WE HAVE shown several hints designed to keep a horse from bogging his head and bucking, and they all have their advantages. They are effective on most horses but some determined ones learn to set their heads hard against the rig and come down stiff-legged, so that some part of the rig eventually breaks. A reader in Montana has come up with a solution to the problem. He says that a short length of sash chain used over the head will discourage most any horse from repeating an attempt to buck. To have the best effect, the chain should be close to one ear. The headstall is equipped with one ring on the strap over the nose to which the chain can be snapped and another ring at the crown through which the chain can be run. The strap can be buckled to a ring at the end of the chain, and the end of the strap wrapped around the horn to keep the horse's head up.

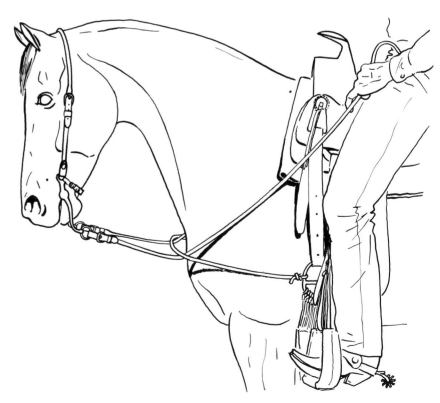

THIS SIMPLE SUBSTITUTE will take the place of a running martingale. My drawing pretty much explains how it is rigged, with the addition of a piece of light rope or sash cord, tied as shown.

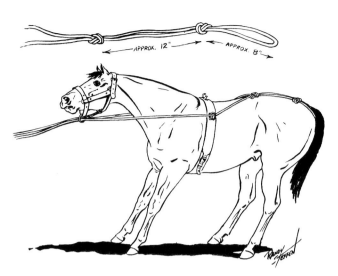

FENCE jumpers and runaways, besides being a blamed nuisance to the owner and his neighbors, are dangerous to themselves. Here's a method to put a stop to this foolishness. Buckle a surcingle with a ring on the bottom around the culprit, fasten a stout leather strap with a ring around each foreleg just above the knee, then run a length of strong rope from one leg, through the surcingle ring, to the other leg, adjusting the length so the animal can walk, lie down, get up, and trot, but can't run fast enough to jump. If you try this, be sure to tie the ropes to the leg straps with knots that can be jerked loose in an emergency.

HERE'S A come-along made from a suitable length of large-diameter, soft cotton rope that will help cure a stubborn pull-back, or break a young horse to lead in a hurry. Somewhat of a variation of the tail-hitch I've described before, this one is used with a surcingle to keep it from falling out of place. A simple overhand knot is tied in the doubled rope to form a crupper about eight inches long. Another overhand knot is tied about a foot in front of the first knot; then the two ends of the rope are passed through the rings on the sides of the surcingle and on up through the halter ring. A few gentle tugs on this outfit will convince most any horse that it doesn't pay to pull back against it. A horse can be tied to a tree or post with this rig with almost no chance of it falling off.

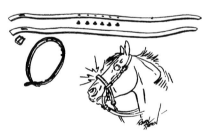

ONE OF our contributors uses this rivet noseband on high-headed horses to help get their heads down where they belong. He uses two identical pieces of $1/2$- to $3/4$-inch leather, the same length as a noseband, punches holes in the center piece to accommodate a half-dozen rivets (hollow copper type) so they protrude about $3/16$ of an inch beyond the leather, then sews the other strip of leather to the first piece so the heads are secured in place. By attaching a buckle at one end, and punching holes in the opposite, he has a rivet noseband that will discourage a horse from sticking his nose up in the air when he works, without hurting him.

THERE'S NOTHING quite so irritating to a horseman as a horse that lays down and defies all efforts to get it up on its feet—and all from pure orneriness. Here's a tried-and-true way to make him scramble to his feet in a rush, without resorting to violence, and without harm to the animal in any way. Take a small tin cup, half-filled with water; hold his head in a upright position, as shown in the drawing, and pour it slowly in one nostril. You'll be amazed to see how quickly he'll scramble to his feet. A word of caution—don't pour any more than a pint of water—you may drown him with a larger quantity.

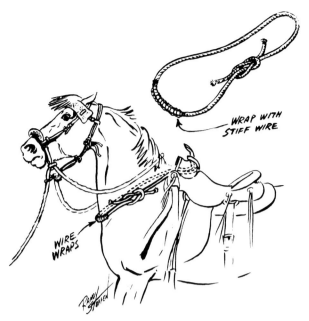

HERE'S A TRICK I picked up from a young bronc snapper who used to be a neighbor of mine in Nevada. He always had a few rough horses in his saddle string, and he used every trick in the book to keep one step ahead of them. When he had one that was pretty sure to pitch with him, he used this neck rope gadget. It consists of a stout 3/4- or 1-inch rope placed around the horse's neck as I've shown here, right where the throat meets the brisket, and is tied tight. This tension prevents a horse from getting his head down; and, of course, you already know that an old pony can't do much but hop around a little if he can't get his head down to put his heart in it. The wraps of stiff wire help discourage his straining his tender throat against the restraint of the rope. With this gadget you can sure help yourself to break them of the pitching habit, and not hurt them a bit in doing so.

AN ARIZONA rancher has a different trick that he uses on a horse he knows is going to be bad to ride. He carries a piece of 1/4-inch rope on his saddle regularly, and when a horse humps up badly when he's saddled, he rigs it like I've shown in my drawing, making sure it goes high over the teeth on the gums. He makes it fairly tight with just a single wrap around the head, and secures it with a slip hitch alongside the jaw. Then he lets the horse soak for about ten minutes before he slips off the rope, steps aboard, and rides off. He says very few horses ever bucked after this treatment. This is very similar to an old Indian trick I've used a number of times, and it does seem to completely bewilder a horse.

A MONTANA horsebreaker has another method of dealing with an old pony that's liable to break in two every time he's saddled. He works by himself most of the time, so he can't have someone snub his horse to the saddle horn. He straps a front leg up, as shown in my drawing, and leads the horse around until he begins to break into a sweat—then removes the strap and steps aboard. Unless you have a sure-enough outlaw on your hands, this should remove all desire to buck, because, as our friend says, it takes plenty of good, fresh energy to make a horse really want to buck.

AND ONE more hint to keep a horse from pitching. This will discourage any horse but a rank outlaw from getting his head down low enough to do a decent job of bucking. Tie a fairly heavy piece of rope around the middle of the neck, using a bowline; then tie the free end to the saddle horn. An old bronc's antics won't last long if he tries anything with this rig—his wind gets shut off in a hurry.

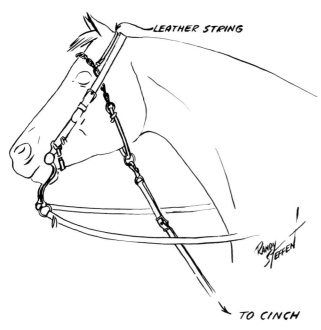

IF YOU HAVE a horse that's bad about throwing his head, here's a tie-down that should effect a quick cure without skinning the pony's nose. Rig a short piece of chain just above the eyes, as shown, and hold it in place with a leather string over the poll. Another stout piece of leather, or flexible wire fastened to the ends of the chain, provides a place to hook to the end of the tie-down strap that fastens to the cinch, as with all tie-downs.

A FOOT CHAIN can be the solution to the problem of horses that are hard to catch in a big corral or night pasture. And, before we go any farther, let me tell you most emphatically that I endorse this stunt wholeheartedly—it certainly works. I've used it a jillion times on horses that I had to pasture with a bunch of cattle. Many horses develop a habit of chasing cows and calves, which sure takes off pounds of valuable weight. A "clogchain,"—for that's what I've called this rig—will certainly break them of this habit in a hurry. Used to use it, too, on mustangs that I'd caught and had to drive in a bunch; works as good as tying a forefoot to the tail and sidelines. And a horse that's had this cure won't be shy about anything around his ankles. Be sure you do fasten the chain to the ankle with a piece of large diameter, soft cotton rope, or with a leather strap that's lined with felt or sheepskin. I once saw a horse clogchained by wiring the chain in a loop around the bare ankle. After a week of the chain biting into his flesh, the ankle became infested with screw worms and the horse had to be destroyed. I can't impress on you enough that a bare chain will result in a dead or worthless horse.

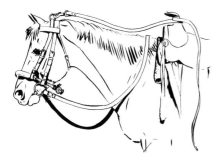

YOU'VE HEARD of tie-downs but here's a tie-up that will interest owners of horses that like to drop their heads and buck a little. This one comes from an eastern reader who uses a heavy head-stall on a rawhide bosal, slips a ring over the headstall at the poll, ties a rope to it and the other end to the saddle horn. A couple of dallies, or two half-hitches, will keep the horse from getting his head down far enough to do much more than jump around a little. You'll have to adjust this rope to suit your horse's dimensions. A heavy leather rein can be used instead of a rope, as I've shown here.

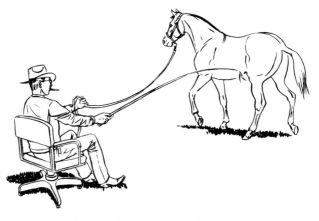

THIS ONE IS bound to bring a grin, and it sure made me snicker when I first heard of it, but darned if it isn't a pretty good idea at that. A racehorse trainer who was crippled for awhile used a swivel chair to longe some of his string. Bet there's more than one reader over the nation who will give this one a whirl.

I HAD A LETTER from a cowboy in California who was working in the Paso Robles area. I learned that he was riding an old saddle horse of mine in contest roping on the west coast; but his suggestion was born of necessity, like most inventions are. He was laid up for awhile after a bronc riding match, and while recuperating, he had a couple of catty colts he wanted to break. With a leg in a cast, he was at a disadvantage until he dreamed this one up. He took a couple of old tires, fastened a chain around each, then snapped them fast to snaps set in the ends of a stout nylon rope run through the fork of his saddle as shown here. He tells me that a colt gentles himself in a hurry with this rig, and has no way to injure himself. Of course you should place the tires high enough to keep him from kicking a hind foot through one of them. He says this rig also works well on an old, spoiled horse that likes to come unwound every time the saddle is cinched on him.

A TRAINER in Colorado uses this method to put the finishing touches on halter breaking his colts. The lead rope is fastened to a two-gallon bucket filled with concrete and run through a hole in a corral board or arranged as shown. When the colt is tied to this arrangement he can pull back some, but he doesn't get any slack until he steps up to the fence. He says this finish sure makes them lead better and it's seldom that any of his colts get hurt this way.

A READER IN Oregon has a simple method that might cure some horses from throwing their heads. She merely slips an old bar snaffle bit over the reins, under the horse's jowls, and lets it ride there. When the horse throws his head the bit slides up, from centrifugal force, and slams him under the jaw. When he lowers his head and goes on normally, the bit slides back down the reins, and there's no punishment. This is the best kind of cure; the horse punishes himself the instant he does wrong—there's no time lag where human reaction has to be considered.

I HAD A letter from a horseman in Connecticut who told me that this is the way he taught a 12-year-old hot-blooded gelding to work on a longe line. The horse was halter broke, but scared of a whip; with the normal longe line procedure he'd either come up to his owner or try to escape by running away. By using a stout pole in the center of his training corral he was able to keep him at the end of the longe line, urge him forward from behind, and keep him going in a perfect circle, all at the same time. As the horse learned to bend his body and adjust to the course the circle demanded, the handler was able to approach him gradually at a more perpendicular angle until the post was eliminated.

THIS IS A FINE rig to teach young horses to stand tied, and was made by hands on a ranch near Gallup, New Mexico. The posts are sections of utility poles set deep in the ground, and the cables were discarded by the telephone company—$1/2$-inch or $3/4$-inch cable will do. Cable clamps set on the outside of each pole, and at intervals along the length of the cable, prevent the harness rings on the cable from moving too far along the cable, and prevent the colts from getting snarled up with each other. A turnbuckle at one end of the cable, where it fastens to a "deadman" set deeply in the ground, will allow the cable tension to be kept tight.

THIS IS one of the handiest training stunts I've seen in a long time. A reader in California who has been around many good horses for many years described this method of bitting and neck reining colts to me in a letter. He says he used to work many of them this way, and the method really saved time, and what's better, worked well. He used a 30-foot by 12-foot pen. At each end was a tall pole set firmly in the ground, and a $3/8$-inch steel woven cable was stretched tightly between these poles, at a height about a foot taller than a man's head when he was on horseback. A stout iron ring was placed on this cable before it was strung, so it could slide freely from one end of the pen to the other. The colt to be worked was placed in the pen, saddled. A strap with another ring on the end was fastened to the ring on the cable, so it hung about the same height as a man's hand would be if he were mounted on the horse. The reins from the snaffle bit in the horse's mouth were fastened to this ring at the end of the strap, and the colt turned loose to teach himself. Since the pen is only 12 feet wide, the colt could back no farther than 6 feet in either direction. If he starts to leave the cable, the reins will neck-rein him back.

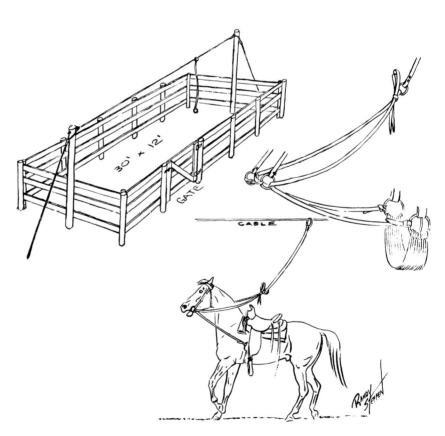

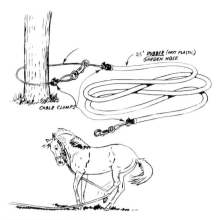

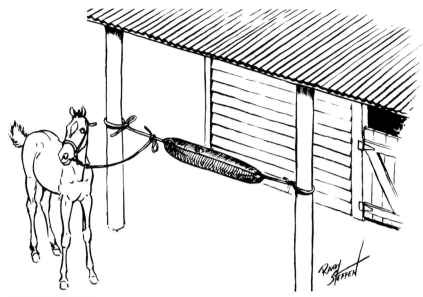

BREAKING A horse to a stake rope is a tough job to accomplish without burning his heels even once. Years ago I used a cow chain inside a garden hose to break a few horses to a stake rope, and it worked real well, although I remember what a job it was to get the chain threaded through the hose. Now a reader in Missouri has come up with a brilliant way to do this touchy job, using a steel cable, rubber (not plastic) hose, some cable clamps, and a couple of swivel snaps. Taping the end of the cable makes it easy to thread through the hose, and by arranging the clamps as I've shown in the drawing, one end of this rig can be fastened to a tree or post, and the other end to the halter ring of the horse. The rubber hose will keep the horse's heels from being burned, and is strong enough to contain the cable so there is no danger of the cable cutting through the hose.

FROM A HORSEMAN in Iowa comes this suggestion for a halter breaking setup to keep very small colts from throwing themselves or pulling their necks down. It's a stout rope tied between two posts of the barn, with an old inner tube tied in the middle. It has enough give to it to prevent injury, and makes a good place for the colts to rub flies from their backs during fly season.

HERE'S another training and breaking rig that makes shoeing a mean horse or a kicker a fairly simple job. The leg straps should be lined with woolskin to keep from burning the hide when the horse fights the rope; and don't forget to use slip-hitch knots that you can jerk loose in an emergency.

EVER TRY TO load a deer or elk carcass or quarters on a spooky old pack horse? To make the job easier, rub a little blood from the game on the horse's nose before you try to pack out the meat. This will give ol' spook a chance to get used to the smell before you try to drape the meat over his back.

A READER IN New York tells us that her husband came up with this cure for a mare they board that is a bad barn kicker. The mare is exercised every day but, in spite of that, as soon as she's tied in her stall she tries to kick it to pieces. They cured her by suspending a heavily padded weight above the place where the mare stands when she kicks, and just a few inches above her rump. Every time she raises her rump to kick, the weight bumps her and she changes her mind in a hurry.

8 TRUCK AND TRAILER TIPS

WE HEARD FROM A trainer in New Mexico who says he runs across a horse now and then that's tough to load in a trailer. This is the way he handles the situation when he has no help. He backs his trailer up to a gate so one post acts as a wing, swings the gate open against the trailer gate for the other wing, then uses a long rope from the horse's head through the manger tie-ring and back to himself, well back of the animal's heels. Patience and the judicious use of a training whip will soon make the most reluctant horse scramble to get in. This is not the time to pit your strength against the horse's power—you just haven't got what it takes in muscle to drag one in; just keep his head pointed in the right direction with the rope and let the whip let him know you mean business. There's never any need to stand there and beat him—a pop or two at the right time will get the job done.

YOU CAN use a plastic shoe bag, the type you can buy from the mail-order houses, as a container for grooming tools, medicines, and almost anything else small enough to fit in the pockets. The bag can be hung on three small metal hooks welded to the inside of the tack compartment of your horse trailer. Sure keeps in order the miscellaneous plunder that generally accumulates in a trailer.

THIS ONE COMES from a Cuban horseman who says that he's had a lot of success loading reluctant horses with this rope-under-tail method. While one man steps into the trailer with the lead rope in his hand, two others use a large-diameter, soft cotton rope as indicated. The horse usually chooses the lesser of two evils and stomps into the trailer. Of course, there's no gimmick that works with every horse, but this should load its share of balky horses.

THIS IS ANOTHER method of loading a gentle but stubborn horse in a trailer. Use eight to ten feet of soft rope, tie each end around a front pastern with a bowline knot, and then gently pull one foot at a time until the horse is in the trailer. The hind end will follow after the front end gets in. I've used this same method many times and can vouch for its effectiveness.

ANOTHER METHOD of getting the hard-to-load horse in a trailer is to drive him in. There are plenty of horsemen who break all their colts to drive with long lines before they ever climb aboard them. If a colt's been driven before, this method of getting him into a trailer is worth trying.

CHANGING A tire on a pickup or car hitched to a trailer can be a dangerous job if the rig should shift and spill off the jack. A simple set of wood chocks can be made to make absolutely sure the outfit can't budge a fraction of an inch. The way the chain is fastened to the chocks makes adjustment simple.

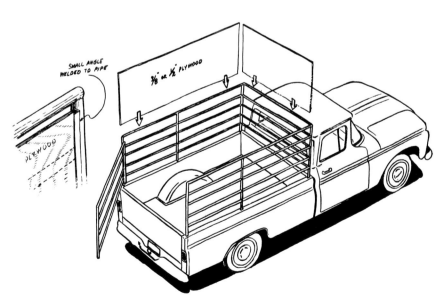

EVERY horsemen has a different idea as to what he wants in his horse trailer. But this little gimmick will benefit anyone who has to haul young horses. It is the addition of an extra tie ring on each manger, located at the rear near the horse's chest. When a young horse is tied as shown in the drawing, it becomes almost impossible for him to try to climb into the manger with his front feet. As you know, this often happens when hauling a young horse for the first time. I would recommend the addition of such a ring to any trailer you buy, or may already have.

HORSEMEN WITH pipe stock racks on their pickups may get some good from this one, especially those who live in cold country. Some ³/₈-inch plywood cut to fit between the vertical pipe stakes will do the trick. Weld a small angle iron in each corner to hold the plywood against the rack, and you've got a windbreak that can be removed at will. It will certainly make riding a lot more comfortable for a horse in the winter.

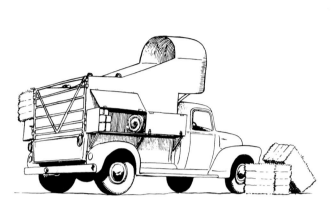

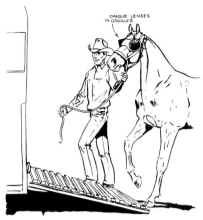

A PAIR OF long, narrow boxes, either metal or plywood, fastened to an angle-iron rack mounted on either side of your pickup truck will provide a good storage place for your bedroll, horse gear, medicines, groceries, and the other things needed for an outing on horseback. Bales of hay can be stored atop the boxes. Just make sure that the boxes you select (many can be found at surplus stores) won't make the total width of your truck more than the legal limit in your state.

HERE'S A different twist on loading a horse. A friend writes that he's had mighty good luck loading a horse in a trailer for the first time with goggles fitted with opaque lenses, or solid covers over the regular lenses so the horse can't see a thing. He says the horse has to depend on you, and will follow you into the trailer.

HERE'S A TIP from a hoss-trainin' friend who has rigged up a series of mirrors on one of his trailers so that he can see his horses through the front trailer window at any time. He says it's real tricky to get the mirrors aligned just right, so don't be in too big a hurry. It's best to have plenty of help, at least one man on each mirror before mounting them to the trailer. Then, when everything is just right, and the man in the driver's seat can see just what he wants, mark 'em accurately and fasten them in place.

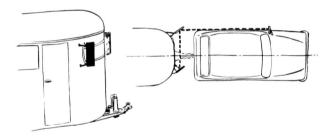

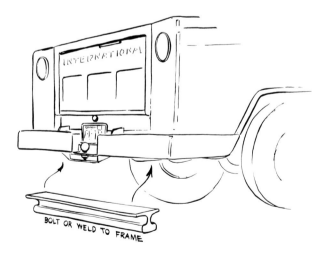

HAULING A tandem-axle horse trailer with a pickup in rough country can be exasperating if no ballast is in the bed to give it traction. Several horsemen I know install a permanent ballast where it can't be seen or interfere with any load they might want to carry in the bed. Those of you who haul your horses in single-axle trailers usually have enough weight on the hitch to give your pickup suitable traction.

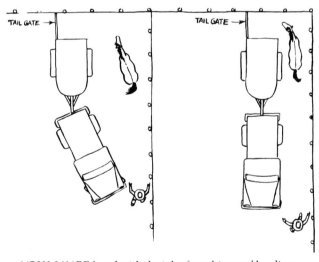

YOU MAY BE faced with the job of catching and loading a horse in a big pasture. If the horse can't be walked up to and caught easily, and there's no pen or loading chute available, here's a way to park your trailer and car that will allow you to drive the horse into the trailer.

ONE OF our readers got tired of burning her hands on the pulley rope used to lift the end gate on the family stock truck. So she made a handle by tying an old narrow-tread stirrup to the end of the rope. No more rope burns, and the handle makes gate lifting much easier for the ladies.

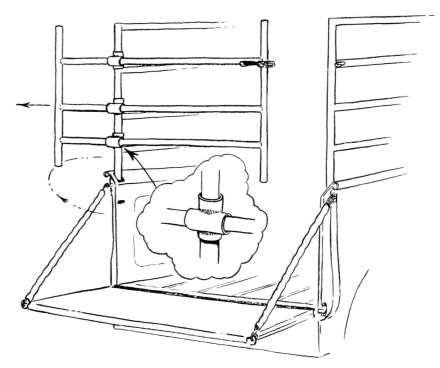

THERE'S NO DOUBT that pickup stock racks made of welded pipe are practically indestructible, and this gate that will either slide open to the side, or swing open like an ordinary one, is also stout as a bull. The illustration shows how short pipe nipples, the right size to slip freely over the horizontal gate members, as well as the vertical rear rack posts, are welded up and fitted to both rack and gate before assembly.

11" TRAILER STABILIZER STAND (USE TWO)

A FRIEND of ours in Houston is an avid hunter. Like most Texans, he'd rather do his hunting horseback than afoot, so his camp is a horse camp in every sense. It gets pretty cold when those blue northers whip down from the panhandle country, and horses used to the shelter of a box stall in a good, tight barn can get mighty cold. So our friend bought a pair of low, house trailer stabilizing jacks, which he sets under each back corner of the horse trailer, after it's been unhooked from the pickup. In seconds, with the front jack and the two rear ones, he levels the trailer, and makes it a rock-steady stall for protecting the horses at night. Side curtains on the trailer are let down, and a rear curtain across the opening at the back makes them as snug as bugs in a rug. Some rocks, put in front of and behind the tires, help keep the trailer from rolling.

IF YOU EVER need a padded cell—I mean trailer—for your horse, here's a way to make it quick and easy. A pair of old mattresses with straps sewn to the top can be hung on each side of the trailer to make injury to a horse nearly impossible.

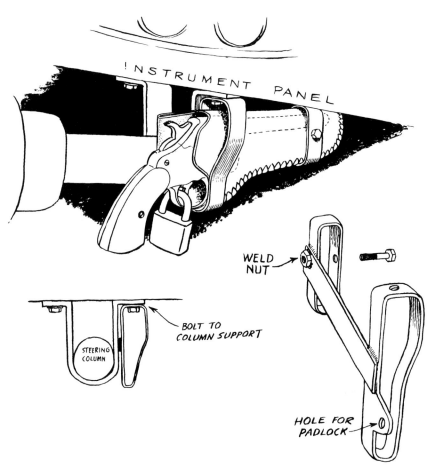

INSTRUMENT PANEL

WELD NUT

BOLT TO COLUMN SUPPORT

STEERING COLUMN

HOLE FOR PADLOCK

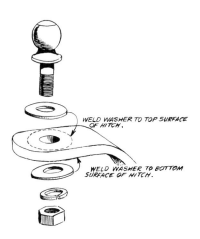

WELD WASHER TO TOP SURFACE OF HITCH.

WELD WASHER TO BOTTOM SURFACE OF HITCH.

A TRAILER hitch that is used day in and day out, such as the hitches on ranch pickups that are used to transport horses from one section of the ranch to another, sometimes receives excessive wear on the flat surface of the hitch under the ball. To avoid this wear and make the hitch last as long as the pickup, weld a proper-size steel washer to both the upper and lower surfaces of the flat hitch. These surfaces are generally much harder than the material in the hitch, and last much longer.

IF YOU CARRY a handgun in your pickup, here is a clever method of locking it to the steering column for security. Made from strap iron, there's a little welding to be done, but with an old holster, it's simple to install, and it's about as theft-proof as any I've seen.

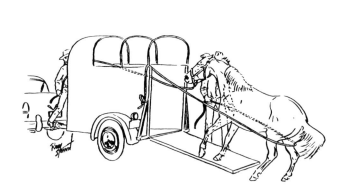

HERE'S HOW to rig a 20-foot rope to snake a reluctant horse into a trailer. You'll need a partner to handle and take the slack out of the lead rope as you persuade the old stag to get in where he belongs. The trick here is to inch him in slowly. Of course, it may not work exactly alike on all horses, but it's worth trying the next time you have one that's hard to load.

SOME HORSES are bad about trying to rear in a trailer or pickup. A good strong rope, a couple of half-hitches around the saddle horn and then tied to the racks on each side will keep his feet on the floor.

HERE'S AN EASY way to change a flat tire on a trailer. A section of six-inch beam is beveled as shown to provide a ramp to raise the wheel off the ground for removal. This method is easier than using a jack and it will work on either the front or the rear axle.

NOW HERE'S A different western design for a pickup stock rack. This one is made from old implement wheels and pipe; the materials are welded together to form this unique and very practical rack. Sure would dress up a pickup, wouldn't it?

ONE OF our readers frequently takes off on the show circuit or cross-country trips for extended periods of time. Enough storage space has always been a problem so he mounted a luggage carrier on top of his horse trailer. A good idea for metal top trailers.

THIS DESIGN for a pickup gate latch keeps the gate closed tightly with no rattles. The working parts of the latch are made of 1/4-inch by 1 1/2-inch steel straps which hinge on 1/2-inch rivets. The latch straps are mounted on 1/4-inch boiler plate which is welded to the pipe members of the gate. Scrap steel stops are welded to the boiler plate in the correct position to prevent the latch handle from dropping below the horizontal. Overall length of each latch should be about 24 inches.

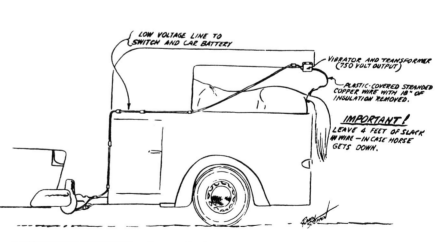

A HORSE THAT KICKS and raises the devil every time he gets in a trailer is a blamed nuisance, and here's a method that should cure him. A word of caution—don't use this on colts or frightened horses, just on those so and so's that are trying to get your goat. Look over this rig; be sure that you have it wired properly, and that you have at least four feet of slack in the lead that goes to the tail, as a safety measure. Now, when the horse starts to kick, press your switch up in the driver's seat for no more than a half second—all you want is a momentary jolt—and holler at the same time, loud enough to make sure the horse hears you. One or two applications should cure the most cantankerous of the trailer kickers.

9 AND MORE TIPS

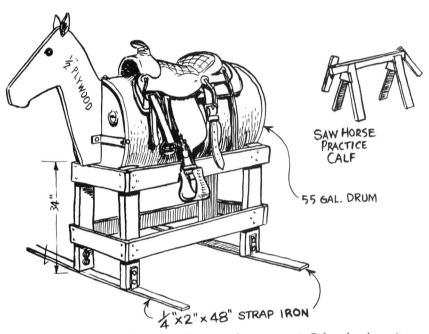

½" PLYWOOD

34"

¼"×2"×48" STRAP IRON

SAW HORSE PRACTICE CALF

55 GAL. DRUM

WE HEARD from an enthusiastic calf roper and team roper in Colorado who writes that when he doesn't have time to use livestock to sharpen his roping, he uses this oil drum horse and a sawhorse calf, similar to the one Toots Mansfield used. The horse doesn't take much effort or materials to build and he claims it pays for itself many times over. He adds that it's good for the man who wants to practice getting off from the right side.

I RECEIVED A letter from a couple in Michigan who own and show some fine Quarter Horses in their part of the country. They included a clipping that tells about the use horsemen in the Detroit area are making of old foot lockers, trunks, and large suitcases. I know some of you will think this is a good idea, so here's the dope. These trunks, old as they may be, from the old round-topped trunks of grandma's era to the more modern, large steamer trunks, have been cleaned up, painted with the owner's stable colors, and decorated with various degrees of fancy designs and names. A really good place to keep bridles, brushes, shoeing equipment, stable sheets and blankets, and all the other horse gear so necessary at a show. The old round-toppers make real fine places to set a saddle, too.

AN ORDINARY can opener of the type I've pictured here will serve as a hoof pick in an emergency. It will do the job, is inexpensive, and small enough to carry in a shirt pocket.

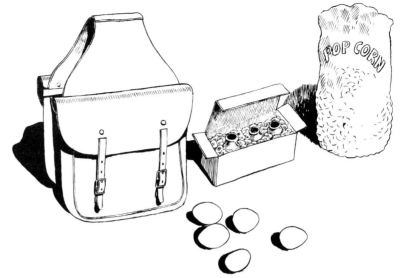

HERE'S A GREAT IDEA for protecting fragile items that must be packed in saddle bags or pack panniers for transportation on horseback. Popcorn can be used to ensure the safe arrival of any hard-to-pack items such as vaccine bottles, eggs, and even light bulbs.

THIS IS A handy trick to store away in your "war bag." A flashlight secured to the lower arm with a couple of big rubber bands makes bridling and saddling a horse in the dark much easier. In fact, this is a handy one for any number of jobs that require the use of both hands.

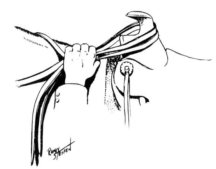

SHORT LEGS and tall horses make a poor combination for climbing into the saddle. This method of looping the reins over the saddle horn allows the rider to take up the reins enough to maintain control of his horse before mounting, but also allows him to give himself a real boost without pulling on the horse's mouth. I think this is an idea many young riders will be able to put to good use.

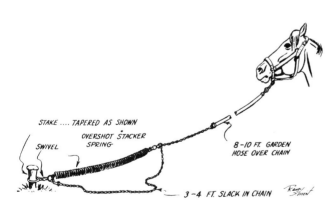

STAKE .... TAPERED AS SHOWN
OVERSHOT STACKER SPRING
SWIVEL
8-10 FT. GARDEN HOSE OVER CHAIN
3-4 FT. SLACK IN CHAIN

HERE'S A DIFFERENT slant on the stake-breaking rig I showed some time ago. This idea comes from a reader in Hardin, Mont., who sent us a sketch of the rig he uses to break his colts to stake—so we are passing it on to you. He uses a heavy spring about 42 inches long and 3 inches in diameter (from an overshot stacker) to take the jar out of the rig when an ol' colt hits the end of the chain. The drawing shows just how the whole outfit is put together, so if you can dig up an old spring that is stout enough to stand the pull, rig it up. I believe you'll like it.

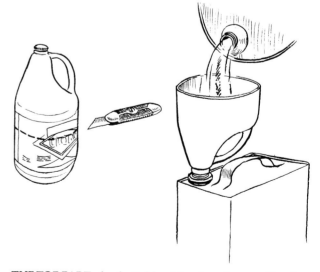

THE TOP PART of a plastic bleach bottle makes a real handy funnel around the ranch. Use a sharp knife to cut it off about as shown, remove the cap, and it's ready to use.

THIS IS a good way to keep that ol' "thirty-some-odd" saddle carbine securely in the boot in rough country. Take a strip of inner tube rubber two or three inches wide, and about two feet long, and rivet it to the open end of the saddle boot. By slipping the loop of rubber over the end of the stock, you make sure it's there to stay until you flip the rubber keeper off when you're ready to draw down on a good eatin'-size deer or a sneaky coyote (four-legged, that is).

THIS TIP WILL make your horse more visible during hunting season. Tie several long, bright-colored ribbons to the horse's halter and to short pigtails plaited in his tail. Stay away from white ribbons since they could be mistaken for the tail of a deer; yellow, orange, and red are excellent.

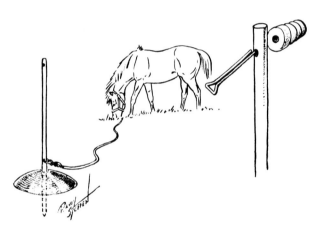

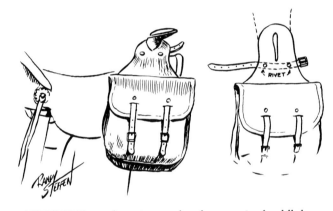

THIS DISK AND rod outfit is a handy way to stake out horses to graze. You'll need to weld a sharpened iron rod to an old disc blade so about a foot of the sharpened end sticks below the base of the disc. A hole with a ring through it near the base provides a place for a long tie-rope to be snapped for grazing. The maker of this one uses the same post for temporary electric fence posts. He inserts a pin and insulator through a drilled hole near the top of the rod, then fastens his electric wire to the insulator.

A FRIEND likes to hang just one bag from a pair of saddle bags to the horn on his saddle. He cuts a slot in the leather web that separates the bags, rivets on a small strap with buckle, and buckles the bag to the horn. He claims that this is a much better way to carry a bag with a pack string than behind the saddle, and it keeps the lead ropes from fouling. He balances the weight of the bag by strapping his carbine scabbard on the opposite side.

YOU'VE gotta hand it to the cowgirls near Union, Missouri. When they've got a touchy horse to doctor for an injury on a hind leg, they get a board fence between the one that's going to be horse-nurse and the patient, have another girl back the animal up against the fence, then hold its head around so the horse can see what's going on at the south end. This is good horse psychology. When a horse can see what's going on, he's not so apt to throw a fit while being doctored.

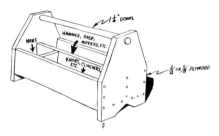

THIS SHOWS the basic design for an easy-to-make, and sturdy, farrier's box. Most any 3/4-inch lumber will do, but 3/4- or 5/8-inch plywood makes a stronger box. And be sure to use wood screws instead of nails. Built this way, your shoeing box should last forever.

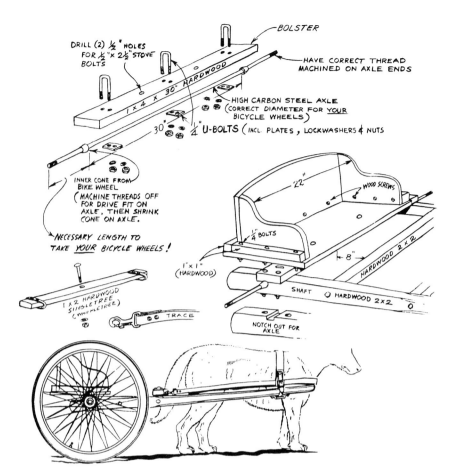

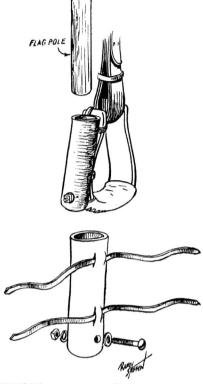

HERE'S A DOG cart that I remember seeing when I was a kid. I don't remember exactly how the axle was fastened to the body and shafts of that one, but here's how you can make one for your kids. If you use a goat, you'll want to rig a bridle much like a horse bridle, with a snaffle bit. But if you use a dog, rig an outfit that fits his head like a muzzle; fasten the lines to each side. For the first time or two that your kids drive him, you tag along with a long switch. When they want to turn left, have them pull and slack on the left line; at the same time you reach up and tap him alongside the face with the switch, to help him learn to turn. He'll get the idea pretty quick. My wagon was a little wood-wheeled Studebaker that was common for children then.

IF YOU have to carry a flag in a parade or rodeo grand entry and don't have a shop-made flagpole boot, then try this one. Get yourself an eight-inch piece of automobile radiator hose, a couple of pieces of whang leather, a bolt long enough to go through the tubing, and a washer and a nut. Do as I've shown in the drawing and you'll come up with a boot as good as any.

NOW HERE'S a different and new use for a horse halter if I ever saw one. A reader in Calgary, Alberta, writes that an old halter placed upside down on her Doberman, as shown here, and used with a couple of rope traces with snaps, made an ideal rig for pulling her children on a light toboggan. If you live in snow country, try it on your Fido.

HERE'S AN easy way to grain your horse on a trail ride or a hunting trip when you can't take a feed trough with you. Grain is usually too precious at times like this to chance wasting a lot of it by feeding on the bare ground. Just take a gunny sack or two with you, cut as shown on my sketch, tie the long ends together back of the horse's ears, and you have a good, serviceable *morral*.

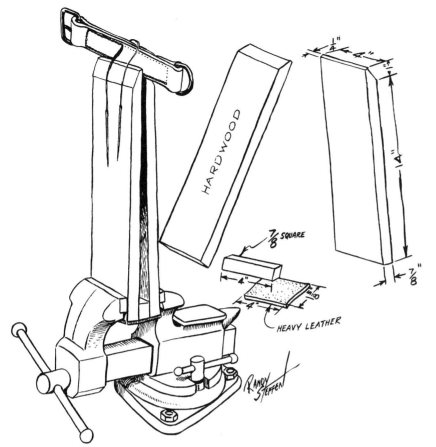

ANY HORSEMAN who does even a little of his own repair work on horse equipment will find this stitching clamp design as handy as any extra pair of hands. This one can be used in a vise, as shown, and takes only a few minutes to make. Be sure to use hardwood for the clamp sides and spacer. The leather hinge can be nailed or screwed to the bottom of the clamp sides, and in minutes it's ready to do your bidding on large and small jobs.

A READER in Minnesota believes in taking care of his saddle when it's raining. He uses a four-foot-square piece of rubber sheeting with a hole cut in the center to cover his saddle when he's off on a rainy season trail ride. He slips a rope with a loop on one end through the hole in the sheeting, runs the loop through the fork of the saddle and over the horn, then ties the whole works to the limb of a tree so it's up off the ground. He reinforces the hole with an extra piece of rubber cemented to the sheet, and advises that any water-repellent material can be used.

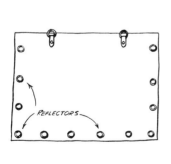

THIS HINT MIGHT cause a snicker or two at first glance, but if you live in a heavily populated area where traffic is fast and furious, and if you have occasion to ride along busy streets after dark, don't take this lightly. It could prevent a bad accident to you and your horse. A reader who lives in California participates in quite a few parades and other horse activities after dark. Her "tail light" rig is practical and easy to use. Made from a piece of white cloth or canvas, with rings to attach to the saddle strings, it features a row of small red reflectors around the cloth that pick up and reflect the headlights of traffic from the rear and both sides. A mighty good safety precaution.

DURING THE SPRING rainy season we all get more or less disgusted with our horses when they seem to delight in rolling in the mud like a bunch of hogs. It's usually quite a grooming job to scrape and brush all the mud from them, and here's where a common household item will help cut the job short. Take an old, fairly stiff broom, saw about two feet off the handle, and get after old Blizzard with the business end, after the mud has had a chance to dry. You'll be surprised how fast the dust and clods will fly.

118

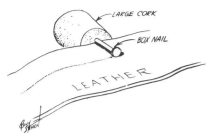

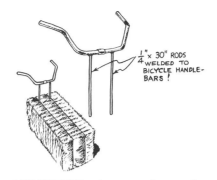

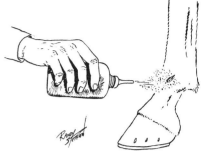

TACK ROOM repairs often require cutting a string or strip of leather from a large piece. A cork and nail make a simple marking gauge. The head of a box nail makes an easy-to-see mark on the leather to guide your knife for a neat, even job.

NOW HERE'S a clever practice steer for the team roper. The horns are a pair of old bicycle handlebars, to which a couple of $1/4$-inch rods have been welded. This whole assembly is stuck into a bale of hay to make a mighty fine roping dummy.

NEXT TIME the women in your house finish with some of their cosmetics that come in those flexible plastic bottles, save 'em—they're handy as an extra hand around the horse barn. Many come equipped with a small, nozzle-like cap, which makes the best applicator for healing powders, sulfa, and other forms of medicine in either wet or dry form that you've ever seen. One time, I took my two daughters to a beauty salon in Abilene, Tex., and saw one of the operators using a little plastic bottle like the one in the drawing. I took a close look, and saw it was a container for neutralizer used in the permanent wave process. Well sir, I begged a half-dozen empties, filled them when I got home with blue, barbed wire ointment, another with sulfa powder, one with a screwworm smear, and another with a boric acid solution. I'd been treating my stud's eye, and man, how easy it was to put that solution right where it belonged instead of all over him and me, too.

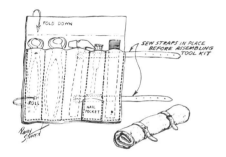

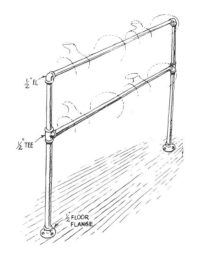

THIS HORSESHOER'S kit can be made from leather or heavy canvas. It certainly would keep essential tools and nails in a compact bundle; it's easy to stow, and is protected from dirt and weather. You can have your local saddlemaker stitch the canvas or leather if he has a harness stitching machine, or you can hand stitch it with an awl or an awl and two needles.

THIS SIMPLE saddle rack is made of $1/2$-inch pipe and standard pipe fittings. It bolts to the floor and will support four heavy saddles.

A SUBSCRIBER north of the border in Ontario enjoys training his own jumping horses. But it seems as though he could never accumulate enough jump standards to put under the jump bars, so he dreamed up this idea. He uses broken fence rails and cedar poles, cuts them to about six-foot lengths, drills a hole about a foot from the top of each, then assembles them in groups of three poles to a standard. Using heavy, smooth fence wire about 18 inches long for tying each unit, he runs the wire through the holes in three posts, leaves about two inches of slack, then twists the wire up so it will hold securely. These tripods are easy to set up and adjust for height and they knock down to store in a mighty small space.

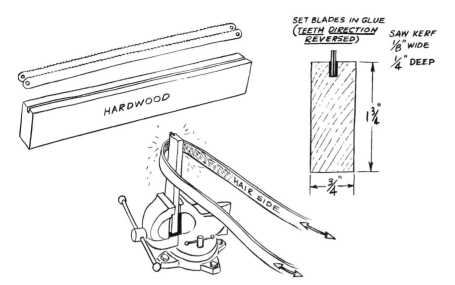

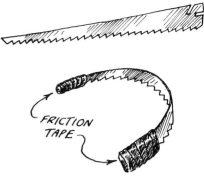

A BLADE from an old coarse-toothed keyhole saw, bent in an arc with the ends taped, makes a handy tool for scraping dried mud from heavy-coated horses.

THIS IS A combination tool that should prove mighty useful to every horse owner. Its primary function is to strip the old hair from a horse at shedding time in the spring, but it can also be used as a means of removing the hair from rawhide strips used for braiding or making repairs around the ranch. Two new hacksaw blades are set with the teeth running in opposite directions in a strip of hardwood with a saw kerf running its full length. The best way to get the blades to stay in the groove permanently is to use epoxy cement. As a shedding tool, it can be used with either one or two hands, and pulled with the lay of the hair. When stripping hair from strips of rawhide, fasten the tool in a bench vise as shown and work the rawhide strip back and forth against the teeth of the blades, being careful not to remove the surface layer of hide, for that's the part of rawhide that gives it its strength. The rawhide should be wet enough to be flexible but not soggy.

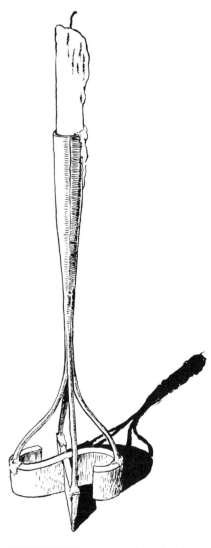

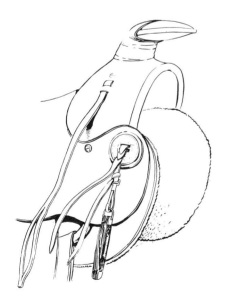

AN ARDENT trail rider in Minnesota finds packing a knife in her pocket too uncomfortable so she ties a simple over-hand knot in the eye of a small snap with one of the saddle strings at the fork of her saddle, and hangs her knife at this spot. It's always there when she wants it—with no discomfort to her.

OF ALL THE rain gear I've ever owned, I believe the old army poncho is the one I like best. It's feather-light, completely waterproof, and the parka-type hood on mine can be pulled up over the hat to keep out blowing rain. It covers the saddle as good as a slicker, and can be rolled into a mighty compact bundle to carry behind the cantle.

HERE'S ONE I sure never thought of, and I have quite a branding iron collection. The old-type irons that were made to be used with a wooden handle make mighty nice western candle holders.

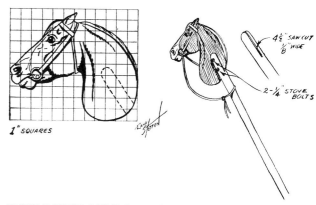

FOR THOSE OF you who have a problem in making a horse back up, here's a simple trick that I've used for years that seldom fails, if it's used with a little horse sense. Of course, you can just up and scare one to death with it and have a runaway, but if you use an assistant with a little sense, and have him open the umbrella on your cue, then pull and slack on your reins firmly but gently, telling the horse to back at the same time, chances are you'll meet with pretty good success. This lesson repeated a couple of times a day for two or three days should get most any horse to backing with a little rein pressure and verbal commands. But sit up straight when you're pulling on the reins; don't rear back in the saddle and throw all your weight on the horse's hindquarters. Keep your weight over the stirrups as the rider in the drawing is doing.

THE NEXT TIME you have an orphan foal to foist off on a foster-mother mare, try rubbing some Vicks VapoRub in the nostrils of the mare and squirt a little of the mare's milk on the orphan himself. The mare should be fooled enough to let him suck without a big hassle.

EVERY LITTLE COWBOY needs a good stick horse, and here's one that will please the little fellers. If you mark off a sheet of paper in one-inch squares, it'll be real easy for you to copy this design on the paper, and later transfer it to a piece of $1/8$-inch tempered masonite. A coping saw, or motor jigsaw, will make short and easy work of cutting the head to shape, and then painting doesn't take long. Don't forget the $1/4$-inch hole that's to be drilled in the masonite horse head, at the edge of the snaffle bit ring. The reins will pass through this hole after you're finished with the painting job.

First of all, give the whole horse a coat of flat white. Now, after the white has dried completely, use a buff, sand, or dark ivory to paint everything except the mane, foretop, and the blaze face; leave these parts white. Next, using your paper pattern again, rub graphite from a soft pencil all over the back, and trace on the cutout head—all black lines. The graphite backing acts like a carbon paper. You can turn the pattern over and trace the reverse on the opposite side, using the graphite pencil marks from your original design as the transferring carbon. I'd suggest you do the opposite side first, then rub the pencil all over the back to make your transfer.

Now use some reddish-brown paint to fill in the leather parts of the bridle, and when that's dry, take a small brush and paint in the outlines of all the details: eyes, nose, bridle, bit—everything. A piece of leather lacing will make a good set of reins, and get your stick horse ready to be topped off by your little buckaroo.

THERE ARE SEVERAL practical ways to sling a carbine scabbard on a saddle, but the two most used in the West are those shown here. The top drawing shows the butt-to-the-back method of slinging, which is the most popular way in Texas, at least. The butt of the carbine should be as close to even with the top of the horse's hip as possible. With the rifle in this position, it's possible to dismount and withdraw the carbine from the scabbard in one smooth motion, using a backward movement of the right arm as you come out of the saddle. It's equally as simple to draw the rifle from the boot while sitting in the saddle, for a shot while mounted.

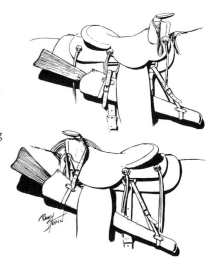

The lower drawing shows the booted carbine slung butt forward on the near side of the horse, with the front sling strap through the fork of the saddle, and the rear one fastened through the rear D ring. While this is a popular way of mounting the saddle gun, it's not near as handy to withdraw the rifle from this position, mounted or coming off. Contrary to Hollywood fashion, very few *horsemen* sling a carbine on the off side with the butt forward and sticking through the coils of the saddle rope. This would be all right for a southpaw, but unhandy as all get out for a right-handed cowboy.

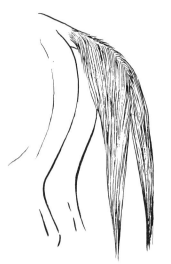

TYING UP A horse's tail so it will stay is a tough job. If it isn't done correctly, the knot will soon slip, letting the tail dangle. This is the way a Sioux Indian friend of mine ties up a tail, and he tells me that this same method was used by his ancestors when they tied up their ponies' tails for war. The tail hair is first divided into halves, and separated at least as far up as the end of the dock, or tail bone. Then, as shown in the center drawing, a simple overhand knot is tied with the two halves, and drawn up snug against the dock. The two remaining ends are wound, in opposite directions, tightly against the remaining hair, as shown by the directional arrows, and another overhand knot tied where the ends meet. The ends of this knot should be tucked under the last wrap, with a length of cloth, or suitable length of leather string, wrapped around the tail at the last knot and tied to keep this one from coming undone. The bulk of the first overhand knot at the bottom of the dock keeps the other wraps from slipping down.

THOSE TRUCK flares that are used as emergency flares at the scene of highway breakdowns or accidents are handy for lighting fires in wet or snowy weather. They come in a small metal box, flat enough to carry in your saddle bags, and they light by striking a friction cap at the spike end. Each flare will burn with a hot flame for 15 to 20 minutes. They will help ignite small twigs and branches that are too wet to light any other way. They're mighty good for trail riders to carry as part of their regular gear, for these flares will also make fine emergency signals that can be seen a long way off.

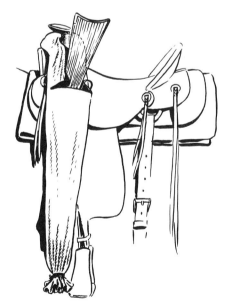

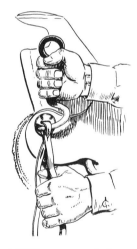

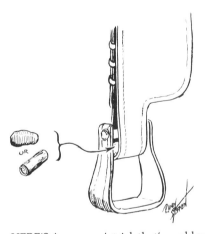

A READER who rides and hunts in the Corvallis, Ore., country, tells us that this is a real fine way to make an emergency rifle scabbard. She takes an old inner tube, wires one end together after cutting it to the right length, makes a slit clear through the other end to hang on the horn, then a slit through one side only to slip the rifle inside. This is a good one to remember.

IF YOU'VE ever struggled to get a set of conchas off a saddle, you'll appreciate this method of loosening the saddle strings from their set positions in the Spanish braid that's used to fasten the strings through the slots in the conchas. The reader who sent this one uses a common hoof pick to pull the strings through the slots. He says the best way is to shove the hoof pick in up to the bend, work it around, and pull up while pulling down against it with the other hand. If the strings are hard and dry, use a drop or two of water or oil to soften them first.

HERE'S A cowman's trick that's as old as the hills, but there may be many of you who have never seen it. Shortening a pair of laced stirrup leathers runs into time and effort, and if you're like me, you don't want anyone messing with the length of your stirrups, anyway. If it becomes necessary to shorten your stirrups temporarily, just insert a section of stick, or a chunky rock of the right size, between the bottom of the stirrup leather and the stirrup cross bolt. This trick had grey hair before Blevins became a byword for quick change of stirrup lengths.

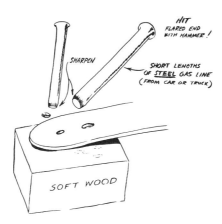

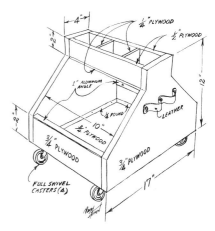

COMES A word of caution from a reader in California, and we're passing along her experience in the hope that you may profit by it. She wrote that hay bales on their spread had always been broken with an ax until three years ago when two operations had to be performed on expensive cows as a result of their swallowing small pieces of wire that had been broken off by an ax. It seems that the wire doesn't always sever where the ax strikes it, but that occasionally the wire will break on either side of the blow. The small pieces flying off into the feed are a serious hazard to both horses and cattle, so she advises against breaking bales open with an ax. She says they broke bales for eight years with an ax without any trouble, but then lost one cow, and came near losing the second a short time later.

AN OLD-TIMER tells me this makes a good leather punch. He salvages a few *steel* gas or brake lines from an old car or truck, gets them in several different sizes, retains the swaged end to hit with the hammer, cuts them off in a suitable length, sharpens the ends, and with a piece of soft wood as a base, knocks out holes in leather easily and quickly.

NOW HERE'S a piece of equipment that will make a back-breaking chore a little easier. The contributor who built this box designed it with the help of a professional farrier. He sent us photos of the finished box, along with the dimensions. Advantages of this piece of equipment are many—it's strong enough for rough treatment; tools can be taken or replaced in either end of the open box; the height is just right for easy access to nails while working on a horse's foot; casters allow the box to be nudged around freely on any reasonably level surface; and its value has been proved in actual use. Made of several thicknesses of plywood, aluminum angles, and a small strip of leather, it should be assembled with screws. If you do any work at all on your horse's feet, this box is well worth making.

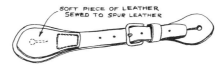

TO KEEP spur buttons from catching in the seams of Levi's, sew a soft piece of leather over the button holes of the leathers. I show just one button hole covered. This will also keep the buttons from catching on a wire fence should you ride just a little too close.

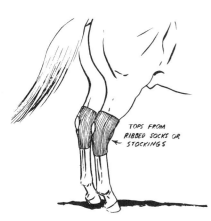

HERE'S A handy way to keep salve or other kinds of medicine on the hocks of a horse. A friend reports that it was nearly impossible to keep a bandage on the hocks of a mare that needed medicine applied daily to some wounds, until he cut the tops off a pair of ribbed socks, cut a two-inch slit in the center of each one to fit over the point of each hock, and slipped them into place. Really keeps the salve on the wound, and stays in place perfectly, he tells us.

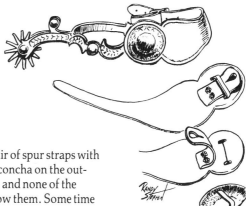

I HAVEN'T seen a pair of spur straps with a big, good-looking concha on the outside for many a year, and none of the catalogs I've seen show them. Some time ago, I borrowed a pair to use as models for a historical illustration I had to do, and here's the way the concha is attached to the spur strap. I'm making a pair of straps now, and have a pair of 2^1/$_2$-inch

silver conchas ordered for them. Rigging the straps this way is no job at all, and they really do look good.

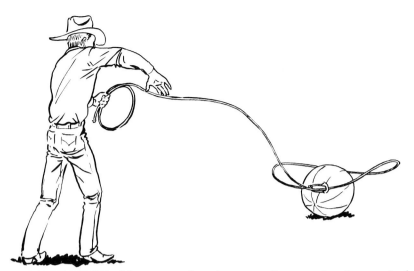

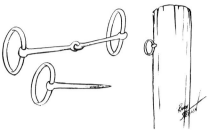

THE CONTRIBUTOR of this one must be quite a roper. She wrote that she soon tired of walking ten miles a day taking her rope off things she'd roped while on the ground practicing, so she soon abandoned draping her loop on posts and other solid objects. Instead, she caught things like loose round or oval rocks, big beach balls, and the like, so a simple jerk of the rope would free her loop. This is an ideal way to practice and perfect the old horse catch, or *hoolihan*, as it's called in some parts of the cow country. Since a perfect horse catch is one where the loop settles in a circle straight over the object being roped, a big beach ball is a perfect target.

THIS IDEA comes from a former cavalryman and this broken-snaffle hitching ring is a trick he used in the cavalry. He takes a jointed snaffle, grinds the mouthpiece to a sharp point, and drives it into a post or tree for a place to tie up a saddle horse. If you make use of this idea, be certain the post or tree you select is good and solid, so the pin won't pull out the first time your pony leans on his reins or tie rope.

BURLAP FEED SACK

WHO CAN think of anything worse than being in a remote camp for a week or two with a mess of canned goods whose labels have been torn off? Well, here's a simple solution to the problem. Wrap your cans in a feed sack before packing them in a pannier and it'll keep the labels from wearing off in a hurry. And, they'll stack like cordwood.

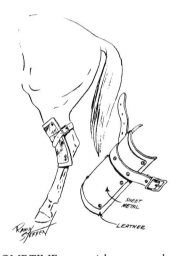

SHEET METAL
LEATHER

SOME TIME ago, a girl wrote me about a problem she was having with her horse cow-kicking while she was working around the animal. Here is the way to solve this problem. The rig I've drawn here isn't original for I've seen it used many times. I made one the other day to make sure my design would work, for I haven't seen one recently; this one does work real well. Be sure the sheet metal you use is heavy enough, and the leather shield should be at least as heavy as good skirting leather. Sole leather, without the metal, will also do nicely. Use two-piece copper rivets to assemble the parts. When used properly, your horse won't be able to bend his leg enough to do any kicking.

THIS SIMPLE stunt will save some cinch galls, especially in the winter when the hair is long and coarse. Straighten out the twisted hair under the cinch after saddling by lifting and pulling first one leg, then the other as though shaking hands with ol' Paint. This makes the hide and hair stretch under the cinch and helps smooth it out.

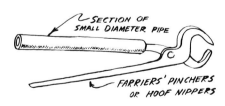

SECTION OF SMALL DIAMETER PIPE

FARRIERS' PINCHERS OR HOOF NIPPERS

HERE'S A way to get a better leverage on a pair of pinchers or nippers when you get a dry, hard hoof to trim. Slip a length of small-diameter pipe over one handle—it fits your hand better and affords a much firmer grip. Anything that makes any part of shoeing faster and easier is for me.

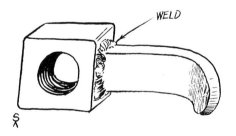

WELD

A FELLER finds many places around a horse establishment where large nuts have to be removed or screwed down quite frequently. Here's a simple gimmick to make this often aggravating chore an easy one. Weld a bent handle on the nut, and turning it will be a snap, even when the nut is dry and tight.

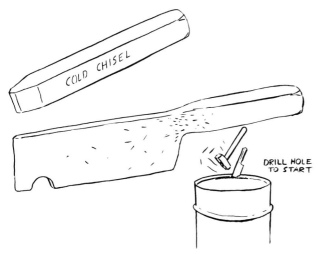

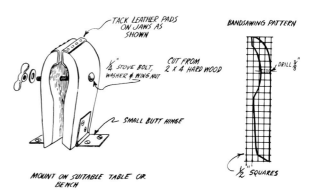

HERE'S A MUCH better way to cut the ends out of steel drums than using a cutting torch, according to one of our readers. He beats an old cold chisel to the shape shown, on a forge and anvil, then re-tempers it. After drilling a starting hole in the top of the drum, he uses a hammer to pound the cutter around the edge of the drum, making a cleaner and faster cut than is possible with a torch. He claims it follows the line better, too. Of course, the half-round depression in the edge of the cutter is the cutting surface.

THIS IS A dandy idea for a small saddler's stitching vise. The jaws are band-sawed from a hardwood 2x4, ten inches long, according to the pattern I've shown here. The jaws are drilled so that a 1/4-inch bolt will be loose in the holes and then fastened to a suitable work surface with wood screws and a pair of small butt hinges. A wing nut on the bolt allows you to clamp a piece of leather firmly in the jaws for sewing with an awl and needle. I'd advise tacking a piece of leather on each jaw to keep from scuffing any good leather you're working on. This is one of the handiest tools a leather worker can have in his shop.

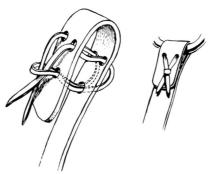

A READER from Canada tells us that this method of lacing a latigo beats any other he's ever tried. He says he guarantees this type of lacing will not work loose, as some others will.

ONE OF our rancher friends sometimes uses this method to slow down calves and grown cows to keep from having to chouse them all over the place during the cow works. He uses a strap or a pigging string, buckles or ties it just above the hock as shown, and it hampers the use of the large tendon enough to do the trick. But don't tie this tight enough to cut off the circulation.

BLANKET-hipped Appaloosas, leopards, and some solid horses—light grays, palominos, etc.—are mighty hard to get clean when they've been wallerin' in a wet corral. One solution is the use of a deluxe car-washing brush that attaches to a garden hose. The fancy ones are ideal since some include an inner brush that revolves with the pressure of the water and even include a place in the handle for a liquid detergent. With one of these gadgets, you can stand out of the splash and give that ol' pony a shampoo, a couple of rinses, and have him sparkling clean in nothing flat.

HERE ARE A couple of tips for leather workers. The small end of a shoeing rasp makes a mighty fine punch for large holes in leather. Use a hammer, as shown, with a block of wood. Another tip is this awl made by grinding to a smooth point the worn end of an old Phillips-head screwdriver.

HERE'S THE way I've been earing a horse for quite a few years. It takes less pressure to get his attention with the ear folded double, and won't hurt him a bit. It comes in handy when a horse's attention needs to be taken off a needle or other medicinal application.

THIS DIAGRAM shows a method of stacking railroad crossties to form a steady loading ramp where there are no regular loading facilities. This method was devised many years ago by the U.S. Cavalry, and was used to load horses into railroad cars during maneuvers and actual campaigns on the Mexican border.

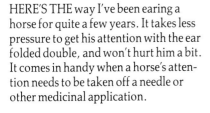

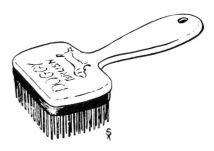

AN EX-JOCKEY friend does a lot of leather work in keeping his tack in good repair. Here's the way he cuts leather laces or strings, a method that requires no special equipment aside from a sharp knife. He drives two nails into a board, as shown, sticks the point of the knife down into the board at the correct distance to get the size lace he wants, and pulls the leather strips through. If you are careful, and pull steady, you can cut almost perfect strings this way.

A DOG grooming brush, the kind with rather blunt teeth set in rubber, makes an ideal brush for slicking up a horse in summer or winter coat, or for combing manes and tails. These brushes are inexpensive and are readily available at pet supply shops.

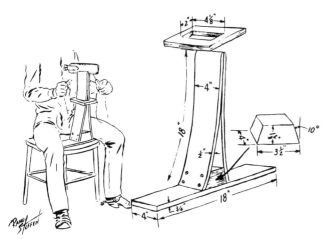

SADDLER'S STITCHING horses are getting rather scarce these days, and when you can find 'em they come rather high. While most of us haven't much use for a regular stitching horse, all of us do occasionally find ourselves with a repair job of some kind or another in the tack room when we'd give our eyeteeth for a good rig to hold our work steady and firm. Here's a stitching "colt" that's easy to make from scrap lumber, and will sureenough hold without a wiggle whatever you clamp between its jaws. The frame part can be made as big or small as you please, but the dimensions I've given here work out real nice for a big variety of jobs. Use a piece of 3/4-inch plywood to make the clamping piece, and 1/2-inch soft lumber will work out nicely for the rest of the outfit.

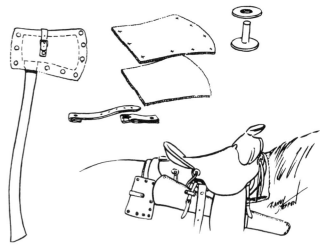

A FRIEND and old-timer is back with another good idea for the working horseman. This time it's an easy-to-make protective sheath for a long-handled ax that must be packed on the saddle. Made from pieces of heavy canvas belting cut to shape, then riveted together, it protects the cutting edge of the ax as well as the horse and rider. A small strap and buckle riveted to the sheath keeps the belting cover in place at all times. He recommends carrying it in a rifle boot fastened to the off side of the saddle, with the opening turned toward the rear of the horse, as I've shown in my drawing.

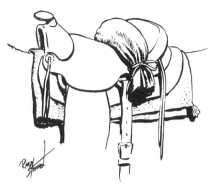

I HEARD from one of our readers in the Midwest who says that to help a person who always rides a saddle like a chair and can't seem to get a forward seat, tie a rolled-up saddle blanket or slicker in the seat, using the short jockey strings. This will make the rider stay up front and not depend on the cantle. This works very well, especially for those saddles with a sloping seat and high cantle which naturally force a person to the rear of the saddle. A person who has thick hips and thighs can learn to grip with the upper part of the leg by using the blanket, too.

A COAT hanger makes a good sweat scraper when there's no regular wood or aluminum scraper handy. I remember this tip from having seen it used in washing down the horses on the grueling Tevis Cup Ride in California.

WE'VE ALL seen tire carcass bumpers placed on the barrels used in barrel racing. However, instead of a tire, an inner tube can be fitted over the barrel and then inflated. It makes a softer bumper if you hit it.

THEY SAY "a word to the wise is sufficient." So here are a couple of words that may save you a lot of grief and loss, if you sometimes use a *morral* or nosebag to feed your horse. *Always* punch a few holes in the bottom of it so water can run out. I've heard of several horses that drowned in their nosebags, either through dunking it in the water in an effort to get a drink, or in a hard downpour of rain where there was no shelter. A leather punch is the best tool, the single punch type that is used with a hammer, but a large nail will also do the trick.

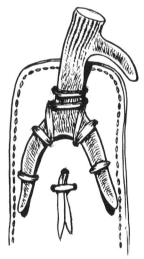

JOE BACK'S book, *Horses, Hitches, and Rocky Trails* has for years been the bible of packers who ride the back country. When the book first appeared, it was the most complete work on packing ever published. Joe has been a packer all of his life, and I doubt that there are many tricks of that trade he hasn't used. His book is filled with wonderfully detailed pen-and-ink drawings and down-to-earth instructions on the art of packing. This deer-horn lash-cinch hook is one of many emergency repair hints in the book. All it requires is a leather punch, a piece of horn shaped like this, and a few pieces of whang leather.

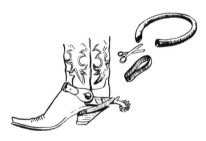

THIS IS another version of the rubber spur tie. By cutting ³/₄-inch sections from a bicycle inner tube, you get inexpensive but highly satisfactory tie-downs. They're not rock hard like leather or wire—they have a certain amount of give and spring to them, which makes them better.

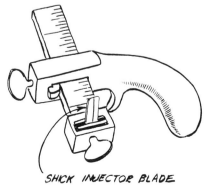

SHICK INJECTOR BLADE

HERE'S A tip for those who do a lot of leather work. When replacing the blade on a leather draw gauge, a Schick injector blade works real fine. These blades are inexpensive and you can afford to throw them away when they get dull.

127

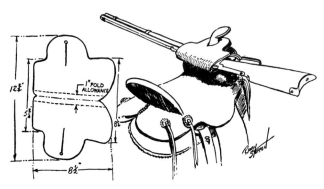

IF YOU LIVED 30 miles from town, by yourself, had a big horse but no saddle, and there just wasn't anyone to give you a boost up, what would you do? Well, here's how a reader in Arizona's desert country solved the problem, and it's a good trick to know for any of you who do crawl up on one bareback at times. She places a bench beside a fence, with just enough room between the fence and the bench for her to walk in. It was rough trying to get that old horse up next to the bench so she could climb on, until she worked out a definite pattern. I show her tracks and those of the horse. She starts leading the horse toward the bench, then makes a turn to the right and completes the circle so the horse comes up alongside the bench while she ducks behind it and up on it. What made this one tough for her was that the horse had been schooled to step up on anything he was led up to, including benches.

THIS SADDLE HORN rifle boot is a ghost from the past. While I'd seen one my grandfather had used in his younger days, that's the only one I'd ever remembered seeing until I made one for an old-time parade. It felt so good, and appeared to be so practical that I used it hunting in open country, and I'm sure sold on it where the timber or brush is not too thick. The dimensions I show here will make a boot that will fit any of the Model 1892 or 1894 Winchester rifles, or the Marlin lever actions. You'd best use medium-weight sole leather or heavy saddle skirting. When the carbine is shoved firmly into the boot it will stay put without much help from you, and will leave both hands free most of the time. But when a big mule deer jumps out in front of you, believe me, you can have that rifle to your shoulder before he can make two jumps. If you'll look at some Frederic Remington or Charlie Russell prints, you'll see one of these boots occasionally.

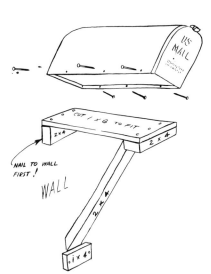

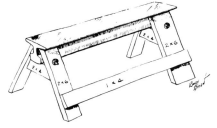

I SAW THIS anvil made from a piece of railroad track at a friend's shop. It looked like such a practical gadget for most any horseman who putters around with his own repairs and maintenance that I made a sketch of it. He used a 36-inch section of old rail, and a sawhorse-like base that clamps the rail solidly by means of two long $1/2$-inch bolts, with the washers and nuts recessed into the 2x6 legs. He uses it for everything from shoeing to making fence and gate hardware, and I'm sure there are a hundred other chores around his place this anvil makes easier.

WE'VE SHOWN many different kinds of saddle racks, but here's one of the most unusual. It is made from a discarded rural mailbox with the flag and keeper removed from the right side, and mounted on the wall as shown. The lid swings open easily even with the saddle on it and makes a good place to store any equipment small enough to fit inside.

HERE'S A hint that's as old as the hills, but the people who need it are usually the ones who don't seem to know about it. When you are having trouble getting a horse to take the bit in his mouth (and little children who can't reach an old wise pony are plagued with this one), just put a little honey or jelly on the mouthpiece of the bit and see how fast ol' Paint comes running with his mouth wide open next time you shake a bridle in his face.

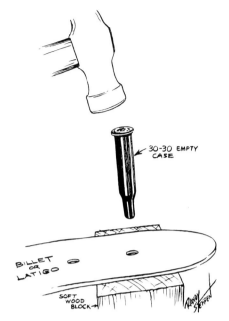

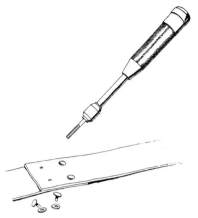

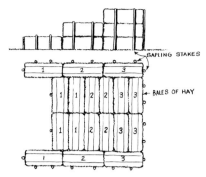

ONE OF our readers in Texas has come up with an easy way to punch those extra-large holes in a latigo or off-billet. He takes an empty 30-06 or 30-30 cartridge case, backs up the latigo with a block of soft wood, and uses a hammer to drive the case through the leather. Smaller cartridge cases can be used for punching smaller holes in other pieces of leather.

SEVERAL TIMES when a leather punch wasn't right at hand when I needed to punch some holes in leather for riveting, I used a push drill that was close by. It makes satisfactory holes, through thicker material than a punch will handle, for using two-piece copper rivets.

IN DOING some research for my book on cavalry, I ran across this old-time U.S. Cavalry method of building a loading ramp out of stacked bales of hay and sapling stakes. They piled the bales as shown, anchored them in place by driving sapling stakes into the ground, and they had a ramp that would allow them to run their horses into a truck or railroad car where there were no other loading facilities.

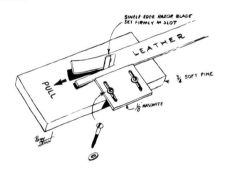

THIS LEATHER thong cutter is a good one. Use a piece of soft pine for the base, then make slots with some small chisels that you can wedge a single-edged razor blade into firmly. You'll probably have to tap the blade in with a hammer, but go easy. A piece of masonite fixed as shown makes a dandy adjustable guide.

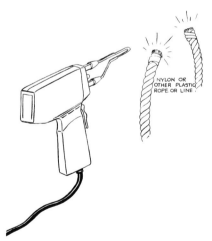

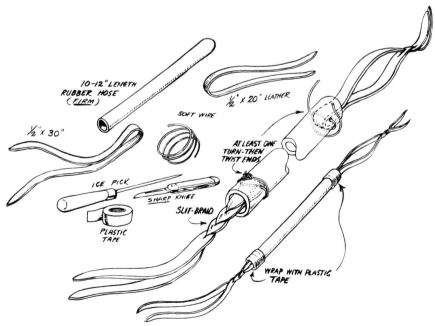

I'VE FOUND that an electric soldering gun is by far the best way to sear the ends of a nylon rope. If an end is to be seared to prevent unraveling, a small piece of most any kind of tape to hold the strands in place temporarily makes the task very simple. After the fibers have been seared, the tape can be removed. The electric soldering gun, or a regular soldering iron, does a much better job than a match or a torch.

A SUBSCRIBER in New York sent in this way to make your own quirt from materials around every horseman's place. I don't know if he knew it or not, but this is exactly the same method the Plains Indians used to make their quirts, but they used bone or antler instead of rubber hose. The drawings show just what you'll need to do. Use your imagination a little, and you can come up with some real attractive variations.

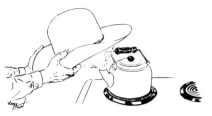

A FRIEND had a couple of mares that were hard to catch, even with grain. So she used a hook made from heavy wire to snag the ol' gals—after shaking a bucket of grain to get them within range of the hook. However, it is extremely dangerous to leave halters on loose horses. Many horses have been killed or seriously injured when the halter catches on something like a branch, post, spigot, nail, door latch, even a back foot being used to scratch an ear. If you must leave a halter on the horse, use a breakaway halter, or cut the halter in several places, about ³/₄ way through, so if the horse hangs it up on something, it will break loose.

THE OLD cow country method of blocking a new hat was to throw it into the horse trough, then shape it while it's still wet. When the hat was dried slowly, it kept its shape from then on, if the hat wasn't one with a lot of sizing to give it body. But you just can't beat an old tea kettle on top of ma's kitchen range for blocking a hat these days.

The trick is to get up a real good head of steam, then steam just a small area at a time. I usually start out by doing one front quarter of the brim first, then the other front quarter. Next comes the back of the brim, so it will slope down and not look like some TV dude hat. The crown comes last and several passes are necessary to get it steamed enough to stay the way you want it. It helps, after the felt has absorbed the steam, to hold the shape you want with your hands and wave the hat around in the air until it cools and dries, which takes only a half minute or so.

I USE photography a lot in my work—mostly for reference. At times, it's necessary for me to make shots of a horse prior to doing a painting of that particular horse. I used to have a heck of a time getting an old pony to stand alert, with his ears up and his eyes sparkling. So many just loll around, lazy as a hog in the sun. Believe me, I tried all kinds of stunts to wake 'em up—some of which did the job so well it took an hour to catch 'em and calm 'em down, like the time I waved a buffalo robe at my old stud. But this little umbrella trick works fine almost every time, if it isn't overdone. The good thing about an umbrella is that it can be opened a tiny bit, just shaken a little, or opened up wide like a hippo about to devour a bale of hay. When the photographer's all set, with the camera set and focused, he tells the umbrella operator, "Now," and he does the rest. But, as I said, use a little discretion; you don't want a stampede, just some attention.

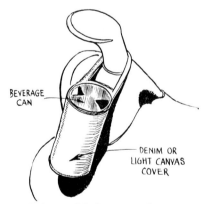

THIS IS one of the best contributions to our national conservation that I've seen. Many fires have been started by careless riders who toss away a cigarette before it is completely snuffed out. This saddle ash tray is something that every rider who smokes should carry with him at all times. It's simple to make; a light piece of canvas or denim sewn to hold a common beverage can. Looped over the saddle horn, it's right there to receive the ashes as well as the smoked-out butt. And there are always plenty of replacement cans around when one gets too full.

HERE'S A way to spread the heels of a shoe when you have to do a cold-shoeing job. Spread the jaws of your hoof nipper between the heels of the shoe. You'll have to put a little muscle into it, but it works.

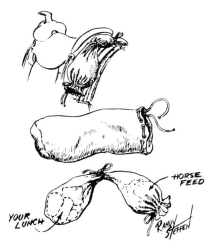

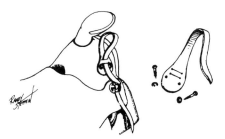

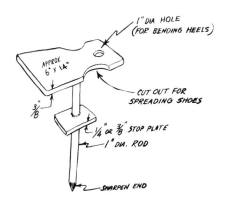

A READER who rides in and around Salem, Ore., packs her own lunch and a grain ration for her horse in this unique makeshift saddlebag. She uses a canvas ice bag or an old army duffle bag, packs her own lunch in the bottom, ties a stout cord securely around the middle, uses the open end to hold a good grain ration for her horse, pulls up the draw string, and ties it to the saddle with the saddle strings.

THIS ISN'T an original idea, but it's a real simple way to rig a quick-release rope strap for that second loop in competition, or for carrying your rope while riding pasture or working stock during roundup. If you use a fairly heavy latigo leather and make the tongue fit the slot pretty snug, it'll hold as well as any rope strap. Be sure to use escutcheon-type washers under the screw heads when you screw it to your saddle tree, to keep the leathers from tearing at the screw heads.

THIS PORTABLE shoeing anvil is easily made by welding a few pieces of iron or steel together, as shown in the drawing. It allows the shoer to place it just where he wants it without having to lug a big heavy anvil all over the place. Of course, this one is handiest when cold shoeing is done; it may not be steady enough to make shoes on.

HERE IS the old cow-country method of holding split reins while mounting. The left rein is pulled snug and some slack is left in the right rein. Should the horse start to move as the rider mounts, a twist of the wrist on the hand that is holding the left rein—along with a chunk of the horse's mane—will put pressure on the rein. This will spin the horse toward the rider, making mounting easy.

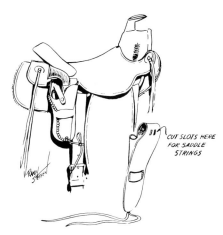

THIS ONE comes from a subscriber in California who was raised in the Dakota country. He's been a horse and gun buff all his life and this method of carrying a holstered handgun on the saddle is a trick he picked up during his years of security and law enforcement work. The drawing shows how the slits in the back of the belt flap accommodate the saddle strings of the upper jockey. These strings are tied good and tight so they won't slip, and this position places the grips of the revolver just where your right hand falls naturally. It's a good idea to have a safety strap on whatever holster you use. It would be easy to lose a pistol without one.

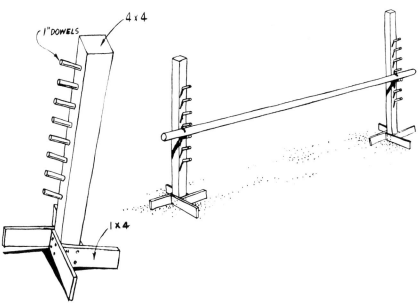

HERE'S HOW TO make inexpensive jump standards with just ordinary tools that most every household has. The standards themselves are suitable lengths of 4x4 lumber, drilled in the appropriate places for the dowels, which should be slanted slightly upward.

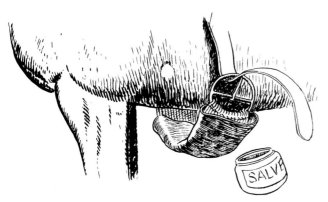

I'VE HAD SEVERAL visits with an old-time *vaquero* of the California-Nevada country and I've never run across a man who knows so much about Spanish-Californian horse gear and horse lore. Here's a little trick he mentioned—a method of curing a cinch sore while you're riding the animal. Cut a length of old inner tube and slip it over the cinch. After daubing a little salve on the galled spot, cinch up just tight enough to keep the saddle in place and go on about your business. He says this has worked well for him on the few occasions his cinch has rubbed a raw spot on one of his horses.

ONE OF OUR contributors reported that she had a horse with a good-looking mane and tail, but almost no forelock. She wasn't very proud of his appearance in parades and shows until she hit on this way to make a horsey hair piece. She pulled and cut enough hair from the underside of her horse's tail to make a good-looking hair piece, arranged it as shown in the drawing, and ran it through her sewing machine several times until it stayed flat. She used a few bobby pins to attach it back of the poll to the mane, slipped on the headstall to help hold it in place, and had a magnificent forelock where there had been none.

A HORSEMAN from British Columbia uses a squirt oiler to apply medicine to injuries on his horses' legs. Either the metal or plastic types, available most everywhere at a nominal price, will do the job. He tells us this type squirter sends a single, solid jet for a great distance, letting you stay away from those dynamite-packed feet. He recommends cleaning the squirt cans every few days with alcohol or some other solvent to keep the medicine from clogging the mechanism.

MUFFIN PAN
FOR SMALL PARTS

FOR THOSE of you who do a lot of leather work or work with small parts of any kind, including shirt snaps, grommets, or rivets, you might consider swiping the little lady's aluminum or tin muffin pan for a small parts bin. This will keep the little parts separated and save a lot of temper.

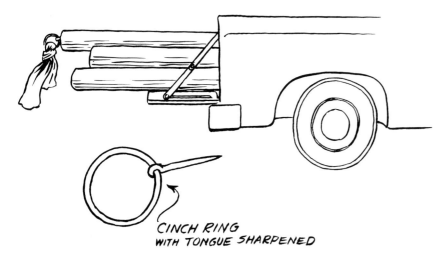

CINCH RING
WITH TONGUE SHARPENED

HERE'S AN EASY-to-make gadget that's a good one to keep in the tool box of the pickup. An old cinch ring, with the tongue sharpened on a grinder, makes a dandy attachment for a red flag on the end of a load of posts, or other wood that hangs out over the end of the pickup bed. A few taps with a hammer on the clinched end of the tongue will drive it into the wood far enough to hold a red rag tied in a square knot as a flag. Another few sideways taps of the hammer will loosen it enough to remove it when the job is done.

AN EMPTY liquid shoe polish container and applicator is a handy item to have for dressing your horse's hoofs. Of course, you'll need to determine what kind of a solvent will cut the shoe polish. Clean both bottle and applicator thoroughly before using it with the hoof dressing.

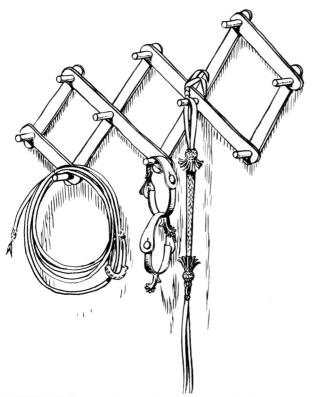

AN OLD-TIME accordion-type hat rack, or clothes hanger, makes a fine place to hang miscellaneous horse gear in the saddle room. This kind of rack used to be seen in almost every hallway years ago, and if you look around, I'll bet you can find one tucked away in the attic or barn.

YOU MAY GIGGLE when you see this old mare standing here with a pair of bib overalls on, but, if you live in country where horn flies and other types of flying critters swarm on your horses' legs, go ahead and grin, but try it. The contributor of this idea says, "the overalls look sad, but they sure do keep the flies from gnawing at my light-colored mare's legs and chest."

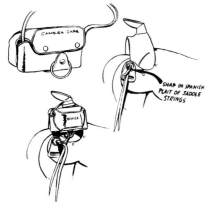

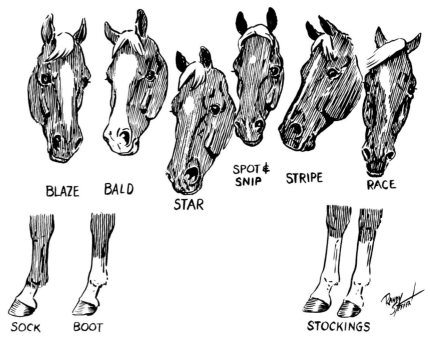

SOME TIME ago, a reader wrote and asked about a good way to carry a camera on horseback. Here's the way I've carried a 35mm camera a number of times on trail rides, and I think it would work equally as well with a twin lens reflex. Undo one loop of the Spanish braid used to fasten your saddle strings to the saddle. Insert a small snap, then redo the braid. Place a small ring on the back side of your camera case, toward the bottom. Wrap the carrying strap around the horn several times to keep the camera as high up and as tight against the fork as possible. Then snap the snap into the ring, and it sure won't do much bouncing around, even at a trot or lope.

I HELP OUT WITH a 4-H horsemanship project, and it's surprising how many times I catch youngsters on questions dealing with the markings of the horse. For the benefit of new young horsemen, I thought this set of drawings might be useful. In addition to the above markings, most bay horses have black points; these so-called points are black mane and tail, black legs from the knee or hock, or slightly above the knee or hock, down to the hoof. The exceptions to this are the bays that have socks, boots, or stockings, and sometimes black muzzles and black areas around the eyes. A great many bays also have black tips on their ears.

133

SOMETIMES IT is difficult to burn a brand on a horse or cow in a branding chute without moving the iron and blotching it a little. Here's a way to use a plain board so it will help steady the iron and make the brand a perfect one. Place the board against the side of the animal, then slide the hot iron down the board until it rests against the hide. The weight of the iron itself will put enough pressure on the hair and hide to make a neat brand without burning too deeply.

A READER WHO SHOES his own animals has devised these stands for clinching and final rasping of the hoofs. The one at the top is nothing more than an old washing machine agitator, or rotor. The other is one he made himself by shaping a piece of hardwood as shown, then fastening it solidly to an old disc with a lag screw up through the middle. With either of these stands, he can place his own feet on the rims, and hold it steady when the horse pulls his foot back.

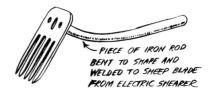

— PIECE OF IRON ROD BENT TO SHAPE AND WELDED TO SHEEP BLADE FROM ELECTRIC SHEARER

HERE'S A gadget to help thin your horse's tail the easy way. It's made from a worn blade from an electric sheep shearer with a bent rod or bolt welded to the blade to form a handle. By varying the angle, you can pretty well control the amount of hair removed with each stroke.

A FRIEND of mine some 20 years is pretty much of a horseman, and the last time we talked, he mentioned an easy-to-make breeding hobble that requires only a length of cotton rope and an old feed sack. This is how it's rigged, and it is most effective. Properly placed on a mare, it prevents her from kicking at the stallion. Depending on the mare, the position of the hobbled foot should be as relaxed as possible, and not hiked off the ground as far as I've shown in this drawing.

THIS IS a way a reader from Fort Worth makes up low-cost horse troughs from 55-gallon drums on his horse outfit. He cuts the drums open at the ends and along one side, as shown here, and bends the two halves back to form the trough. Angle iron or small scrap pipe is welded around the edges to prevent injury from rough edges. This split drum is then welded at the four contact points to the top of another drum, which is buried in the ground for a third of its length. This makes a real sturdy and inexpensive trough, suitable for water, feed, or minerals. Several coats of good paint should be added to prevent corrosion.

MANY TRAIL riders carry a line and a few hooks in their saddle bags. If you do, here is a handy tip to help with the scaling of your catch. The old familiar saw-toothed curry comb that you probably have in your saddle pockets will do a nice job of a messy chore.

A READER IN Sacramento has come up with a good wrinkle on driving metal fence posts. He made this hand pile driver from a 30-inch section of 6-inch pipe. A ½-inch plate welded to the end makes a good solid pounding surface. The ¾-inch pipe handles on the side make it easy to handle. He also suggests that you tie a piece of string at the point on the post where it should be underground, then just tap it down with the 40-odd pounds of the driver doing the biggest part of the work.

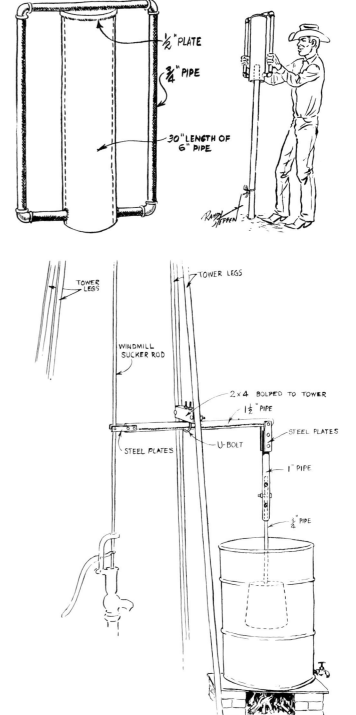

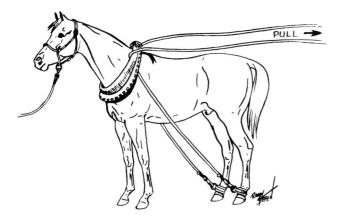

HERE'S another suggestion for downing a horse. Ropes are fastened to leather straps on the rear legs of the horse and run through a leather collar. The lines are pulled from the rear, casting the horse to the ground. It is desirable to have an assistant pull sideways on the lead rope of the horse as his feet are drawn up; the horse does not have time to struggle that way.

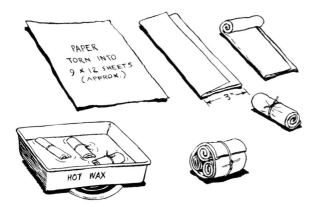

THIS IS AN EASY way to make fire-starters that won't fail. The contributor of this one makes up a supply of these for use on trail rides and hunting trips. She tears newspaper into sheets about 9x12 inches, folds each sheet into thirds so it makes a piece 3 inches wide and 12 inches long, then rolls them fairly loosely, and ties them with a small piece of twine. When enough rolls are made, she melts wax in a suitable flat pan and soaks each roll in the hot wax. Then she takes three of these waxed paper rolls and wraps another folded sheet around them, ties it with twine, then soaks the triple roll in wax. Several of these starters will start a fire with almost any kind of damp wood, as long as it isn't wet enough to be soggy. It's possible that these little starters could save a life.

THIS WINDMILL CLOTHES washer comes from a line camp rider on the Big Springs Ranch outside of Wells, Nevada. The dimensions he gave for this outfit were for a pump whose sucker rod had an 8-inch stroke. The drawing shows how the component parts are rigged. The washer tub is a 55-gallon drum with the top cut out. A faucet on the bottom allows the water to be drained quickly and easily. The washer plunger is a two-gallon milk pail welded to a piece of ¾-inch pipe that fits up inside the 1-inch pipe that actuates the plunger. The fire chamber under the drum allows the water to be heated so that clothes will get really clean. This outfit will not only wash clothes, but it'll pump water at the same time. I've seen other windmill washers, but this is the best design I've run across.

135

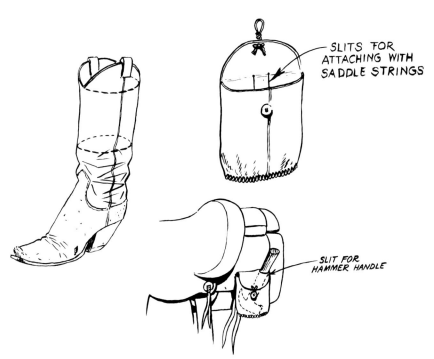

SLITS FOR ATTACHING WITH SADDLE STRINGS

SLIT FOR HAMMER HANDLE

BEDROLL TARPS that have snap fasteners to close up the top are expensive as the dickens. Any ordinary tarp that's the right size, and a lot less expensive, can be made into a real fine close-up job by using the buckles off an old pair of galoshes, arctics or rubber overshoes—whatever you prefer to call them. The buckles can be cut off with a razor blade and fastened to the tarp with rivets.

A LONG TIME AGO, we did a feature on things to make from old boots, but here's just a little different wrinkle submitted by a reader in Denver. She makes up a pouch from the top of an old boot, using a button and a piece of whang leather to fasten the top down. A pair of slits in the back provide a way to fasten the pouch to the saddle strings on the upper jockey. If the pouch is used to carry a hammer and staples, a slit in the top allows the handle to stick out with no danger of losing the hammer.

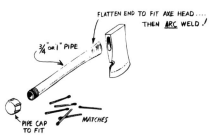

FLATTEN END TO FIT AXE HEAD.... THEN ARC WELD !

3/4" OR 1" PIPE

PIPE CAP TO FIT

MATCHES

THIS PIPE handle on an ax could be a lifesaver. The cap end allows matches to be kept bone dry when the ax is used in snow country during the winter. And the ax is just as handy to use as one with a conventional wooden handle.

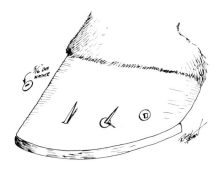

THIS TIP ON shoeing comes from a friend in Cheyenne. His method of preventing nail clinches from chipping away the horn of the hoof directly below them is to use a thin iron washer on the nail before the clinch is made. The washers should be about 5/16-inch in diameter, and should have a slot in the center to fit the flat section of the nail. After the nail has been driven, the washer is placed on the point and lightly tapped down against the hoof. The nail is then turned down and cut. Using a washer eliminates weakening the horn from the inevitable groove formed by the clinched nail, and distributes the strain over the entire surface of the washer.

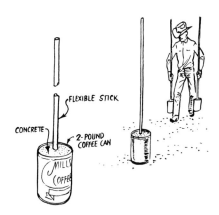

FLEXIBLE STICK

CONCRETE

2-POUND COFFEE CAN

THE POPULARITY of gymkhana-type competitions has put the spotlight on pole bending and other similar events. Here's how one of our contributors makes up pole bending standards. He uses a light, flexible stick for the pole, fills a two-pound coffee can with concrete, sticks in the pole, and, after making sure it's vertical, allows it to set overnight. These standards are light enough to be handled easily, and are practically indestructible. And they'll tip over if a horse hits them without injuring the horse.

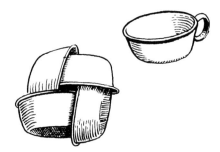

HERE'S ONE way I discovered for nesting tin cups for packing. I can't think of anything simpler, and it allows you to nest four together so they take up little more room than a single cup. A wrap or two of a terry cloth towel will help eliminate a lot of the rattle if it annoys you as much as it does me.

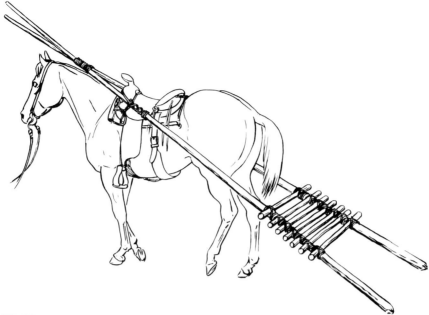

IF YOU'RE EVER FACED with bringing a big game animal, or some other heavy, unwieldy object, out of the back country with a saddle horse, it will be well for you to remember the old Indian travois, and how to rig it on your saddle horse. Two fairly straight poles, each about 20 feet long, and several smaller sticks; about 30 feet of light, strong cord, and 30 minutes of lashing will result in a travois that will enable you and your horse to drag a mighty big hunk of meat, or anything else, a long ways.

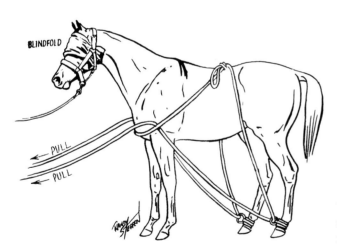

THERE ARE MANY ways to put a horse down on the ground. One method is to use a large diameter, soft cotton rope to prevent burning the hide; about 55 to 60 feet of rope will be needed. One turn is taken around the horse, from the chest to a point midway between the withers and the croup, as shown, and a simple overhand knot is tied in the rope at the top of the horse. The two free ends are run through rings set in sheepskin-lined straps fastened to each rear ankle. A blindfold is recommended, too. Now the ropes can be run to the front of the horse, and a pull will draw up the rear legs so the horse can be toppled with little effort. If you want to prevent the horse from kicking, run the free ends of the rope through the collar rope and tie.

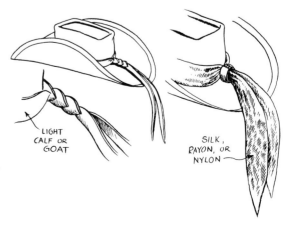

ONE OF OUR readers who lives near Cheyenne is conscious of style and fashion. She makes a ponytail hatband by Spanish-splicing a piece of lightweight calf or goatskin around her hat so the ends hang a good foot below the edge of the brim. She also uses bright silk or nylon, and draws it together at the back of the hat with a keeper made of a loop of leather laced together.

137

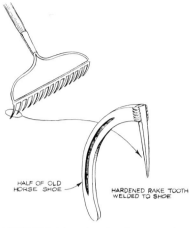

TRAIL RIDES, ESPECIALLY overnight trail rides, are becoming more and more popular. Any trail ride will be improved considerably if the food is good, and cooking is so much easier and more pleasant when a proper fire is built and maintained. Outdoor cooking is accomplished best over a bed of hot coals, not in direct flames. The "keyhole" type of fire is one that's been used for years. The big fire is built so the prevailing wind will blow the smoke away from the smaller bed of coals and the grill. As the coals are formed, they're scraped into the small pit, allowing you to keep a somewhat constant temperature on the bed of coals.

THIS IDEA for a hoof pick is a good one, and allows one to be made up from materials that are usually around every horse outfit, large or small. Half a horseshoe is welded to a tooth from an old garden rake. These teeth are hardened steel, so if the pick is quenched in cool water as soon as it is welded, the tooth will retain its hardness, and won't bend out of shape with repeated use.

AN OLD spur, fastened to the wall as shown with a washer and wood screw, makes a mighty good-looking hook on which to hang gun belts or catch ropes.

THIS IS an idea that will save you and your horse bruises and skinned places if you plan to start training a horse for barrel racing. One of our Canadian readers cuts a section from one side wall of an old tire to make it fit over the end of a 55-gallon drum; the remaining wall holds the tire in place. If your horse runs too close to this barrel your shins and your horse's hide will be protected.

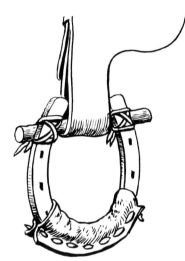

THIS emergency stirrup is another dandy from Joe Back's *Horses, Hitches, and Rocky Trails*. Stirrups do get smashed in falls, and this combination of a spare horseshoe, a stout stick of green wood, and some leather strings makes a real practical temporary stirrup.

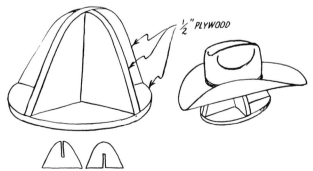

THIS ONE COMES from a collector of military equipment, especially cavalry equipment and uniforms. This hat rack is a design he makes up with a jigsaw and a glue pot from scrap pieces of plywood. He uses the racks for his military hats, caps, and helmets, but his design works equally well for storing western hats so the brims don't get pushed out of shape lying flat on a shelf. Shaped to fit any size hat, the two vertical pieces are slotted to fit together, glued, then fastened to the round base piece with small nails and glue. Painted a bright color, they add a lot to a horseman's closet or shelf.

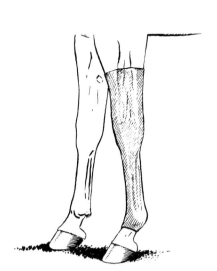

MOWER SECTION

WELD PIPE HANDLE TO *FLAT* SIDE OF MOWER SECTION SO EDGES CAN BE SHARPENED EASILY BY FILE OR GRINDER.

KEEPING wound dressings and liniment-soaked cloths on a leg of most any horse is a tough thing to accomplish. A lady in Michigan tells us she's had considerable success by cutting the legs out of old leotards, panty hose, or tights, and using these close-fitting tubes of cloth to hold medication in place.

HERE'S AN IDEA for an efficient tool with which to flesh any size of hide preparatory to tanning or cutting into rawhide strips. Made by welding a suitable length of ½-inch pipe to the flat surface of an old mower section, it affords two sharp surfaces with which to scrape the fat and flesh particles from a fresh hide. By welding the handle to the flat side of the blade, it enables one to sharpen the edges quickly and easily with either a file or a grinder.

THERE'S A NEED for some kind of safety precaution if you ride in traffic-filled areas at night. One friend of mine, who has a flashy Appaloosa stud with a hind end which is almost a reflector in itself, drapes an old auto tail light on her pony's posterior. This reflector boot idea is a little neater. My drawing pretty much shows how you can make a couple of them up for your pony. I'd suggest that you use one on each hind leg so that cars coming from either side will be sure to see you and your horse.

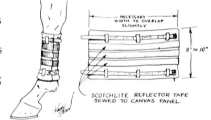

NECESSARY WIDTH TO OVERLAP SLIGHTLY

8" to 10"

SCOTCHLITE REFLECTOR TAPE SEWED TO CANVAS PANEL

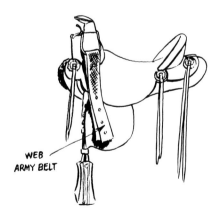

WEB ARMY BELT

WHEN A friend's daughter's horse has been saddled and bridled, it's still a long way from the ground to the seat so she devised this mounting aid. One of Dad's old army web belts was folded in the middle, the buckle ends cut off, and a leather thong used to tie the halves near the loop end. Another stout leather string loops over the horn, and the whole rig gives a strong but soft handhold up to the saddle, and it's never in the way.

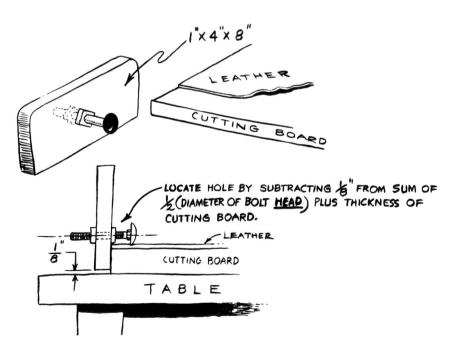

1"x 4"x 8"

LEATHER

CUTTING BOARD

LOCATE HOLE BY SUBTRACTING ⅛" FROM SUM OF ½ (DIAMETER OF BOLT **HEAD**) PLUS THICKNESS OF CUTTING BOARD.

LEATHER

CUTTING BOARD

⅛"

TABLE

FOR THE LEATHER worker, here's an easy-to-make marking gauge that does a real fine job of marking good straight lines on leather for most any kind of repair. My sketch pretty much shows how to make and use this gauge.

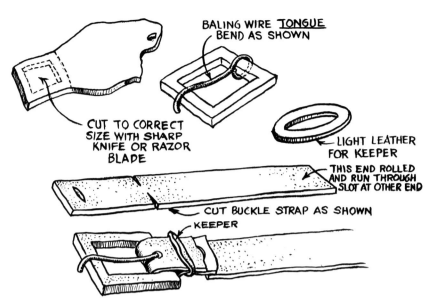

BALING WIRE **TONGUE** BEND AS SHOWN

CUT TO CORRECT SIZE WITH SHARP KNIFE OR RAZOR BLADE

LIGHT LEATHER FOR KEEPER

THIS END ROLLED AND RUN THROUGH SLOT AT OTHER END

CUT BUCKLE STRAP AS SHOWN

KEEPER

THIS IS AN INGENIOUS way of improvising a buckle in an emergency with some of your horse gear; or a dandy way to make a good-looking buckle on a leather project you may be working on. The drawing shows how to cut the parts from scrap leather, and how to form the tongue of the buckle from a short piece of baling wire. The way that the buckle strap is cut makes it stay put when the simple leather keeper is slid into place. And this buckle works like a charm—try it.

FROM A reader in California comes a suggestion that sure can save your horses from injury if you keep them in a wire corral. He writes that he's had several experiences with horses being cut up on wire enclosures because they were unable to see the wire quickly enough when running and playing in the pen. So he's equipped his pens with white cloth pennants that flutter in the wind. He used old sheets and tore them into strips about two inches wide and twenty inches long, then tied them four or five feet apart all around the top strand of wire. Of course, the strips need replacing every once in a while, as they wear out or are torn off by the horses.

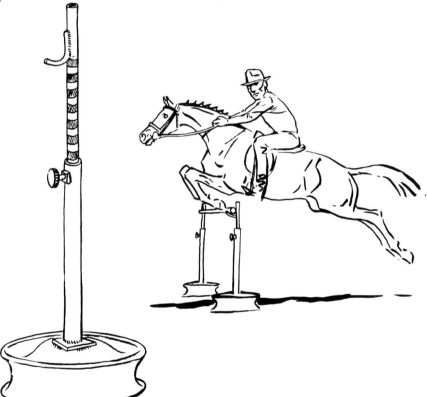

HERE'S ANOTHER VERSION of a set of adjustable standards for training hunters or jumpers. A section of pipe is fitted into a second section just loose enough so it will slide up and down easily. A metal plate is then welded to one end of the larger pipe, and the plate is welded or bolted to an old car or truck wheel. At the other end of the large pipe, a hole is drilled a short distance from the opening. A nut is welded over the hole so an adjustment bolt can lock the inner pipe at the desired height. A rest for the jumping bar is welded at one end of the small pipe. Inch-wide stripes, painted one inch apart on the small pipe, will make it easy to adjust a pair of these standards to equal heights. The crossbar should be long enough to allow setting the standards a safe distance apart.

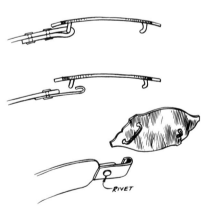

RIVET

ONE OF our readers in New Mexico objected to the bulk that results from the conventional way of fastening a belt to a trophy buckle. So this is the way he does something about it. Instead of doubling the end of the belt back on itself and riveting, as is the usual way, he shapes a piece of brass so that it acts as a hook and rivets it to the end of the belt with a single rivet as shown. By doing this on each of several belts, he can change belts at will, using the same favorite buckle each time. This eliminates half the bulk that he found so objectionable before.

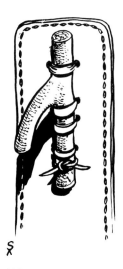

HERE'S AN emergency pack-cinch hook that may save the day for you sometime. A small crotch of tough brush is lashed to the pack cinch with a leather thong through holes punched in the cinch. If the brush is tough enough it'll get you home.

IF YOU SHOULD be caught away from shelter in a rain heavy enough to soak your clothes and boots, wait 'til the sun comes out, strip down, rig a pole like I've shown here, and cut a couple of stakes for your boots. Build a *small* fire that's practically flameless, and let the low heat and time dry 'em out. Be sure the boots are far enough from the fire to keep them from scorching and becoming brittle—that's mighty easy to do.

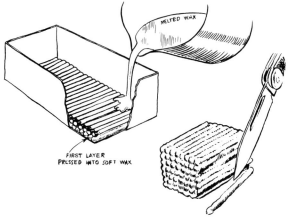

YOU WOULD BE real smart to hinge your barn or cabin door in country where there are heavy snowfalls so it swings *in* instead of *out*. When the door swings out, you're liable to wake up some morning and find you've been locked in your cabin as securely as though there were a padlock on the door. Not many cabin doors do swing out, but a great many barn and feed shed doors do. That same big snow could make you do a heap of shoveling before the stock could be tended if all your doors on the buildings swung out.

ONE OF OUR Idaho contributors does a lot of horseback camping and hunting. She is fully aware of the importance of dry matches in all kinds of weather, and her ability to start a fire under almost any circumstances. So this is the way she prepares a supply of waterproof matches that do not require any special care or handling. Using a box of large kitchen matches, she empties the box and pours a thin layer (about $1/8$-inch) of melted wax into the bottom of the box. Then while the wax is still warm and pliable, she presses a layer of matches into the wax. Another layer of wax is poured on top of the matches, and so on until the box is full. Chunks of waxed matches can be broken off and they can be carried in saddle bags with no danger of getting wet. Single matches are easy to pry from the chunk of waxed matches with the blade of a pocket-knife. The wax not only keeps the matches completely dry, but makes them burn with a larger flame, making fire-starting easier.

141

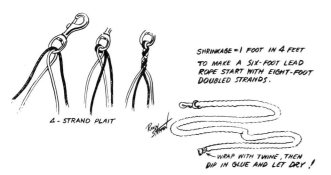

SHRINKAGE = 1 FOOT IN 4 FEET

TO MAKE A SIX-FOOT LEAD ROPE START WITH EIGHT-FOOT DOUBLED STRANDS.

4-STRAND PLAIT

WRAP WITH TWINE, THEN DIP IN GLUE AND LET DRY!

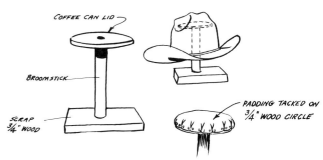

COFFEE CAN LID

BROOMSTICK

SCRAP 3/4" WOOD

PADDING TACKED ON 3/4" WOOD CIRCLE

ONE OF OUR Iowa readers plaits his own halter lead ropes from four doubled strands of baling twine. I show the fundamental steps here in doing the four-strand plait. Be sure you allow for one-fourth shrinkage if you plan to give it a try. Our friend says he plaits up longer ropes the same way for working with colts; the ropes are soft and not apt to burn.

THIS BUNKHOUSE hat rack isn't much to look at, but it'll sure keep the brim from curling the wrong way, and is easy to make. You can also use a circle of 3/4-inch wood and tack some padding on it for a deluxe job.

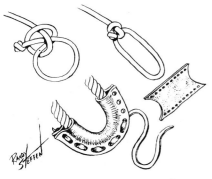

HERE'S THE most common way of tying a honda in your saddle rope, and of attaching a chafe, or wear leather, to prevent the strands of the rope from wearing through from long and hard usage. The drawing shows a terminal knot in the end of the rope that goes through the common overhand knot,

and this terminal knot can be any kind that provides enough bulk on the end to keep it from slipping through the overhand knot. Many stockmen use the single or double Matthew Walker knot, while others merely tie a tight overhand knot in the end. If you can tie the Turk's head, that's a real good one to use.

After the honda is tied, wet it slightly in a container of water, and stretch it so it assumes and holds the shape shown in the drawing. Attaching a chafe is a simple matter—cut a piece of rawhide or durable latigo leather to the shape shown, then punch an odd number of holes with an awl or leather punch along both edges. Lace this in place as shown, using tightly drawn overhand knots at the start and finish to hold everything in place.

THIS ONE comes from a subscriber in Sacramento who uses this bib to keep her horse from chewing on his stable sheet or gnawing at a wound. The leather used should allow free jaw movement for eating, but should be heavy enough to keep him from bending it over too easily. Three snaps are riveted to the bib so it can be snapped in place quickly. *Remember:* If you must leave a halter on a horse, for safety's sake, use a quick-release halter, or cut 3/4 way through it in several places so it will break free if the horse catches it on something.

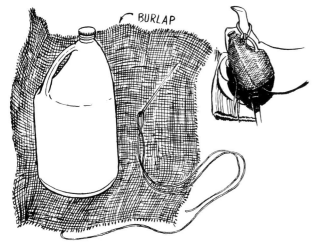

BURLAP

THE PLASTIC bleach bottles that have been on the market for many years have attracted a lot of attention from gadget-minded horsemen. I've shown a couple of different ways to cut these containers for use as grain scoops, as suggested by a number of readers. Another twist is to cover one of these bottles with burlap for use as a saddle canteen. The burlap would keep the water cool if it were wetted occasionally.

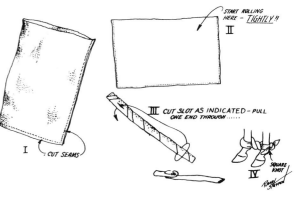

START ROLLING HERE – *TIGHTLY*!!

I   CUT SEAMS

II

III   CUT SLOT AS INDICATED – PULL ONE END THROUGH......

IV   SQUARE KNOT

THOSE OLD BURLAP feed sacks found in any horse barn can be mighty useful pieces of material. The gunnysack hobbles shown here are quick and easy to make and certainly won't chafe a colt's heels. The drawing shows how to fold and slit the sack. Be sure to pull the long end through tightly to keep it from coming undone. A wrap or two with binder twine near the ends will also accomplish this purpose nicely.

HERE'S A good grooming hint from a reader in Arkansas. After grooming with a brush and currycomb, use a piece of damp foam rubber to gather up all the dirt and dust the brush missed. Our friend says this leaves the coat much glossier.

HERE'S another picket-line hitch that will not slip in either direction along the picket line, and will not jam so as to be hard to untie, even if it becomes wet. I checked this out and found it a good hitch to use with a horse that slobbers a lot.

THIS SUGGESTION is for a retainer plate to use when it's necessary to pack a horse's foot for thrush or injury to the sole or frog. Cut a thin piece of leather, using the bottom of the foot as a pattern, and tack in place under the shoe. Use as few nails as possible to hold the shoe firmly in place, for it will be necessary to remove this shoe in a comparatively short time.

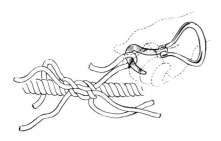

A FOLDING hoof pick is a helpful tool when splicing rope. The pick end is handy to open tightly wrapped strands, and the handle allows you to pull one strand through the splices, using thumb pressure as shown in my drawing.

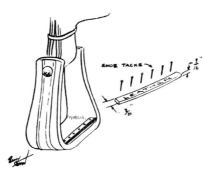

FOR THOSE of you who use the wide-tread roping stirrups, and have a hard time keeping your feet in the stirrups when working cattle or riding a cutting horse, here's a simple homemade remedy that will make it easier to keep from blowing a stirrup at the wrong time. Use cobbler's tacks to nail a piece of heavy leather, 3/8-inch wide, to the back edge of the stirrup tread. This affords the shank of your boot a much more secure hold on the stirrup.

LOOSE STOCK on a road at night can be dangerous to a driver. One remedy is to make sure your fences and corrals are stout enough to keep your animals in, but if there is question that one could get out, a few strips of reflectorized tape on neck straps will help the motorist see the animal before it is too late. A dark animal often blends into the background at night, but the tape will pick up the glow of the headlights.

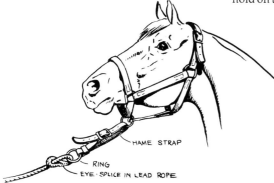

A RANCHING COUPLE in Alberta writes that they've had trouble for years with halter shank straps breaking and coming apart. Of course, once the snap is ruined it's a chore to remove it, no matter how it's fastened to the shank. So they've gone to making up their own leads with the arrangement I've shown here, using a hame strap, a metal ring, and an eye spliced in the lead rope end. If any of these components breaks, it is easy enough to replace.

STARTING A FIRE in snow and rain can sometimes be a mighty serious problem. One of our packer friends tells us that he carries a can of miner's carbide in his outfit; and, if the weather's wet, he sprinkles the carbide in a little pile on the wet ground or snow, wets it well, lights it with a match, and then keeps it wet as it burns. Carbide needs moisture to burn, and it will flame plenty long enough to light whatever dry material you've been able to gather.

Western Horseman Magazine

Colorado Springs, Colorado

The Western Horseman Magazine, established in 1936, is the world's leading horse publication.
For subscription information and a list of other Western Horseman books, contact:
Western Horseman Magazine, Box 7980, Colorado Springs, CO 80933-7980; 719-633-5524.